The One Show
1984

The One Show

Judged To Be Advertising's Best Print, Radio, TV

Volume 6

A Presentation of
The One Club for Art and Copy

Published by
Rotovision S.A.
Geneva

The One Club
For Art and Copy

Ron Berger
PRESIDENT

Allan Beaver
CHAIRMAN, PUBLICATIONS COMMITTEE

Beverley Daniels
DIRECTOR

Seymour Chwast and Michael Aron
Pushpin Lubalin Peckolick Inc., New York
DESIGNERS

Terry Berkowitz, New York
LAYOUT AND PRODUCTION

Elise Sachs
EDITORIAL COORDINATION AND INDEX

Beverley Daniels
ADVERTISING SPACE SALES

Sunlight Graphics, New York
TYPESETTING

Dai Nippon Printing Co., Ltd., Tokyo, Japan
COLOR SEPARATIONS, PRINTING AND BINDING

PUBLISHED BY
Rotovision S.A.
10, Rue de l'Arquebuse
Case Postale 434
CH - 1211 Geneve 11
Switzerland
Telephone 22 - 21 21 21

IN ASSOCIATION WITH
The One Club for Art and Copy, Inc.
251 East 50th Street
New York, New York 10022
(212) 935-0121

U.S. DISTRIBUTION:
R.M. & R.E. Silver
95 Madison Avenue
New York, New York 10016
(212) 686-5630

WORLDWIDE DISTRIBUTION:
Rotovision S.A.
10, Rue de l'Arquebuse
Case Postale 434
CH - 1211 Geneve 11
Switzerland
Telephone 22 - 21 21 21

First Printing.
ISBN 0-960-2628-6-5
ISSN 0273-2033

Contents

The Board of Directors

President's Message

This message isn't dedicated to the copywriters or art directors whose work is represented in the 1984 One Show Annual.

And it isn't dedicated to the agencies.

Or to the photographers. Or directors. Or retouchers. Or engravers.

Or to any of the other people who contributed to the work you'll see in the pages that follow.

Instead, this message is dedicated to the one group of people without whom good advertising would never get done.

Those people are affectionately known as clients.

It's dedicated to those clients who had the guts to say "yes" to ideas to which others would have said "no."

Those clients who, when the research numbers said one thing, had the confidence to listen to their judgment that said something else.

Those clients who had the trust to give their agencies and creative people all any agency really wants: the opportunity to fail on its own terms.

How can I write about clients in a book that's supposed to be an example of what it takes to do good creative work?

Well, when you think about it, how can I not?

Ron Berger

The one on the left has claimed more victims.

A nice, comfy floral-patterned armchair? What possible harm could that do to anybody?

According to the latest medical opinion, the answer is plenty.

The people at risk, we're told, are the retired (and nowadays that can mean mere youngsters of 55 or so).

They've worked hard all their lives. Now they feel they deserve to take things a bit easy.

Quite right, too.

The trouble begins when 'taking things easy' turns into lazing in an armchair all day.

Too many naps, too many snoozes, and the body can suddenly decide it's simply not worth waking up again.

The message from the doctors is loud and clear. Don't just sit there. Do something.

Opt for an active retirement, in other words.

You're always daydreaming about the things you wish you'd done with your life.

This will be your chance to do them.

Go ahead, build your ocean-going catamaran. Start up your vegetarian restaurant on Skye. Open that donkey sanctuary in Wales.

There'll be nothing to stop you.

Except money, of course.

And that is why you should be talking to Albany Life.

Not later on in your career. But right now, in your thirties or forties.

Start putting a regular sum into one of our high-growth savings plans and you can build yourself a very nice wodge of capital indeed.

We'll collect every penny of tax relief due to you. We'll then lump the two sums together and invest them on your behalf.

And our investment advice is arguably the best there is.

We retain the services of none other than Warburg Investment Management, a subsidiary of the merchant bank S. G. Warburg & Co. Ltd.

If you'd like to hear more about our retirement savings plans, post off the coupon.

We'd hate to see you sitting in a chair just because you couldn't afford to do anything else.

To learn more about our plans, send this coupon to Peter Kelly, Albany Life Assurance, FREEPOST, Potters Bar EN6 1BR.
Name
Address
Tel:
Name of your Life Assurance Broker, if any:

Albany Life
A member of the American General Corporation group.

1 GOLD

DON'T SQUANDER YOUR DISPOSABLE INCOME ON A DISPOSABLE CAR.

At BMW, we assume cars are bought with funds earmarked for investment, not disappearance. And we build them accordingly.

Which is why few cars in the world resist disintegration into scrap metal as determinedly as the BMW 318i.

The resistance is provided by the 4,700 spot welds that fuse the body elements into a taut shell. And by a 40-stage paint process during which layers are baked no fewer than four times.

Flaws are corrected through exhaustive inspections. Including spot-checking by a laser measuring device that checks 2,170 points on the car.

The 318i's engine was proved through a testing process that's not only exhaustive but traumatic:

One-thousand hours of running at wide-open throttle in the lab. Then 10,000 km at top speed on the BMW test track in Nardo, Italy. Then 10,000 km of race-style driving on the Nürburgring, with the car loaded to maximum weight.

Given such powers of endurance, it isn't surprising that the 318i carries a 3-year/ 36,000-mile limited warranty and a 6-year limited warranty against rust perforation.*

Nor is it surprising that, over the past few years, 3-Series BMW's have enjoyed a higher resale value than the vast majority of cars.**

What is remarkable is that all this accompanies a genuine performance car—one "so good," Motor Trend wrote, "it's pure, delightful sin."

And in the long run, that may be its greatest virtue of all.

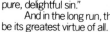

THE ULTIMATE DRIVING MACHINE.

The typical executive fitness program.

Monday   Tuesday   Wednesday   Thursday   Friday

Look familiar?

You went out and bought every paperback on jogging.

Your wife got you the designer warm-up suit.

You sprang for those sneakers that were supposed to be designed expressly for jogging.

The sneakers might have been. But you weren't.

You're sitting there, knowing you should exercise. That's the trouble. You're just sitting there. And about all you ever do regularly is lift the phone receiver.

Muscles should be exercised. And the most important muscle of all to exercise is your heart.

That's where we come in.

We knew what we were doing when we called ourselves Cardio-Fitness. We offer individualized programs designed to strengthen your heart and lungs. To reduce your weight and lower your pulse rate and blood pressure. To increase your physical and mental endurance.

A program of safe exercises done under professional guidance. We review your progress and constantly set new goals for you. All this takes place in a modern, attractive environment. Not a scene from Rocky I, II or III.

Which may be why we boast over 100 chief executive officers. Corporate memberships which include, American Express, Bankers Trust, First Boston Corporation, Time Inc., Revlon and Seagram. And many individual members as well.

One reason why over 90% of our members renew is that we make it so easy. Come at your convenience. You never have to wait. You're in and out in less than an hour.

There's no gym bag to lug around. We supply the fresh shorts, shirts and socks daily. And a permanent locker to store those hardly worn jogging sneakers.

For more information call:

Cardio Fitness Center

Midtown: 345 Park Avenue, entrance on 52nd Street, (212) 838-4570.
1221 Avenue of the Americas, McGraw-Hill Bldg. at Rockefeller Center, (212) 840-8240.
Wall Street Area: 79 Maiden Lane, (212) 943-1510.

Advertisement prepared by Korey, Kay & Partners   1983 Cardio-Fitness Systems, Inc.

3 GOLD

"Junk" food, "health" food, and your food

It costs 272 percent more to feed a family today than it did in 1967. North Fulton Medical Center's course on nutrition can show you ways to hold the cost down, while raising the value of what you eat.

How much thought do you give to the food you and your family eat?

Chances are your diet is reasonably balanced, but you could stand some improvement; everybody could.

So what are we saying: should you be eating nothing but bran and yogurt? Should you try and live on a diet of fast-food burgers?

On the contrary; North Fulton Medical Center wants to help you find a little sanity in the crazy world of nutrition.

And just as variety is the spice of life, it is the way to a balanced diet.

Moderation is the key

Most foods contain nutrients that your body can use for energy. But no single food contains everything you need. It's a matter of eating the right amounts of all kinds of foods, so you get the proper combination of vitamins, minerals, protein and carbohydrates.

What is food?

Food is anything that can provide your body with the materials it needs to produce the energy used in the repair and maintenance of body tissues, or regulation of your body systems.

The jobs are performed by various substances in food, known as nutrients. And different nutrients are provided by different kinds of food.

The best diet is a blend of nutrients, a mixture of all the things your body needs: protein, carbohydrates, fats, vitamins, minerals and water.

What are nutrients?

PROTEINS provide the raw materials for your body's growth and maintenance. The main sources are meat, poultry and fish, dairy products and nuts (peanuts are higher in protein than some meats).

CARBOHYDRATES are the basic source of energy. They're important in the functioning of your internal organs and your central nervous system.

FAT is the most concentrated form of energy. Fats contain the same elements as carbohydrates, combined in a different way.

VITAMINS are needed for the regulation of the chemical processes in your body. They are constantly taking place in your body. They aid in growth and development, and in protecting you against disease.

What about vitamin supplements? A proper diet provides sufficient quantities of vitamins for our needs. So if you eat right, you do not need to take vitamins (unless your doctor tells you otherwise).

MINERALS help regulate your body fluids and the balance of chemicals.

They include calcium, found in dairy products, phosphorus, found in liver, kidneys and cheese, sodium and chlorine found in salt, and potassium, found in bananas, meat, fish, vegetables, chocolate, and instant coffee.

Iron, found in fish, liver, eggs, raisins, pecans and oatmeal, is essential for the growth and maintenance of red blood cells (the average body contains about as much iron as that contained in a 5-inch nail).

Iodine can be poisonous in large amounts, but it's important in the functioning of your thyroid gland (that's why table salt is often "iodized").

Flourine is needed in the bones, teeth and skin. It has been shown to help prevent tooth decay.

Then there is the forgotten nutrient: WATER. It makes up over 60% of your body. Without it, none of the other functions can take place. We can actually live longer without food than without water.

Another item in our diet that isn't exactly a nutrient, but is proving to be important, is FIBER. It's an important part of fruits, vegetables, whole grains, beans and peas. It helps in digestion. People in areas of the world where fiber is a major factor in food show fewer problems with cancer of the colon, digestive tract disorders and even heart disease.

The dreaded calorie

In today's world, the calorie takes a lot of bumps. The truth is, a calorie is nothing more than a measurement of energy. Carbohydrates and fats are the main sources of this energy. How many calories do you need?

The average daily requirement for an adult woman is approximately 1700 to 2400 calories; for a man, it's about 2300 to 2800. But this can vary widely, depending on your size, sex, age, metabolism, and the amount of regular physical activity you include in your routine.

Everything we do uses calories. While this sentence is being written, calories are providing energy to the writer's fingers. And as you read these words, your body is using up fat (just sitting actually uses about 20 calories per hour).

Calories provide energy. But unused calories are stored in your body in the form of fat. That's why overeating, especially of high calorie foods, causes us to gain weight.

If you are overweight, how do you lose? There are no miracles. You need to take in less food, without cutting out any of the foods you need. And you need to exercise regularly. The importance of this for good health and the right kind of weight loss cannot be over-emphasized.

A word about "Wellness"

This is an example of what you'll be seeing a lot of soon—The Wellness Program from North Fulton Medical Center. Through ads like these, brochures, pamphlets and special classes, we'll be giving you information on how to live healthier, better, and more safely. Working with your doctor, we hope to add a benefit to the community that you might not expect from a hospital.

Besides classes on nutrition, you'll be able to learn more about CPR, having a baby, exercising properly, taking care of your heart, dealing with stress, living with diabetes—even being a better babysitter.

While North Fulton Medical Center won't be open till November, the classes are going on right now. For a schedule of available programs and times, call now.

Interesting facts about what you eat

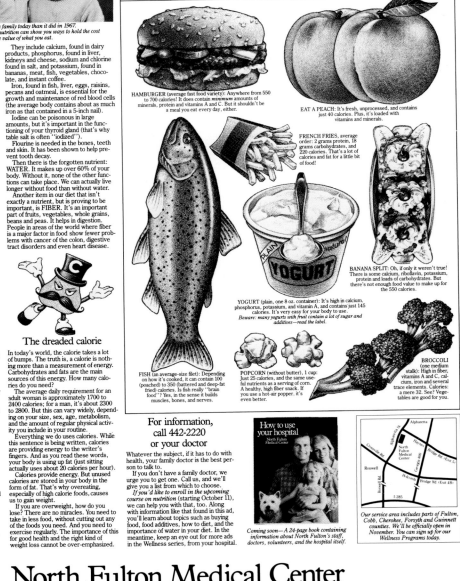

HAMBURGER (average fast food variety): Anywhere from 550 to 700 calories! It does contain *minimum* amounts of minerals, protein and vitamins A and C. But it shouldn't be a meal you eat every day, either.

EAT A PEACH: It's fresh, unprocessed, and contains just 40 calories. Plus, it's loaded with vitamins and minerals.

FRENCH FRIES, average order: 2 grams protein, 18 grams carbohydrates, and 220 calories. That's a lot of calories and fat for a little bit of food!

BANANA SPLIT: Oh, if only it weren't true! There is some calcium, riboflavin, potassium, protein and loads of carbohydrates. But there's not enough food value to make up for the 550 calories.

YOGURT (plain, one 8 oz. container): It's high in calcium, phosphorus, potassium, and vitamin A, and contains just 145 calories. It's very easy for your body to use. *Beware: many yogurts with fruit contain a lot of sugar and additives—read the label.*

FISH (an average-size filet): Depending on how it's cooked, it can contain 100 (poached) to 350 (battered and deep-fat fried) calories. Is fish really "brain food"? Yes, in the sense it builds muscles, bones, and nerves.

POPCORN (without butter), 1 cup: Just 25 calories, and the same useful nutrients as a serving of corn. A healthy, high fiber snack. If you use a hot-air popper, it's even better.

BROCCOLI (one medium stalk): High in fiber, vitamins A and C, calcium, iron and several trace elements. Calories: a mere 32. See? Vegetables are good for you.

For information, call 442-2220 or your doctor

Whatever the subject, if it has to do with health, your family doctor is the best person to talk to.

If you don't have a family doctor, we urge you to get one. Call us, and we'll give you a list from which to choose.

If you'd like to enroll in the upcoming course on nutrition (starting October 11), we can help you with that, too. Along with information like that found in this ad, you'll learn about topics such as buying food, food additives, how to diet, and the importance of water in your diet. In the meantime, keep an eye out for more ads in the Wellness series, from your hospital.

Coming soon—A 24-page book containing information about North Fulton's staff, doctors, volunteers, and the hospital itself.

Our service area includes parts of Fulton, Cobb, Cherokee, Forsyth and Gwinnett counties. We'll be officially open in November. You can sign up for our Wellness Programs today.

North Fulton Medical Center
Your hospital

11585 Alpharetta Street, Roswell, Georgia 30076
A health care center of AMI.

Six important things every babysitter should know

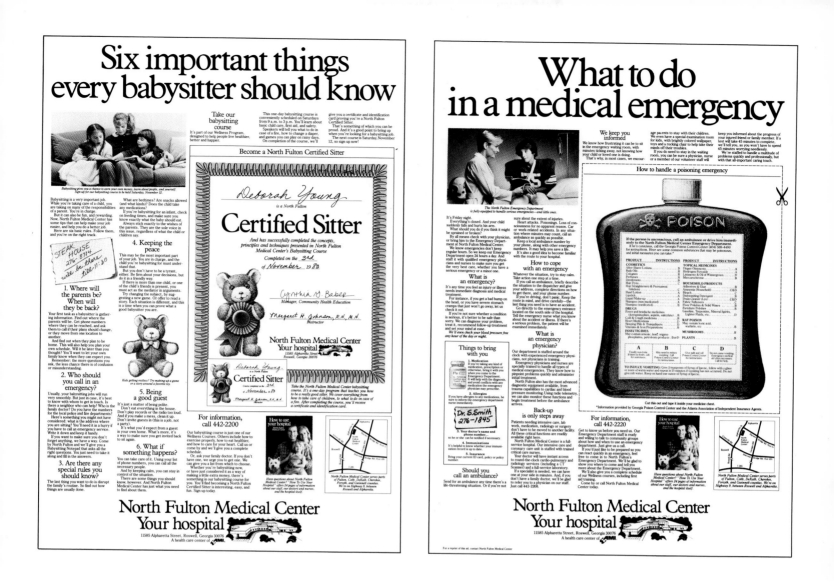

Babysitting gives you a chance to earn your own money, learn about people, and yourself. Sign up for our babysitting course to be held Saturday, November 12.

Babysitting is a very important job. While you're taking care of a child, you are taking on many of the responsibilities of a parent. You're in charge.

But it can also be fun, and rewarding. Now, North Fulton Medical Center has some tips that can help make your job easier, and help you do a better job.

Here are six basic rules. Follow them, and you're on the right track.

1. Where will the parents be? When will they be back?

Your first task as a babysitter is gathering information. Find out where the parents will be. Get phone numbers where they can be reached, and ask them to call if their plans should change, or they move from one location to another.

And find out when they plan to be home. This will also help you plan your own schedule. Will it be later than you thought? You'll want to let your own family know when they can expect you.

Remember: the more questions you ask, the less chance there is of confusion or misunderstanding.

2. Who should you call in an emergency?

Usually, your babysitting jobs will run very smoothly. But just in case, it's best to know with whom to get in touch. Is there a neighbor who can help? Who is the family doctor? Do you have the numbers for the local police and fire departments?

Here's something you might not have considered: what is the address where you are sitting? You'll need it in a hurry if you have to call an emergency service. Write it down and keep it handy.

If you want to make sure you don't forget anything, we have a way. Come by North Fulton and we'll give you a Babysitting Notepad that asks all the right questions. You just need to take it along and fill in the answers.

3. Are there any special rules you should know?

The last thing you want to do is disrupt the family's routine. So find out how things are usually done.

What are bedtimes? Are snacks allowed (and what kinds)? Does the child take any medications?

If you're babysitting for an infant, check on feeding times, and make sure you know exactly what the baby should eat.

Always stick exactly to the wishes of the parents. They are the sole voice in this issue, regardless of what the child or children say.

4. Keeping the peace

This may be the most important part of your job. You are in charge, and the child you're babysitting for must understand that.

But you don't have to be a tyrant, either. Be firm about your decisions, but do it in a friendly way.

If there is more than one child, or one of the child's friends is present, you must act as the mediator in arguments.

Try changing the subject, by suggesting a new game. Or offer to read a story. Each situation is different, and this is a time when you can prove what a good babysitter you are.

Kids getting restless? Try making up a game or a story around a favorite toy.

5. Being a good guest

It's just a matter of being polite.

Don't eat everything in the house. Don't play records or the radio too loud. And if you make a mess, clean it up. Don't invite guests in (this is a job, not a party).

It's what you'd expect from a guest in your own home. What's more, it's a way to make sure you get invited back to sit again.

6. What if something happens?

You can take care of it. Using your list of phone numbers, you can call all the necessary people.

And by keeping calm, you can stay in control of the situation.

There are some things you should know, however. And North Fulton Medical Center has just what you need to find about them.

Take our babysitting course

It's part of our Wellness Program, designed to help people live healthier, better and happier.

This one-day babysitting course is conveniently scheduled on Saturdays from 9 a.m. to 3 p.m. You'll learn about basic child care, first aid, and safety.

Speakers will tell you what to do in case of a fire, how to change a diaper, and games you can play on rainy days.

On completion of the course, we'll give you a certificate and identification card proving you're a North Fulton Certified Sitter.

That's something of which you can be proud. And it's a good point to bring up when you're looking for a babysitting job.

The next course is Saturday, November 12, so sign up now!

Become a North Fulton Certified Sitter

Take the North Fulton Medical Center babysitting course. It's a one-day program that teaches you how to be a really good sitter. We cover everything from how to take care of children, to what to do in case of a fire. After completing the course, you'll receive a certificate and identification card.

For information, call 442-2200

Our babysitting course is just one of our Wellness Courses. Others include how to exercise properly, how to eat healthier, and how to care for your heart. Call us or come by and we'll give you a complete schedule.

Or, ask your family doctor. If you don't have one, we urge you to get one. We can give you a list from which to choose.

Whether you're babysitting now, or have just considered it as a way of making a little extra money, there's something in our babysitting course for you. You'll find becoming a North Fulton Certified Sitter is interesting, easy, and fun. Sign up today.

Have questions about North Fulton Medical Center? "How To Use Your Hospital" offers 24 pages of information about our staff, our doctors and nurses, and the hospital itself.

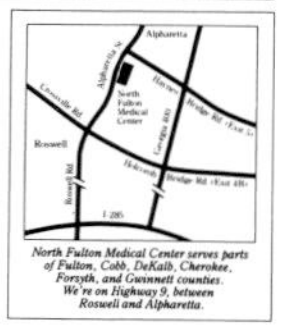

North Fulton Medical Center serves parts of Fulton, Cobb, DeKalb, Cherokee, Forsyth, and Gwinnett counties. We're on Highway 9, between Roswell and Alpharetta.

North Fulton Medical Center
Your hospital
11585 Alpharetta Street, Roswell, Georgia 30076
A health care center of AMI.

What to do in a medical emergency

The North Fulton Emergency Department is fully equipped to handle serious emergencies—and little ones.

It's Friday night.

Everything's closed. And your child suddenly falls and hurts his arm.

What should you do if you think it might be sprained or broken?

By all means check with your physician, or bring him to the Emergency Department at North Fulton Medical Center.

We know emergencies don't keep regular hours. So we keep our Emergency Department open 24 hours a day. And staff it with qualified emergency physicians and nurses to make sure you get the very best care, whether you have a serious emergency or a minor one.

What is an emergency?

It's any time you feel an injury or illness needs immediate diagnosis and medical treatment.

For instance, if you get a bad bump on the head, or you have severe stomach cramps that just won't go away, let us check it out.

If you're not sure whether a condition is serious, it's better to be safe than sorry. We can diagnose your problem, treat it, recommend follow-up treatment and set your mind at ease.

We'll even check your blood pressure free any hour of the day or night.

Things to bring with you

1. Medication
If you're taking any kind of medication, prescription or otherwise, bring it with you when you come to the Emergency Department. It will help with the diagnosis, and avoid conflicts with any medication the emergency physician may prescribe.

2. Allergies
If you have allergies to any medications, be sure to inform the emergency department nurse immediately.

3. Your doctor's name and phone number...
so he or she can be notified if necessary.

4. Immunizations
It's helpful to know whether your immunization record is up to date.

5. Insurance
Bring your current ID card, policy or policy number.

Should you call an ambulance?

Send for an ambulance any time there's a life-threatening situation. Or if you're not sure about the extent of injuries.

Heart attacks. Poisonings. Loss of consciousness for no apparent reason. Car or work-related accidents. In any situation where minutes may count, call an ambulance as quickly as possible.

Keep a local ambulance number by your phone, along with other emergency numbers. It may help you save a life.

It's also a good idea to become familiar with the route to your hospital.

How to cope with an emergency

Whatever the situation, try to stay calm. Take action one step at a time.

If you call an ambulance, briefly describe the situation to the dispatcher and give your address, complete directions on how to get there, and your phone number.

If you're driving, don't panic. Keep the route in mind, and drive carefully—the last thing you need is to have an accident.

Go directly to the emergency entrance located on the south side of the hospital. Tell the emergency nurse what you know about the accident or illness. If there's a serious problem, the patient will be examined immediately.

What is an emergency physician?

Our department is staffed around the clock with experienced emergency physicians, not physicians in training.

Emergency physicians and nurses are specially trained to handle all types of medical emergencies. They know how to pinpoint problems quickly and administer initial treatment.

North Fulton also has the most advanced diagnostic equipment available, from trauma capabilities to cardiac and blood pressure monitoring. Using radio telemetry, we can also monitor these functions and begin treatment before the ambulance arrives.

Back-up is only steps away

Patients needing intensive care, lab work, medication, radiology or surgery don't have to be moved to another facility. All these critical functions are readily available right here.

North Fulton Medical Center is a full-service hospital. Our intensive care and coronary care unit is staffed with trained critical care nurses.

Your doctor will have instant access to round-the-clock cardio-pulmonary and radiology services (including a CT Scanner) and a full-service laboratory.

If a specialist is needed, we can have one at your side in minutes. And, if you don't have a family doctor, we'll be glad to refer you to a physician on our staff. Just call 442-2208.

We keep you informed

We know how frustrating it can be to sit in the emergency waiting room, with minutes ticking away, not knowing how your child or loved one is doing.

That's why, in most cases, we encourage parents to stay with their children. We even have a special examination room for kids, with brightly colored wallpaper, toys and a rocking chair to help take their minds off their troubles.

If you do need to stay in the waiting room, you can be sure a physician, nurse or a member of our volunteer staff will keep you informed about the progress of your injured friend or family member. If a test will take 45 minutes to complete, we'll tell you, so you won't have to spend 45 minutes worrying needlessly.

We're staffed to handle a multitude of problems quickly and professionally, but with that all-important caring touch.

How to handle a poisoning emergency

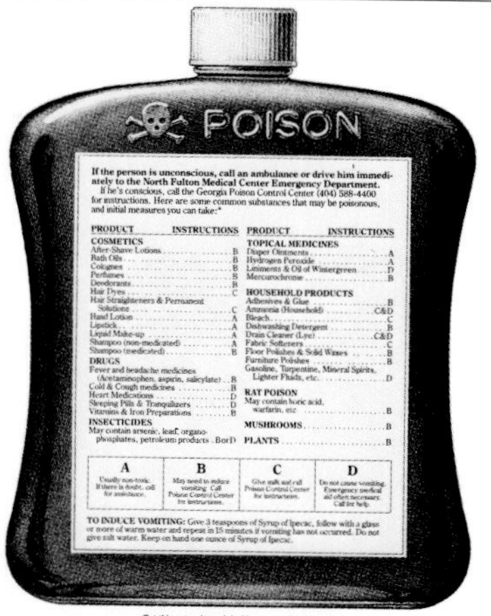

If the person is unconscious, call an ambulance or drive him immediately to the North Fulton Medical Center Emergency Department.

If he's conscious, call the Georgia Poison Control Center (404) 588-4400 for instructions. Here are some common substances that may be poisonous, and initial measures you can take:*

PRODUCT	INSTRUCTIONS	PRODUCT	INSTRUCTIONS
COSMETICS		**TOPICAL MEDICINES**	
After-Shave Lotions	B	Diaper Ointments	A
Bath Oils	B	Hydrogen Peroxide	A
Colognes	B	Liniments & Oil of Wintergreen	D
Perfumes	B	Mercurochrome	B
Deodorants	B		
Hair Dyes	C	**HOUSEHOLD PRODUCTS**	
Hair Straighteners & Permanent Solutions	C	Adhesives & Glue	B
		Ammonia (Household)	C&D
Hand Lotion	A	Bleach	C
Lipstick	A	Dishwashing Detergent	B
Liquid Make-up	A	Drain Cleaner (Lye)	C&D
Shampoo (non-medicated)	A	Fabric Softeners	C
Shampoo (medicated)	B	Floor Polishes & Solid Waxes	B
DRUGS		Furniture Polishes	B
Fever and headache medicines (Acetaminophen, asperin, salicylate)	B	Gasoline, Turpentine, Mineral Spirits, Lighter Fluids, etc.	D
Cold & Cough medicines	B		
Heart Medications	D	**RAT POISON**	
Sleeping Pills & Tranquilizers	D	May contain boric acid, warfarin, etc	B
Vitamins & Iron Preparations	B		
INSECTICIDES		**MUSHROOMS**	B
May contain arsenic, lead, organo-phosphates, petroleum products	B or D	**PLANTS**	B

A	B	C	D
Usually non-toxic. If there is doubt, call for assistance.	May need to induce vomiting. Call Poison Control Center for instructions.	Give milk and call Poison Control Center for instructions.	Do not cause vomiting. Emergency medical aid often necessary. Call for help.

TO INDUCE VOMITING: Give 3 teaspoons of Syrup of Ipecac, follow with a glass or more of warm water and repeat in 15 minutes if vomiting has not occurred. Do not give salt water. Keep on hand one ounce of Syrup of Ipecac.

Cut this out and tape it inside your medicine chest.

*Information provided by Georgia Poison Control Center and the Atlanta Association of Independent Insurance Agents.

For information, call 442-2220

Get to know us before you need us. Our Emergency Department staff is ready and willing to talk to community groups about how and when to use an emergency department. Just give us a call.

If you'd just like to be prepared so you can react quickly in an emergency, feel free to come in to North Fulton's Emergency Department. We'll be glad to show you where to come and tell you more about the Emergency Department.

We'll also give you a complete schedule of our Wellness courses, including first aid training.

Come by or call North Fulton Medical Center today.

Have questions about North Fulton Medical Center? "How To Use Your Hospital" offers 24 pages of information about our staff, our doctors and nurses, and the hospital itself.

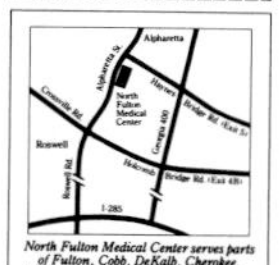

North Fulton Medical Center serves parts of Fulton, Cobb, DeKalb, Cherokee, Forsyth, and Gwinnett counties. We're on Highway 9, between Roswell and Alpharetta.

North Fulton Medical Center
Your hospital
11585 Alpharetta Street, Roswell, Georgia 30076
A health care center of AMI.

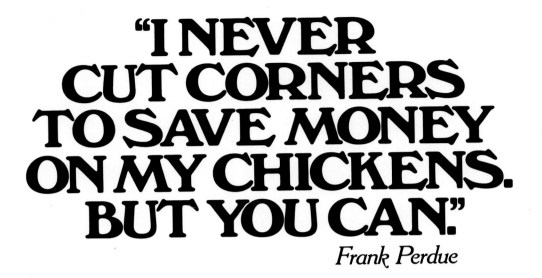

"I NEVER CUT CORNERS TO SAVE MONEY ON MY CHICKENS. BUT YOU CAN."

Frank Perdue

5 GOLD

"I may be one of the few people in the world who has seen a canary given an enema."

So says the secretary to the remarkable, diminutive — five-foot-four, 100 pounds — Dr. Gus Eckstein (1890-1981), expert on animal behavior.

In an original article in the June Reader's Digest, Eckstein's secretary recounts her boss's work with birds, mice, cockroaches, etc. — and his magnetic personality that attracted such notables as Sinclair Lewis, Aldous Huxley, Thornton Wilder, Garson Kanin and Helen Hayes (who, walking into Eckstein's lab, had her mink coat attacked by frenzied canaries).

Eckstein "drew people to him by his intensity" — which is how The Digest" draws 39 million readers.

Genital herpes viruses may live on towels for 72 hours and on toilet seats for four hours. Choose your bathrooms carefully.

The latest news about genital herpes isn't exactly encouraging. The January Reader's Digest reports that this incurable disease doesn't even depend on genital intercourse for transmission: Contact with an infected finger, mouth, towel or toilet seat may be sufficient.

And once someone gets genital herpes, a recurrence can be triggered simply by the stress of *worrying* about it.

This kind of news makes casual sex less attractive. But this kind of reporting helps The Digest® attract 39 million readers.

The only cheese extender we ever use is more cheese.

At Davanni's we use only 100% pure whole milk mozzarella and genuine Sicilian romano.
While other pizza parlors experiment with ways to make their cheese go farther, we're going farther for our cheese.

The mushrooms on some pizzas come from a can. Ours come from a forest.

Mushrooms come to Davanni's fresh. And they go on our pizzas that way.
Go anyplace else and you might get canned.

8 SILVER

It takes bricks to build a better pizza.

Most pizza parlors use ovens that cook pizza unevenly. The crust can be cooked on one half and not on the other. We use even-heating brick ovens at Davanni's. So when your pizza is done, it's all done.

Consumer Magazine Black and White Page or Spread Including Magazine Supplements

9 GOLD
ART DIRECTOR
Dean Hanson
WRITER
Tom McElligott
DESIGNER
Dean Hanson
PHOTOGRAPHER
Bob Adelman
CLIENT
ITT Life
AGENCY
Fallon McElligott Rice/
Minneapolis

10 SILVER
ART DIRECTOR
Roy Grace
WRITER
Irwin Warren
DESIGNER
Roy Grace
PHOTOGRAPHER
Ken Goldberg
CLIENT
Volkswagen
AGENCY
Doyle Dane Bernbach

Consumer Magazine Color Page or Spread Including Magazine Supplements

11 GOLD
ART DIRECTOR
Mike Moser
WRITERS
Brian O' Neill
Steve Hayden
PHOTOGRAPHER
Rudy Legman
CLIENT
Apple Computer
AGENCY
Chiat/Day—Los Angeles

12 SILVER
ART DIRECTOR
Dean Stefanides
WRITER
Stephen Smith
DESIGNER
Dean Stefanides
PHOTOGRAPHER
Harry DeZitter
CLIENT
BMW of North America
AGENCY
Ammirati & Puris

HOW MUCH WEIGHT DO YOU HAVE TO LOSE BEFORE YOUR INSURANCE COMPANY NOTICES IT?

Anyone who's ever tried knows that losing weight can be a real struggle. You go to bed hungry. You wake up hungry. You learn to despise lettuce. You exercise until you ache.

The good news is that according to recent studies, people who stay trim and exercise regularly live longer and are better life insurance risks. So now, ITT Life has come up with a Good Health Bonus* for non-smokers and people who are trim and fit. Which means that if you don't smoke, you could earn a 65% insurance bonus. *With no increase in your insurance premiums.*

If you stay trim and don't smoke, you could get a 100% life insurance bonus. And over half of the non-smokers who apply meet the special underwriting criteria for the Good Health Bonus.

Look. You work very hard to keep your body trim. Isn't it about time you got the trimmer life insurance premiums you deserve?

For more details call free: **1-800-328-2193** and ask for operator 901. In Minnesota call us at 612-545-2100. Or mail the coupon to us today.

ITT Life Insurance Corporation ITT

9 GOLD

Since 1975 we changed a few things on the Rabbit.

Back in 1975 when we introduced the VW Rabbit, *Popular Mechanics* hailed it as a "mechanical masterpiece." And so it was.

But you didn't expect us to rest on our laurels, did you?

Our habit of starting with a revolutionary design and slowly modifying it towards perfection is a Volkswagen tradition dating back to the Beetle.

So eight years after we sold the first Rabbit in America, we astonished the automotive press when we introduced the 1983 Rabbit GTI.

In November, *Car and Driver* called it, "the car we've all been waiting for." It's a new 1.8-liter 90 horsepower fuel-injected engine.

It has a new five-speed close ratio manual transmission.

It has new self-adjusting ventilated front disc brakes.

In fact, it's a culmination of over 15,000 things in a Volkswagen tradition.

But this too is a Volkswagen tradition:

The more things change, the more they stay the same.

Nothing else is a Volkswagen

© 1983 Volkswagen of America.

10 SILVER

Gold
&
Silver
Awards

**Consumer Magazine
Black and White
Campaign Including
Magazine Supplements**

13 GOLD
ART DIRECTOR
Michael Wolf
WRITER
Anita Madeira
PHOTOGRAPHER
Richard Avedon
CLIENT
Danskin
AGENCY
Grey Advertising

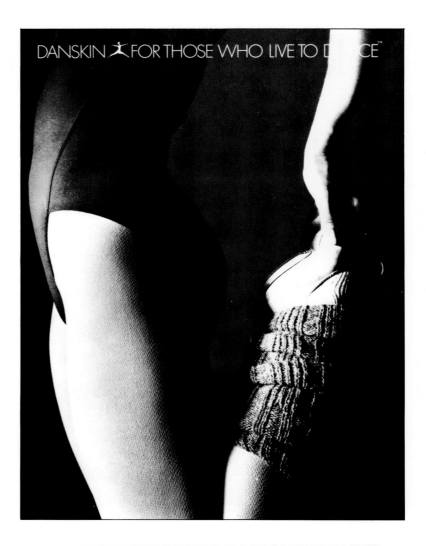

13 GOLD

**Consumer Magazine
Black and White
Campaign Including
Magazine Supplements**

14 SILVER
ART DIRECTOR
Michael Wolf

WRITER
Anita Madeira

PHOTOGRAPHER
Richard Avedon

CLIENT
Danskin

AGENCY
Grey Advertising

DANSKIN FOR THOSE WHO LIVE TO DANCE™

14 SILVER

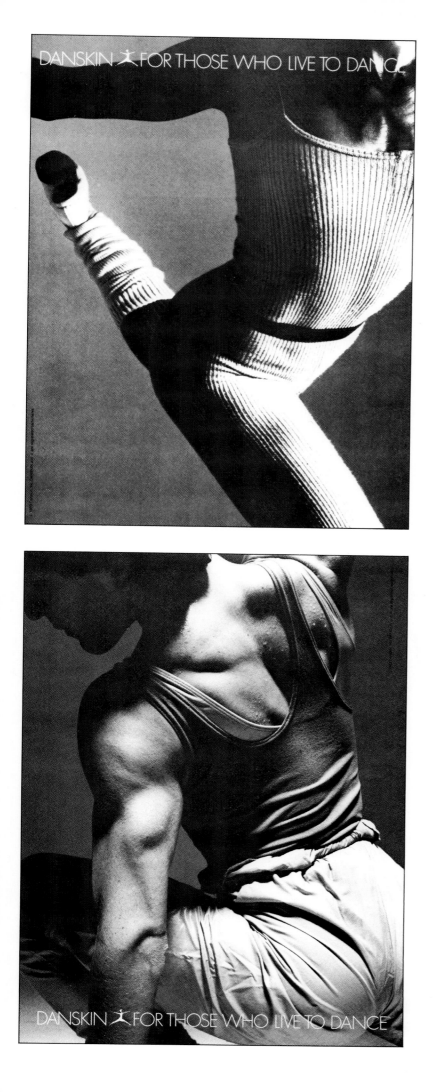

**Consumer Magazine
Color Campaign
Including Magazine
Supplements**

15 GOLD

ART DIRECTORS
Anthony Angotti
Jeff Vogt

WRITER
Tom Thomas

DESIGNERS
Anthony Angotti
Jeff Vogt

PHOTOGRAPHERS
Dick James
Jerry Cailor

CLIENT
BMW of North America

AGENCY
Ammirati & Puris

THE CAR THAT SET THE STANDARD NOW EXERCISES ITS RIGHT TO RAISE IT.

BMW INTRODUCES THE 318i.

The year was 1977. The nation was between fuel crises and the automotive industry had decided that performance doesn't sell.

BMW introduced the 320i, one of those rare automobiles that seems to usher in the era in which it appears. It became "the quintessential sports sedan"..."the sort of car enthusiasts turn into legend" (Car and Driver). And it proved an entire industry wrong.

Now that car has ushered in its successor. And proved an entire industry late.

A REFUSAL TO REINVENT THE AUTOMOBILE.

The 318i is built on the belief that cars that are annually new find themselves at a permanent disadvantage to those that are annually better.

The reason is obvious: There's never time enough to refine something you're forever reinventing.

The 318i is, in contrast, one of the most refined sports sedans BMW has ever built.

Its redesigned fully-independent suspension represents a maturing of a design bred on race-courses, and provides even greater adhesion. "Its handling and roadholding," previewed one automotive journalist, "are magnificent."

A new L-Jetronic fuel-injection system helps extract even more exuberance (and torque) from an already willing engine.

A new power steering system matches the degree of power assistance to driving conditions, providing more at lower speeds and less at higher—while never insulating the driver from a tactile awareness of the road.

Its technology has advanced, with such additions as an analog fuel economy indicator and an electronic system that actually calculates when routine service is needed.

Its aerodynamics are improved, lowering wind resistance without resorting to the wedge-on-wheels architecture that many cars adopted to add a couple of mpg's to a fuel efficiency figure. The 318i has managed that, too—delivering a remarkable 27 mpg, 38 highway.

(EPA fuel efficiency figures are for comparison only. Your actual mileage may vary, depending on speed, weather and length of trip; actual highway mileage will most likely be lower.)

It is also roomier, quieter, and otherwise better in virtually every way an automobile can be better—including the most important way. The 318i is a balanced car, a matching rather than just a gathering of parts and systems, and as close to perfect equilibrium as a car in its price class has ever come.

AN INVESTMENT, NOT A SPECULATION.

BMW recognizes that there's no such thing as a car worth buying regardless of price. That price must be justified—justified when it's bought, while it's being driven, and later when it's sold.

BMW's perform well in all tenses. Free from programmed obsolescence, and supported by a growing body of car buyers better able to recognize and pay for quality, the BMW 3-Series has traditionally retained its resale value far better than most other automobiles. (Source: NADA Used-Car Guide.)

It's also backed by one of the most confident warranties: a 3-year/36,000-mile limited warranty and a 6-year limited warranty against rust perforation.

(Warranty applies to new automobiles purchased from authorized U.S. BMW dealers only. See your BMW dealer for details.)

In short, the 318i is a new car that arrives without the conventional handicaps of the new-and-untried—a car that elevates the admission requirements for all cars asking to be taken seriously as sports sedans.

We invite you to visit and test drive the new standard at a BMW dealer near you.

THE ULTIMATE DRIVING MACHINE.

© 1983 BMW of North America, Inc. The BMW trademark and logo are registered. European Tourist Delivery can be arranged through your authorized U.S. BMW dealer.

Some think its gold nib outweighs its gold body.

The 18-karat Parker Premier fountain pen contains thirty grams of beautifully crafted gold.

Its nib contains less than one gram.

Yet once you put the nib to paper, there is every possibility you will come to consider it the most valuable part of the pen.

It writes with a free-flowing smoothness that is hard to imagine. And it should.

Each nib requires three weeks to make. Along the way, it must pass 131 inspections.

It is not the product of several disinterested people but the handiwork of one craftsman.

He fashions it from the time it is a formless blank of gold.

On the tip he welds a tiny pellet of ruthenium, a metal four times harder than steel and ten times smoother.

He sculpts this tip under a microscope to achieve what has been called "the baby's bottom," which aptly describes the smooth way it writes.

Then he deftly splits the nib so it will conduct ink, using a cutting disk only .004" wide–fine enough to split the edge of a razor.

Only after all this has been done to his satisfaction will the craftsman who made the nib sign the certificate allowing us to sell you this pen.

It will cost you $2,500.

Partly because of the price of gold.

Partly because precious few things in this world are made with this kind of care and attention.

✦ **PARKER**

Our 18K gold nib is handcrafted so carefully, it takes three weeks to get from the first picture to the last.

16 SILVER

This pen took 2000 years to perfect. Its ink took twice as long.

Writing inks have been made since 3,500 B.C. from all sorts of unlikely materials. Today no ink in the world is made like the one used in our Premier Laque Roller Ball.

The Chinese invented the laque finish back in the 2nd century B.C. It occurred during the Han dynasty.

Few finishes are more beautiful to look at. You have no doubt already concluded that.

But there is a second conclusion to be reached now that Parker has created the Premier Laque Roller Ball.

Nothing could be more beautiful to write with.

Not just because we build up layer upon layer of genuine Chinese laque made from the sap of the *Rhus Vernicifera* tree, rubbing and polishing each layer by hand just as the ancient Chinese did.

Even the placement of the gold flecks you see in the depths of the finish is accomplished manually.

There's something even more remarkable about the Premier Laque Roller Ball: the ink.

Its similarity to the inks the Chinese and Egyptians began experimenting with over 4,000 years ago is quite remote. (An early favorite was made from the lampblack of peach kernels.)

In fact, nothing like it existed until now. Even the dyes that supply its deep, glowing color are found in no other ink.

We filter it molecule by molecule, until it contains no particle larger than a micron. (You need 39,370 microns to equal an inch.)

The result is an ink many times finer than even the finest fountain pen ink. One that glides onto paper with liquid smoothness. And dries to the touch almost instantly.

It is an ink so special, only twelve people in the world know its formula.

How much does a pen like this cost?

Because of the authentic Chinese laque, the price of the Premier Laque Roller Ball is $160.

Because of the way it writes, it's worth every penny.

✦ **PARKER**

For the stores near you which carry Parker Premier pens, call toll-free 1-800-356-7007. Or write The Parker Pen Company, P.O. Box 5100, Dept. P, Janesville, WI 53547. © 1983 TPPC.

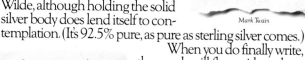

It's wrought from pure silver and writes like pure silk.

You will find writing with the Parker sterling silver Premier fountain pen anything but drudgery.

In fact, it's entirely possible you will find it something of an inspiration.

We can't promise it will give you the wisdom of an Oscar Wilde, although holding the solid silver body does lend itself to contemplation. (It's 92.5% pure, as pure as sterling silver comes.)

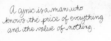

MAN IS THE ONLY ANIMAL THAT BLUSHES. OR NEEDS TO.

Mark Twain

A cynic is a man who knows the price of everything and the value of nothing.

Oscar Wilde

When you do finally write, the words will flow with such uninhibited smoothness there will be nothing to block the way should a profound thought happen to wander along.

Thank the nib for that. And the extremes we go to making it. The nib takes three weeks to manufacture, because we do it almost entirely by hand.

We fashion it from 18K gold to make it flexible to the touch. Then at the tip we mount a tiny pellet of ruthenium, a metal four times harder than steel and ten times smoother.

He is a self-made man and worships his creator.

Disraeli on a fellow politician

The ruthenium tip is sculptured under a microscope—a deft operation any surgeon could envy. But an even more delicate task follows.

The nib must be split with a cutting disc only .004" wide. Literally fine enough to split hairs.

Finally, the nib is tumbled in walnut shells for eighteen hours to leave the gold incomparably smooth.

Only after all this, not to mention 131 inspections along the way, will the craftsman who made the nib sign the certificate allowing us to sell you this pen.

Be civil to all; sociable to many; familiar with few.

Benjamin Franklin

Buy the Parker Premier and even if you never write anything magnificent, at least you will never write anything but magnificently.

✦ **PARKER**

For the stores near you which carry Parker Premier pens, call toll-free 1-800-356-7007. Or write The Parker Pen Company, P.O. Box 5100, Dept. P, Janesville, WI 53547. © 1983 TPPC.

**Consumer Magazine
Less than One Page
B/W or Color
Single**

17 GOLD
ART DIRECTOR
Cathi Mooney
WRITER
Jamie Shevell
PHOTOGRAPHER
Hashi
CLIENT
Mrs. Paul's
AGENCY
Scali, McCabe, Sloves

18 SILVER
ART DIRECTOR
Dan Olson
WRITER
Greg Edien
PHOTOGRAPHER
Gerald Brimacombe
CLIENT
Minnesota Office of Tourism
AGENCY
Colle & McVoy Advertising/
Minneapolis

© 1984 Mrs. Paul's Kitchens, Inc.

An ingredient not found in most other frozen onion rings.

Mrs. Paul's® is the only major brand of onion rings that uses real, whole sliced onions. The others are made from onions that have been ground up, extruded and molded to look like onion rings.

And unlike these other brands, Mrs. Paul's contains no artificial additives.

So every time you bite into a Mrs. Paul's onion ring, you get nothing but real, delicious onion taste.

And Mrs. Paul's onion rings go great with anything from hamburgers and hot dogs, to steak and chicken. Or just as a snack.

So use the coupon and pick up a box. You'll see for yourself how good the real thing tastes.

Mrs. Paul's
It tastes good
because it is good.

17 GOLD

**Consumer Magazine
Less than One Page
B/W or Color
Campaign**

19 GOLD
ART DIRECTOR
Diane Melnick
WRITER
Irwin Warren
CLIENT
Volkswagen
AGENCY
Doyle Dane Bernbach

19 GOLD

It'll feel better in a Volkswagen.

Why? Because every Volkswagen is built to perform in a country where some roads are unblemished macadam masterpieces allowing unlimited speed, and others are little more than 18th Century goat paths.

Nothing else is a Volkswagen.

Seatbelts save lives.

It'll feel better in a Volkswagen.

Why? Because every Volkswagen is built for high speed performance so there is much more directional control engineered into a Volkswagen than in a conventional car.

Nothing else is a Volkswagen.

Seatbelts save lives.

**Consumer Magazine
Less than One Page
B/W or Color
Campaign**

20 SILVER
ART DIRECTORS
John Chepelsky
Joe Kravec
WRITERS
Chuck Husak
Joe Palmo
John Dymun
PHOTOGRAPHERS
Carol Hughes
David Clark
CLIENT
Gulf Oil/National Geographic
AGENCY
Ketchum Advertising/
Pittsburgh

Trade
Black and White
Page or Spread

21 GOLD
ART DIRECTOR
Don Perkins
WRITER
Bob Gardner
PHOTOGRAPHER
Jim Krantz
CLIENT
Petersen Manufacturing
AGENCY
Bozell & Jacobs/Omaha

22 SILVER
ART DIRECTOR
Ervin Jue
WRITER
Mike Rogers
CLIENT
Porsche + Audi
AGENCY
Doyle Dane Bernbach

21 GOLD

Nobody's perfect.

1983 Le Mans results

1st Porsche
2nd Porsche
3rd Porsche
4th Porsche
5th Porsche
6th Porsche
7th Porsche
8th Porsche
9th Sauber/BMW
10th Porsche

There's no tougher endurance race than Le Mans. Over 3,000 punishing miles in 24 hours at speeds often in excess of 200 mph. Last year, Porsche took the first five places. This year, the first eight. Next year, who knows? There's always room for improvement. Even at Porsche. **PORSCHE + AUDI**
© 1983 Porsche Audi   NOTHING EVEN COMES CLOSE

**Trade
Color Page or Spread**

23 GOLD
ART DIRECTOR
Alan Lerner

WRITER
David Miller

PHOTOGRAPHER
Micky Moulton

CLIENT
Ogilvy & Mather

AGENCY
Ogilvy & Mather/London

24 SILVER
ART DIRECTOR
Mark Erwin

WRITER
Jeffrey Epstein

PHOTOGRAPHER
Phil Mazzurco

CLIENT
Nikon

AGENCY
Scali, McCabe, Sloves

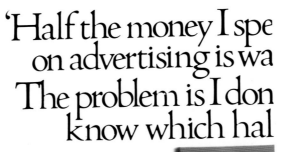

'Half the money I spe
on advertising is wa
The problem is I don
know which hal

23 GOLD

Buy a Nikon lens or FG camera and get these beautiful wallet-size portraits.

The Nikon FG/Lens Rebate.

From May 1 through August 15, 1983, Nikon is giving cash rebates* of $35 on the Programmed FG and up to $40 on some of our most popular lenses.

The Programmed FG is Nikon's most versatile SLR with programmed, automatic, manual and through-the-lens flash metering capabilities. And whether you've been saving for a

	Rebate
Programmed FG Camera	$35
Nikkor 24mm f2.8 wide angle lens	$25
Nikkor 28mm f2.8 wide angle lens	$25
Nikkor 55mm f2.8 micro lens	$20
Nikkor 105mm f2.5 telephoto lens	$25
Nikkor 80-200mm f4 zoom lens	$40
Series E 36-72mm f3.5 zoom lens	$25
Series E 70-210mm f4 zoom lens	$40

wide angle, micro, telephoto or zoom lens, Nikon's got a rebate just for you.

So for beautiful pictures you'll treasure, in your album and in your wallet, there's never been a better time to buy a Nikon. See your participating Nikon dealer for details.

We take the world's greatest pictures.™

*Only on products which include Nikon Inc.'s limited U.S.A. warranty form and are sold by Nikon Inc. in the U.S., U.S. Virgin Islands and Puerto Rico.

Trade
Less than One Page
B/W or Color
Single

25 GOLD
ART DIRECTOR, WRITER
& DESIGNER
Tom McManus
PHOTOGRAPHER
Kiki Bridges
CLIENT
Tom McManus

26 SILVER
ART DIRECTOR
Vincent Ansaldi
WRITER
James Parry
CLIENT
Reader's Digest
AGENCY
Posey, Parry & Quest/
Connecticut

KIKI BRIDGES

HOW LONG CAN THIS MAN GO WITHOUT A DEODORANT?

I'm Tom McManus and after working hard at Needham, Harper, & Steers Advertising as an art director for more than three years, I'm ready for a deodorant. I would also like to work on a bottle of scotch, sink my teeth into some lipstick or get my hands on some dog food.

So, if you're looking for an art director who can not only use his hands but who can also come up with fresh concepts, call 675-0612 and ask for my portfolio. In it you can see award winning ads for Amtrak, Bacardi, Campbell and Xerox.

I might work up a sweat working for you, but you could end up smelling like a rose.

MC MANUS
He can make you look good.

25 GOLD

"I may be one of the few people in the world who has seen a canary given an enema."

So says the secretary to the remarkable, diminutive — five-foot-four, 100 pounds — Dr. Gus Eckstein (1890-1981), expert on animal behavior.

In an original article in the June Reader's Digest, Eckstein's secretary recounts her boss's work with birds, mice, cockroaches, etc. — and his magnetic personality that attracted such notables as Sinclair Lewis, Aldous Huxley, Thornton Wilder, Garson Kanin and Helen Hayes (who, walking into Eckstein's lab, had her mink coat attacked by frenzied canaries).

Eckstein "drew people to him by his intensity" — which is how The Digest" draws 39 million readers.

**Trade
Any Size
B/W or Color
Campaign**

27 GOLD

ART DIRECTOR
Susan Picking

WRITER
Michael Scardino

DESIGNER
Susan Picking

PHOTOGRAPHER
Jerry Cailor

CLIENT
Federal Express

AGENCY
Ally & Gargano

$81.20

$83.55

THERE'S AN ENORMOUS DIFFERENCE BETWEEN FEDERAL EXPRESS AND UPS.

AND IT DEFINITELY ISN'T PRICE.

Actually, price may be the only area where there's any remote similarity.

If you send out a couple of shipments like the above once or twice a week (or as few as one or two packages per day) by UPS 2nd Day Air, we have a pleasant surprise for you.

In most cases, you can use Federal Express Standard Air™ Service for the same price or even less. There, all similarities end.

For while UPS' delivery usually takes at least two days, Federal Express Standard Air schedules delivery on the basis of a two-day *maximum.* In reality, most deliveries are overnight.

And Federal Express has COSMOS tracking, the most

advanced electronic tracking system in the business. So you can locate your shipment in seconds with a phone call, instead of the days or weeks it can take with UPS. It's one of the reasons we've got a record for reliability that's unmatched in the business.

In fact, Federal Express Standard Air gives you just about all the deluxe features you get with all our overnight package and document services. And none of which you get with UPS 2nd Day Air, for just about the same money.

Features like same-day, on-call pickup. Simplified multiple shipment manifests. Itemized proof of performance billing and discounts that accrue against *all* the Federal Express services you use.

So it's easy to see how Federal Express can be the cornerstone of all your important shipping plans, whether they call for premium, first-in overnight delivery (before 10:30 AM to thousands of communities) or economical one- to two-day delivery.

To find out how to get Standard Air Service discounted rates, contact your local Federal Express Sales Representative or call us at 800-238-5355. Or you can send in the coupon to the right.

You'll find that the differences between Federal Express and UPS are even more enormous than you may have thought. Except, of course, when it comes to money.

For a free comparison of Federal Express Standard Air™ versus UPS 2nd Day Air, send to: Standard Air Service Information Center, Federal Express Corp., P.O. Box 727, Memphis, TN 38194-4221

Name _____ Title _____

Company _____

Address _____

City _____ State _____ Zip _____

Telephone # _____ Account # (if any) _____

Estimated number of 2-day air packages per week _____

FEDERAL EXPRESS

Monday through Friday. Saturday delivery and service for Alaska and Hawaii not available with Standard Air™ Service. Puerto Rico available at an additional service charge. Areas served, delivery times, and liability subject to limitations in the Federal Express Service Guide. ©1983 Federal Express Corporation.

TH GOOD 'S IS DERAL EX RESS NOW CARRIES UP TO 125 POUNDS.
THE BAD NEWS IS YOU CAN'T SEND YOURSELF.

IT'S VERY INEXPENSIVE.

Federal Express now delivers packages up to 125 lbs. overnight by 10:30 A.M.* to thousands of communities nationwide. At prices so low you might be tempted to hop in a box and ship yourself. Well, you can't.

But you can save up to $257.55 on a 125-lb. package compared to what Emery is asking. And up to $106.30 compared to Airborne. And since we've eliminated out-of-delivery-area surcharges, your package can go virtually anywhere in the 48 states* for one low price. Even less with our volume discounts.

You can ship any number of Priority 1 heavy packages you like at one time, or drop them off at a Federal Express Convenience Center near you. For very large numbers of heavy packages, give us a call and we'll coordinate a special pickup for you. Even Saturday for Monday delivery.

IT CAN BE EVEN MORE INEXPENSIVE.

If you have to ship something heavy but aren't in such a rush, you can save even more money, using Federal Express Standard Air service for reliable 1 to 2 day delivery. In most cases, your package will arrive overnight. That's faster service at lower rates than you pay with most air freight forwarders.

So if you've got your old kit bag all packed up for a cheap trip out to the coast, we're sorry to disappoint you.

But if you've got up to 125 lbs. of troubles you have to get rid of overnight, now you can call Federal Express and smile, smile, smile.

*Monday through Friday as designated in the Federal Express Service Guide.
Saturday pick up and delivery available at an additional service charge.
Alaska, Hawaii and Puerto Rico service available for a modest surcharge.
Areas served, delivery times, and liability subject to limitations in the
Federal Express Service Guide. Call (800) 238-5355 for any additional information.
© 1983 Federal Express Corporation.

FEDERAL EXPRESS
WHY FOOL AROUND WITH ANYONE ELSE?

"By 10:30 AM? Are you kidding?"

"We'll have it traced by next week."

"On strike."

"What discount?"

"We don't go there."

"We go there but it costs extra."

"Proof of delivery costs extra."

"Pickup is extra."

NOBODY ACCEPTS EXCUSES FROM YOU, WHY SHOULD YOU ACCEPT THEM FROM SOMEBODY ELSE?

Excuses, excuses, excuses. They're everywhere. They get better all the time.

It seems like everybody but you gets to use them.

If you're tired of one standard of performance for you and another for the people you depend on, call Federal Express.

We defined new performance standards for the entire industry. When other companies offered speed, we delivered overnight. When they offered overnight, we scheduled delivery by 10:30 A.M.*

We developed the world's most advanced electronic tracking system. A system which can actually find your package within minutes of your call. Other systems track only paperwork.

We can get your package to more places than any other air express company—more than 37,000, in fact. With a one-price-anywhere policy in the contiguous United States.

We offer simplified procedures and extra services like free automatic proof of performance for every package we carry. And we're constantly working to help you maximize cost efficiencies through a broad range of discounts.

All so we can be the one company you rely on when you simply can't accept any excuses.

Or when somebody can't accept any excuses from you.

FEDERAL EXPRESS
WHY FOOL AROUND WITH ANYONE ELSE?

*Monday through Friday in AA Primary service areas as designated in the Federal Express Service Guide. Service to areas outside the contiguous United States and Saturday delivery by special request, available at an additional service charge. Areas served, delivery times, and liability subject to limitations in the Federal Express Service Guide. © 1983 Federal Express Corporation.

**Trade
Any Size
B/W or Color
Campaign**

28 SILVER
ART DIRECTOR
Mark Fuller

WRITERS
Ed Jones
Allen Wimett

PHOTOGRAPHER
Ralph Holland

CLIENT
The First Colony Coffee
& Tea Company

AGENCY
Finnegan & Agee/
Virginia

Around Here, High Technology Means Having Your Roasters Up On The Top Floor.

We could probably stretch the facts a little and claim that First Colony has been in the forefront of the high technology revolution. After all, our efforts to bring our customers the finest coffees from around the world include the use of the most up-to-date communication systems. And now we've

got a computer hard at work tracking orders all the way from raw product to the retailer's shelf.

But to be perfectly honest, the way we handle the coffee beans themselves just hasn't changed much in four generations.

We still roast our coffees to the right color, not to a fixed amount

of time. Our quality control department still consists of an antique cupping table where we've taste tested our coffees since 1902.

And to guarantee freshness, we send our coffees right from the roaster to the loading dock for same-day shipment.

We'd be happy to change our

ways if customers ended up with a better product in the process. Bring on the laser roasters and electronic flavor analyzers if they'll make a Kenya AA smoother or a Hawaiian Kona richer.

In the meantime, you can be sure that the First Colony coffees

you sell your customers are made using the same methods that made us America's leading specialty coffee company. Every morning, Harvey Groome and his crew will be firing up our trusty old Jabez Burns roasting equipment on the fifth floor.

And until we find better methods or add another floor to our building, that's about as high as most of the technology around here is ever going to get.

The First Colony Coffee & Tea Company

The First Colony Coffee & Tea Company, Inc., Norfolk and San Francisco. Telephone toll-free 800-446-8555.

28 SILVER

Our Boss Spends A Lot Of Time Drinking His Troubles Away.

Stop by First Colony any time of the day, or even some evenings, and there's a good chance you'll find our president sitting down with a cup of coffee. Or two cups. Or half a dozen.

Gill Brockenbrough's got a problem that goes back four generations: how to make sure

nothing but the finest coffees carry the First Colony name. And he still solves that problem the way his ancestors did. By personally tasting samples of each and every candidate for the First Colony label.

From a practical standpoint, it would probably make sense

for the boss to spend a little less time testing coffees at our antique cupping table. The way our business has been growing, there are plenty of other things for him to do. But that's what made us America's leading specialty coffee company in the first place. A commitment to

fine coffees that runs generations deep.

Needless to say, the time Gill Brockenbrough spends testing coffees is not all drudgery. The world's best coffees regularly cross our cupping table on their way to our customers.

Rare Jamaica Blue Mountain. Rich Sumatra Mandheling. The pick of the East African crop—Tanzania Kilimanjaro and Kenya AA.

But even the most distinguished coffee varieties don't always live up to their names.

That's why the president of The First Colony Coffee & Tea Company still insists on drinking his troubles away.

It means you and your customers won't have to.

The First Colony Coffee & Tea Company®

The First Colony Coffee & Tea Company, Inc., Norfolk and San Francisco. Telephone toll-free 800-446-8555.

The Day Our Coffees Reach Drinking Age, We Make Them Leave Home.

And around here our coffees are ready to leave home at a tender age indeed.

Because we know the very thing that improves the flavor of fine wines—aging—has exactly the opposite effect on specialty coffees.

So we ship our gourmet coffees the same day they're roasted. We make sure you get the freshest possible product no matter where you live by roasting at both our East and West Coast plants. We're the only roaster to do so.

Of course, getting a rare Celebes Kalossi or a richly flavored Swiss Chocolate Almond to you quickly is meaningless if it isn't of the highest quality in the first place.

At First Colony, we import only select high-grown coffees from the Carribean, Central and South

America, Africa, Asia and the Middle East.

Then we roast them to just the right color, to the peak of flavorful perfection. And we still taste test every coffee we sell at the same cupping table

our family has used for four generations.

We also work with you on an individual basis to help control your stock, assuring a fresher product and better inventory management.

The First Colony Coffee & Tea Company. Every day we create the finest coffees the world has to offer. Only to leave them homeless.

The First Colony Coffee & Tea Company®

The First Colony Coffee & Tea Company, Inc., Norfolk and San Francisco. Telephone toll-free (800) 446-8555.

**Collateral
Brochures
Other than by mail**

29 GOLD
ART DIRECTOR
Phil Atkinson

WRITER
Alan Wooding

CLIENT
Doyle Dane Bernbach

AGENCY
Doyle Dane Bernbach/
Australia

30 SILVER
ART DIRECTOR
Brooke Kenney

WRITER
Mike Dodge

DESIGNERS
Brooke Kenney
Mike Dodge

ARTIST
Edward Sorel

CLIENT
Robins, Zelle, Larson
& Kaplan

AGENCY
Dodge & Kenney/
Minneapolis

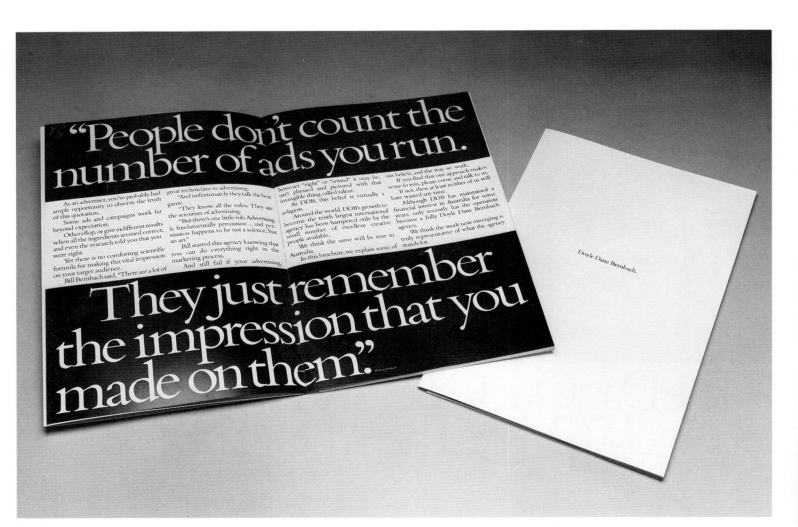

OVER THE YEARS, LAW FIRMS TEND TO GO SOFT.

THIS IS NOT THE TIME FOR THE OLD BOY, OLD SCHOOL, OLD POL APPROACH TO LAW.

The practice of law can be a lovely way of life. It offers a talented and concerned person the opportunity to do a great deal of good in the world.

It also offers the temptation to indulge one's self at the expense of one's ideals. After all, with the right connections and the ability to sound suitably erudite, an attorney can dress exceedingly well. And still have plenty of time for lunch.

Unfortunately, if one's existence is too comfortable for too long, a certain complacency is bound to set in. This happens to individual attorneys. It also happens to entire law firms.

Mind you, this complacency doesn't necessarily diminish a firm's profits. (The legalistic society of ours provides plenty of routine work for lawyers to charge for.) It does, however, diminish a firm's ability to initiate aggressive and innovative action on behalf of its clients.

And this brings us with almost unknowerly haste to our main point. In time, we believe, to inject a new concept into the lawyer-client relationship.

OK, the concept itself is not new at all. It's something people in business and industry deal with every day. You just don't hear lawyers talk about it.

The concept is productivity: the notion that your lawyers should be at least as productive on your behalf as anybody else would have working for you.

There was a time when one might tolerate a pricey paper-shuffling and an exquisite squint or two at the fine print. But those days are gone.

Today, par-one legal counsel can cost you money you can ill afford to squander. The good news is that productive counsel can save you money. We'll be suggesting how this can be done in the pages ahead.

PREVENTATIVE LAW. OR, THE ONLY THING BETTER THAN WINNING IS NOT HAVING TO FIGHT AT ALL.

We're in danger of blowing our image here. You see, although Robins, Zelle, Larson & Kaplan practices law in nearly all its many and wondrous forms, we are best known as litigators.

Indeed, facing Robins, Zelle in court is a little like encountering Genghis Khan on the steppes. To be sure, we are fair, honorable and often courteous. But we are relentless in pursuit of a winning judgment.

Now suddenly the same folks who love to jump up and shout "I object!" are championing an approach to the law, the sole purpose of which is to keep you as far from the courtroom as possible.

If we are to be truly productive on behalf of our clients, we can do no less. And the aggressive practice of preventive law could be one of the best innovations we've made. From our clients' viewpoint and our own.

Preventive law is based upon the realization that within any organization there are potential sources of litigation lurking about like so many smoking time-bombs. The trick is to discover and defuse them before they go off.

There are essentially two ways to do this. One is by employing a technique called the legal audit. At your request, we can survey your situation in order to alert you to your degree of legal exposure and then recommend remedial measures. Having done this, we can continue to monitor the situation to keep the level of exposure from rising.

The other primary technique of preventive law is education. We can conduct seminars and develop programs to make employers more sensitive to potentially litigious situations and learn how best to avoid them.

Our services cover every aspect of preventive law—product liability, insurance and anti-trust compliance—and can be customized for a particular organization. There are other things we can do to help hold the line on legal costs.

Judicious use of paralegals is one thing we can do. Using a combination of partners and associates can also help. There are times when we will undertake work on a contingency basis. Our regional offices can help reduce travel and service costs. We can establish periodic fee-review procedures.

Underlying all this is a distinctive Robins-Zelle quality. It's a willingness to leave the sanctuary of the office, to go beyond the formal procedures of the profession and get involved in the nitty-gritty of a client's business in order to make a real contribution to its success.

Preventive law is not very dramatic. You'd have trouble selling a television series based on the adventures of a hard-working lawyer who spent a lot of time keeping his clients out of court. But the long-term implications for a client-balance sheet are positively thrilling.

There are times when you need to fight, when it would be wrong not to. And there are times when you should do whatever is necessary to avoid litigation. We offer our clients the ability to do either, and the wisdom to know the difference.

AN ATTORNEY'S ABILITY IS NOT NECESSARILY COMMENSURATE WITH THE SIZE OF HIS EGO.

The legal profession has nurtured more than its share of oversize self-images.

It's actually kind of funny when you think about it. What could be more ludicrous than the sight of someone who spent the day finessing a few contracts tending the earth like Clarence Darrow reborn?

We don't cotton to that kind of behavior at Robins, Zelle, Larson & Kaplan. It simply doesn't mesh with the way we practice law.

Our approach is not so much lawyer-centered as it is client-centered. We don't want our people humming away generating legal documents in a vacuum. Each client's business exists in a specific environment in which many things, including legal action, occur. We expect our people to understand that environment intimately.

This means that a Robins-Zelle attorney has to have the wisdom—and the humility—to learn the client's business. And learn it in considerable depth. We give our people every encouragement to acquire this degree of knowledge and insight.

Even in the courtroom, a presumed haven for egomaniacs, we've found that meticulous preparation by a well-integrated team is far more effective than the posturings of an alleged superstar. A major reason for our success in litigation is the ability of our people to work together.

The way we recruit young lawyers is consistent with this point of view. We'll pass up a brilliant student if we have reason to believe he or she is overly competitive or otherwise deficient as a human being. Fortunately, there are some very bright people who are also blessed with the character it takes to practice law in the real world. We've been able to bring a number of them into the firm each year.

We also make sure our associates and partners remember how work is done at Robins-Zelle. All our lawyers have their files reviewed periodically, by other members of the firm. No one, not even the most senior person, is exempt from this invigorating process.

At Robins-Zelle we have a great many gifted people. They've won huge settlements for clients, spearheaded landmark cases and generally been on the cutting edge of the law. But each is expected to function within the bounds of an attitude which can be summarized thusly.

In the lawyer-client relationship, it should always be clear which is which. And, though arrogance and genius are often confused, the confusion is likely to persist only in the minds of the arrogant.

**Collateral
Sales Kits**

31 GOLD
ART DIRECTOR
James Sebastian
DESIGNERS
James Sebastian
Michael McGinn
Jim Hinchee
Bill Walter
PHOTOGRAPHER
Bruce Wolf
CLIENT
Martex-West Point Pepperell
AGENCY
Designframe

32 SILVER
ART DIRECTOR
Pat Burnham
WRITER
Bill Miller
DESIGNER
Pat Burnham
ARTISTS
Bob Blewett
Karla Michels-Boyce
CLIENT
WFLD-TV
AGENCY
Fallon McElligott Rice/
Minneapolis

31 GOLD

**Collateral
Direct Mail**

33 GOLD
ART DIRECTOR
Diane Cook Tench
WRITER
Andy Ellis
DESIGNER
Diane Cook Tench
CLIENT
Advertising Club of Richmond
AGENCY
Siddall, Matus & Coughter/
Virginia

34 SILVER
ART DIRECTOR
Houman Pirdavari
WRITER
Marc Deschenes
DESIGNER
Houman Pirdavari
CLIENT
Marc Deschenes

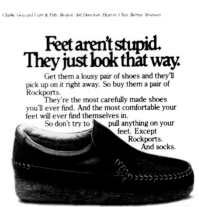

**Outdoor
Campaign**

39 GOLD
ART DIRECTOR
Tony LaPetri
WRITER
George Adels
CLIENT
Pace University
AGENCY
McCann-Erickson

39 GOLD

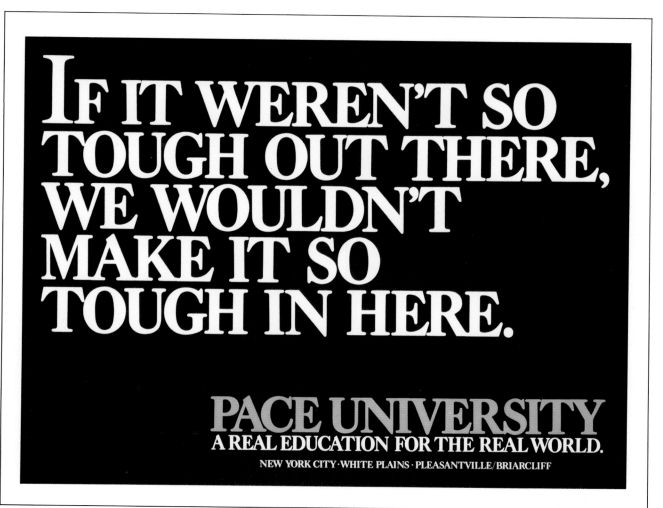

**Outdoor
Campaign**

40 SILVER
ART DIRECTOR
Bob Barrie
WRITER
Jim Newcombe
PHOTOGRAPHER
Bob Barrie
CLIENT
Minneapolis Library
AGENCY
Advertising Au Gratin/
Minneapolis

40 SILVER

How To Steal Books From The Library.

Used Library Books For Sale.
The Friends Bookshop/Minneapolis Library/300 Nicollet Mall

Book Prices So Good, You Can't Put Them Down.

Used Library Books For Sale.
The Friends Bookshop/Minneapolis Library/300 Nicollet Mall

**Public Service
Newspaper or Magazine
Single**

41 GOLD
ART DIRECTOR
John Morrison
WRITER
Jarl Olsen
DESIGNER
John Morrison
CLIENT
Projects With Industry
AGENCY
Fallon McElligott Rice/
Minneapolis

42 SILVER
ART DIRECTOR
Richard Brown
WRITERS
Roger Levinsohn
John Van den Houten
DESIGNER
Richard Brown
PHOTOGRAPHER
Tony Garcia
CLIENT
Herpes Information Council
AGENCY
Richard Brown Associates

41 GOLD

IS THERE SEX AFTER HERPES?

That's a question a lot of people have been afraid to ask themselves lately.

DON'T BE AFRAID TO ASK:

It's also exactly the question one shouldn't be afraid to ask the Herpes Information Council.

We can explain that the answer is enough information to allow you to turn those questions into decisions. Decisions only you can make.

IS IT SAFE TO HAVE SEX?

With herpes, when is it safe to have sex? Can a condom offer protection from the disease? If a woman with herpes is pregnant, how can she protect her unborn child?

And just how long can the virus live on a towel —or a toilet seat?

Only the Herpes Information Council can give you the answer.

NO TRUE CURE:

The truth, there is no true cure. Because herpes lasts a lifetime.

In fact, the only real protection you have against herpes is information.

LOOKING FOR AN ANSWER:

The Herpes Information Council can't give you a simple answer.

But if you write to us at 348 Howland Avenue, River Edge, New Jersey 07661, we can give you enough information to enable you to make the decision a simple one.

And find out everything you always wanted to know about herpes but were afraid to ask.

HERPES.
TILL DEATH DO YOU PART.

Gold & Silver Awards

Public Service Outdoor Campaign

47 GOLD
ART DIRECTOR
Mark Haumersen
WRITER
Lyle Wedemeyer
PHOTOGRAPHERS
Jim Arndt
Kent Severson
Ibid
CLIENT
Minnesota Poison Control
AGENCY
Martin/Williams - Minneapolis

TODAY, JOEY IS FIXING HIS OWN LUNCH. COOKIES AND DRAIN CLEANER.

To a small child, even bad things can look good enough to eat or drink. It's up to you to keep them out of reach.

MINNESOTA POISON CONTROL SYSTEM
TWIN CITIES: 221-2113. MINNESOTA: 1-800-222-1222.

47 GOLD

IF YOU WERE TWO YEARS OLD, COULD YOU TELL THE DIFFERENCE?

When a young child doesn't know a good drink from a bad one, it's up to you to keep the bad ones out of reach.

MINNESOTA POISON CONTROL SYSTEM
TWIN CITIES: 221-2113. MINNESOTA: 1-800-222-1222.

POISONS ARE EASY TO SWALLOW. BUT THE CONSEQUENCES AREN'T.

Don't find yourself regretting a preventable child poisoning later. Keep poisons out of reach now.

MINNESOTA POISON CONTROL SYSTEM
TWIN CITIES: 221-2113. MINNESOTA: 1-800-222-1222.

Gold
&
Silver
Awards

**Public Service
Outdoor Campaign**

48 SILVER
ART DIRECTOR
Rob Dalton
WRITER
Emily Scott
DESIGNER
Rob Dalton
CLIENT
3M
AGENCY
Martin/Williams - Minneapolis

IF YOU'VE GOT A RESPIRATOR, WEAR IT. IF YOU DON'T, GET ONE.

WEAR THIS AND YOUR WHOLE FAMILY WILL BREATHE EASIER.

Occupational Health and Safety Products Division/3M

3M

48 SILVER

IF YOU'VE GOT SAFETY GLOVES, WEAR THEM. IF YOU DON'T, GET SOME.

10 GOOD REASONS TO WEAR YOUR SAFETY GLOVES.

Occupational Health and Safety Products Division/3M

3M

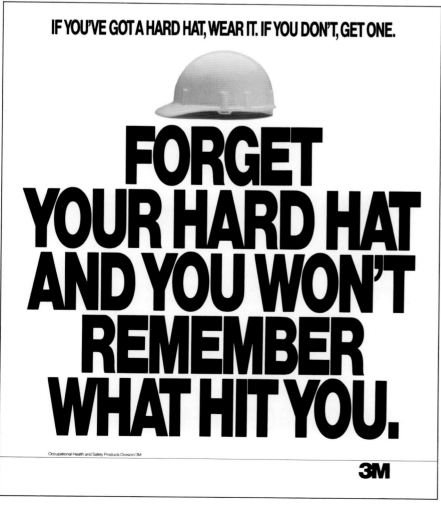

IF YOU'VE GOT A HARD HAT, WEAR IT. IF YOU DON'T, GET ONE.

FORGET YOUR HARD HAT AND YOU WON'T REMEMBER WHAT HIT YOU.

Occupational Health and Safety Products Division/3M

3M

TO APPLY FOR ONE IN AMERICA, YOU GIVE UP YOUR LUNCH HOUR.

IF YOU'RE A SOVIET JEW, YOU GIVE UP YOUR JOB.

Some people think that life is so bad for Jews in Russia that when they apply for emigration, they have nothing to lose.

On the contrary.

They have everything in the world to lose. Jobs, family, security, even freedom. If a Soviet Jew protests too loudly, he'll go to prison. Where he can be alone with his "aberrant" thoughts.

In every case, the Soviets have been clever at making the emigration process a crushing experience. Maybe they'll free a husband, and not his wife. Maybe they'll insist that a young Soviet fulfill his military obligation first. Then decide he knows too many military secrets to leave.

Academics are stripped of titles. Workers are deprived of work. Students are denied entrance to universities. Sounds familiar, doesn't it.

In 1971, the whole world applauded when the first wave of Soviet emigration began.

No one is cheering now.

Last year, only 2688 Jews were chosen people. Last month, just 125 were allowed to leave. The bars on the graph get smaller every year. At this rate of emigration, it will take 1000 years to free them all.

But a curious thing is happening.

Soviet Refuseniks, so named because their appeals are rejected so frequently, refuse to be daunted. They are even more determined to live free as Jews than their government is to prevent them.

So they wait.

And while they wait, they quietly and joyously observe the Jewish holidays. Which is officially discouraged.

They teach Hebrew to their children. Which is banned.

And while the movement out of Russia has virtually ground to a halt, the movement inside is alive and kicking back.

The International Conference on Soviet Jewry is meeting in Jerusalem this week. We'll try to find solutions there. We're running this advertisement to keep you aware of the facts. If you would, please spread them around. Because the more people you tell, the more people will know.

Maybe public outrage can put an end to this madness.

REFUSE TO FORGET THEM.

Use drugs and you, too, can have a monument built in your name.

There are only two ways to learn about drugs. With a clear mind. Or no mind at all.
Tonight at 7:00, turn your channel and your mind to WTCN for a 90 minute documentary titled "Don't Be A Dope."
John Bachman hosts a sobering look at the ups and downs of drug abuse in Minnesota.

NewsCenter 11
WATCH "DON'T BE A DOPE." TONIGHT AT 7 PM.

50 GOLD

CHIAT/DAY IS LOOKING FOR TWO GREAT ACCOUNT EXECUTIVES. WE'RE ALSO LOOKING FOR A UNICORN, THE TREASURE OF SIERRA MADRE AND THE HOLY GRAIL.

We know good AE's really do exist. We actually have a few around here already.

If you have two years experience, some on financial accounts, or five years experience, some on automotive/motorcycle accounts, write (don't call) Barbara Stolar, Chiat/Day, 517 So. Olive Street, Los Angeles, California 90013.

CHIAT/DAY

51 SILVER

WILL IT COME TO THIS?

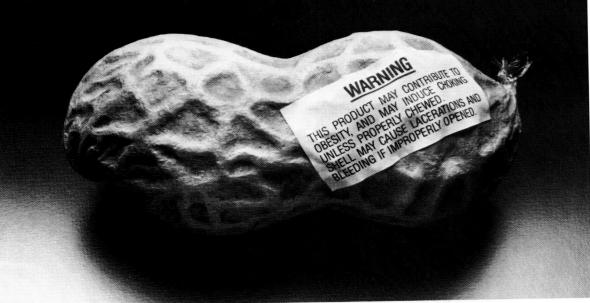

WARNING
THIS PRODUCT MAY CONTRIBUTE TO
OBESITY, AND MAY INDUCE CHOKING
UNLESS PROPERLY CHEWED.
SHELL MAY CAUSE LACERATIONS AND
BLEEDING IF IMPROPERLY OPENED.

Warnings have come a long way since someone had the good sense to put a ☠ on an iodine bottle.

Courts now require warning labels on a whole range of products.

From paint thinner to pajamas.

There have also been rulings on exactly how large such labels should be. And where they should be.

And what they should say.

And it hasn't stopped at labeling, either.

Requirements relating to all aspects of product safety have mushroomed in recent years.

And while these have been a benefit to consumers, they've often been a problem for manufacturers.

Because even a responsible corporation can face liability by unintentionally overlooking a new regulation or an obscure ruling.

That's why at INA, a CIGNA company, we're prepared to do more than just insure our clients against product liability.

We do everything we can to keep them out of court.

To start with, we have a staff of product liability specialists who can examine every step

in the manufacturing and marketing process.

From product design to advertising.

And we're not only likely to spot weaknesses people within a company may overlook, we're also more likely to spot weaknesses general and less specialized loss control examiners might overlook, as well.

We even look for problems before they occur.

We'll help design a product recall program, for example, to have in place, ready to quickly implement if the need for it ever arises.

And, needless to say, on an ongoing basis, we monitor legislation, court rulings, and agency regulations that can affect our client's liability.

If you'd like more information on this topic, please write to INA at 1600 Arch Street, Dept. RA, Philadelphia, Pennsylvania 19101.

Or, if you'd like to know how we can help protect you against product liability exposures, call your agent or broker.

After all, in an area as complicated as this it's entirely possible a consumer isn't the only one who can benefit from a warning.

NOT ALL CORPORATE TAKEOVERS ARE THE RESULT OF WINNING A PROXY FIGHT.

In some places in this world, business people have to worry about losing more than money.

They have to worry about losing their businesses.

To terrorists. Or guerrillas.

Or even governments.

Because a business is just as likely to be lost to a piece of paper as it is to a machine gun.

In fact, at least 25 governments in recent years have legally nationalized the property of foreign corporations in their countries.

And while there is little a business can do to prevent this, at INA, a CIGNA company, we've been a leader in the development of insurance to protect corporations against these kinds of losses.

Our political risk program covers everything from outright seizure of a plant, to the freezing of assets in a foreign bank.

We also offer protection against a variety of other losses that are less dramatic, but equally feasible in a currently unstable political environment. Or in one that suddenly becomes unstable.

We can, for example, cover a company for the losses resulting from an unexpected revocation of an import license.

Or for losses resulting from a government's sudden refusal to pay a supplier for goods he supplied.

We can even insure losses incurred when one country slaps an embargo on another.

And we can usually process claims for these losses in a surprisingly short period of time.

Because with representatives in 140 countries around the world we're never far from a client's problem.

If you'd like more information on the topic of political risk write to Indemnity Insurance Company of North America, 1600 Arch St., Dept. RB, Phila., PA 19101.

Or if you'd like to know how we can specifically address your need for this kind of insurance call your agent or broker.

Because it is unfortunately true that in today's world there is more to learn about doing business overseas than just the language.

IN AMERICA THE ARCHITECTS WOULD STILL BE LIABLE FOR IT.

They might be hard to find.

But they could be liable.

Because in most states architects can be sued for the work they did no matter how long ago they did it.

And so can engineers.

So if a roof falls in or a floor gives out, they, or their firms, or even their estates, can be brought to court over something built 50 years ago.

Or 150 years ago.

In fact, even if a roof doesn't fall in, architects and engineers can still be involved in a suit.

After a crime in a suburban mall, for example, an architectural firm was actually sued for designing a shopping center that was "conducive to kidnapping."

And if that seems absurd, consider this: an engineer was called in as a consultant on a problem limited to the roof at the Hyatt Hotel in Kansas City. He was later sued for failing to notice structural weakness in the skywalk that collapsed there.

The point of all this is that the threat of professional liability is not only real, but growing.

Which is why, at Insurance Company of North America, a CIGNA company, we have a special division dealing exclusively with this risk.

And we'll not only insure architects and engineers for claims made against them while they're our clients, we can even cover their liability for work they did before coming to us.

We'll also provide protection after they retire.

And, maybe most important, we'll do everything we can to help them reduce their likelihood of being sued in the first place.

With seminars and manuals specifically on that topic.

And with a highly specialized in-house claim staff that may well know more about the fine points of design liability than any other group in the business.

If you're interested in this subject and would like more information, write to INA at 1600 Arch Street, Dept. RC, Philadelphia, Pa. 19101.

Or if you're an architect or engineer and would like to discuss your specific situation, please call your agent or broker.

After all, you never know when something might go wrong.

**Corporate
Outdoor Single**

54 SILVER
ART DIRECTOR
Gary Johns
WRITER
Jeff Gorman
PHOTOGRAPHER
Carl Furuta
CLIENT
Nike
AGENCY
Chiat/Day - Los Angeles

**Corporate
Outdoor Campaign**

55 SILVER
ART DIRECTOR
Houman Pirdavari
WRITER
Brent Bouchez
PHOTOGRAPHER
Focus On Sports
CLIENT
Nike
AGENCY
Chiat/Day - Los Angeles

54 SILVER

55 SILVER

**Student Competition
High School**

56 GOLD
ART DIRECTOR & WRITER
Marc McGowan
CLIENT
New York State Returnable
Container Law
SCHOOL
O.F.A. High School/
Ogdensburg, NY

57 SILVER
ART DIRECTORS
Ken Safford
Dan Copeland
WRITERS
Pat Zintel
Mark Popp
CLIENT
New York State Returnable
Container Law
SCHOOL
Perry Central/Perry, NY

GET THE KNACK.

BRING'EM BACK.

Throwing away beer and soda empties is like throwing away money! Look for the New York deposit label on beverage bottles and cans, then return the empties to any store that sells the same brand, type and size and get your deposit back!

CASHING IN EMPTIES MAKES GOOD CENTS.

56 GOLD

For further information on the New York State Returnable Container Law.
Call (212) 267-9800

**Student Competition
College**

58 GOLD
ART DIRECTOR & WRITER
Henry Popp

CLIENT
Manufacturer of
Running Shoes

SCHOOL
East Texas State University/
Texas

Introducing the first running shoe designed to finish last.

When the soles of your running shoes wear out, the shoes are finished. History. And so is the hard-earned money you spent for them.

We developed the Miles running shoe to reach the finish last. Because for us, it isn't enough for a running shoe to look and feel great; it has to be able to last a long, long time.

A while back, the engineers at Miles made a major technological breakthrough that greatly enhanced the durability of our running shoes. It enabled us to produce a shoe capable of lasting well over six thousand miles without major tread wear.

Six thousand miles is a lot of real estate. It's 24,000 trips around the track. Or New York to Buenos Aires. Or almost a quarter of the footwork the average person does in a lifetime.

No other running shoe even comes close.

And the Miles running shoe gets you there in both comfort and style. Our actual shoe design is the result of an intensive five-year research program conducted at major University athletic departments across the country.

But meeting the demands of serious athletes doesn't mean sacrificing looks. With dozens of styles and colors to choose from the Miles running shoe looks just as good running around town as it does running around the track.

So if you're going to pay a premium price for a running shoe, make sure you come out ahead in the long run. Step into a pair of Miles.

A good shoe should always finish last.

miles
more runner for your money

Only one running shoe in the world can do this over five million times.

Ayear or so from now, the running shoes you're wearing probably won't be doing much running. They'll either be collecting dust in the bottom of a closet, or will have made that trip to wherever worn out running shoes go.

It doesn't have to be that way.

At Miles, we believe a running shoe should not only look and feel great, it should last a long, long time.

Several years back, the engineers at Miles made a major technological breakthrough that greatly enhanced the durability of our running shoes. It enables us to produce a shoe capable of lasting well over six thousand miles.

Six thousand miles are a lot of footsteps. At a yard per stride, it takes 10,560,000 steps to cover that much ground. For a pair of running shoes to do it, each shoe has to hit the ground over five million times.

No shoe but Miles can do it.

But for a shoe to stay on your foot that long, it has to be mighty comfortable. Miles takes comfort in stride. An extensive five year research program at major Universities across the country enabled college athletes to tell us what they looked for in a shoe. They told us that a shoe should fit accurately to hold up on the curves, but should flex in a sprint to maximize the efficiency of each stride. We incorporated these ideas into the Miles running shoe. The re-

sult: a running shoe that will go the distance while reducing foot fatigue.

You'd think something that feels so good and lasts so long must look like some kind of orthopedic shoe, right? Wrong. Miles comes in a variety of styles and colors for both men and women. So you don't have to sacrifice aesthetics for performance.

So if you're going to pay a premium price for a pair of running shoes, make sure you come out ahead in the long run.

A journey of five million steps starts with your first Miles.

miles
more runner for your money

How an unknown runner wore out the UCLA track team.

The toughest runner the UCLA track team ever faced was not a man; it was a shoe. The Miles running shoe. And for fifteen weeks, it took everything a track team could dish out.

UCLA helped us test the Miles runner by participating in an extensive five year, nation-wide research program. The program was originally aimed at testing the endurance of this remarkable runner, though it ended up becoming more of a test for UCLA.

Fifteen track team members tried their best to wear out a single pair of Miles running shoes. Each took turns logging mileage, 8 hours a day, 5 days a week.

After 15 weeks, and over 6,000 miles, our runner was still in pretty good shape. But the UCLA athletes looked like they weren't going much farther.

We decided to end the test.

Now the Miles running shoe is available for everyone. Tests like the one at UCLA proved to us that our shoe is the most durable you can buy, at any price.

Miles comes in a variety of styles and colors for both men and women. But don't let the good looks fool you. Beneath that pretty veneer, there's a serious runner ready to wear you out.

more runner for your money

**Consumer Television
60 Seconds Campaign**

68 GOLD
ART DIRECTORS
Brent Thomas
Lee Clow
WRITER
Steve Hayden
CLIENT
Apple Computer
DIRECTOR
Adrian Lyne
PRODUCTION CO.
Jennie
AGENCY PRODUCER
Richard O'Neill
AGENCY
Chiat/Day - Los Angeles

68 GOLD

(SFX: SOLO CLARINET)

ANNCR (VO): Some business people don't have their
best ideas sitting at a desk.

(SFX: GUY MAKING NOTES.)

(SFX: MORE CLARINET.)

ANNCR (VO): At Apple, we understand that "business
as usual" isn't anymore. That's why we make the
most advanced personal computers in the world.
And why, soon, there'll be just two kinds of
people.
Those who use computers.
And those who use Apples.

ANNCR (VO): The way some business people spend
their time has very little to do with a clock.
At Apple, we understand that "business as
usual" isn't anymore. That's why we make the
most advanced personal computers in the
world.
And why, soon, there'll be just two kinds of
people.

GUY: Hi.

ANNCR (VO): Those who use computers...

GUY: Yeah. I'll be home for breakfast.

ANNCR (VO): and those who use Apples.

(MUSIC: THROUGHOUT)

ANNCR (VO): The three-martini lunch wasn't legislated out of existence. It died of natural causes.
At Apple, we understand that "business as usual" isn't anymore. That's why we make the most advanced personal computers in the world. And why, soon, there'll be just two kinds of people in business.
Those who use computers.
And those who use Apples.

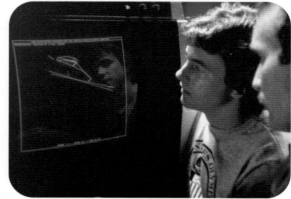

**Consumer Television
60 Seconds Campaign**

69 SILVER
ART DIRECTOR
Bob Steigelman
WRITER
Charlie Breen
CLIENT
Miller Brewing/
High Life
DIRECTOR
Don Guy
PRODUCTION CO.
Dennis, Guy & Hirsch
AGENCY PRODUCERS
Eric Steinhauser
Sally Smith
AGENCY
Backer & Spielvogel

69 SILVER

(MUSIC UNDER)

(SFX: CAR, ALLEY CAT)

ANNCR (VO): That kid's out there again
But he's not alone.
He's got a dream with him and every night
after work he chases that dream, the one that
says someday you're going to watch him run
400 meters faster than any other man in the
summer games.

(MUSIC UP)

In the past it probably would have been just
a dream but we have an Olympic training center
now in Colorado Springs
And he can go there and learn how to run faster
than he's ever run before.
So maybe he'll become as good as he believes he
can be.
And maybe one summer day when you're
watching the '84 games you just might
say... that kid's out there again.

(CHANT: USA... USA... USA)

ANNCR (VO): This American Dream was brought to
you by Miller High Life...
Sponsor of the U.S. Olympic Training Center

ANNCR (VO): They say it's not an American sport but
they forgot to tell him.
Because he's got a dream that says one day the
world's going to watch him jump farther than
any other man in the winter games.
In the past it probably would have been just a
dream...
But we have an Olympic Training Center now in
Colorado Springs and he can go there and find
out what he's doing right, what he's doing
wrong, and how to fly off a mountainside
farther than he's ever flown before.
So maybe it's not just a dream.
And maybe, on a winter day in 1984...

(CHANT UNDER: USA, USA, USA)

VO: They'll stop saying "It's not an American Sport."
This American dream was brought to you by
Miller High Life...
The sponsor of the U.S. Olympic Training
Center.

(SFX: STREET NOISES)

1ST GUY: Hey, hey here he comes, Tiny...

2ND GUY: Yes, here he is ladies and gentlemen, the up and coming...

ANNCR: One inch farther that's how far he wants to throw it today.
And tomorrow an inch farther than that.
Because he's got a dream that says some day he's gonna throw that 16 lb piece of iron farther...

SHOT PUTTER (VO): Ugh.

ANNCR: than any other man in the summer games.

1ST GUY: You're not gonna win any gold medals doin' that, man.

2ND GUY: Shh, Shh

(MUSIC UP)

ANNCR: In the past it probably would have been just a dream but today he just might become as good as he believes he can be...

SHOT PUTTER (VO): Ugh.

ANNCR: Because today he can go to the U.S. Olympic Training Center in Colorado Springs. And maybe on a summer day in 1984...
He'll go up against the best in the world and he'll throw it...one inch farther.

(CHANT UNDER: USA, USA, USA)

ANNCR: This American Dream was brought to you by Miller High Life...
The sponsor of the U.S. Olympic Training Center.

**Consumer Television
30 Seconds Single**

70 GOLD
ART DIRECTOR
Rich Martel
WRITER
Al Merrin
CLIENT
Pepsi Cola/Diet Pepsi
DIRECTOR
Steve Horn
PRODUCTION CO.
Steve Horn Productions
AGENCY PRODUCER
Gene Lofaro
AGENCY
BBDO

71 SILVER
ART DIRECTOR
Dennis Hearfield
WRITER
Greg Alder
CLIENT
Pepsi Cola/Diet Pepsi
DIRECTOR
Patrick Russell
PRODUCTION CO.
The Film Business
AGENCY PRODUCER
Jan Smith
AGENCY
John Clemenger Pty./
Australia

70 GOLD

SINGER: *Sip into something
      irresistible.
      Sip into Diet Pepsi.
      Sip into something
      irresistible.
      Sip into Diet Pepsi.
      Put your lips
      to that Pepsi taste.
      Sip into that
      one calorie waist.
      Sip into
      something
      irresistible.
      Sip into Diet Pepsi.*

71 SILVER

*Now you see it
Now you don't
Here you have it
Here you won't
Oh, Diet Pepsi!
One small calorie
Now you see it,
Now you don't.
That great Pepsi taste.
Diet Pepsi won't go to
your waist.
So now you see it
Now you don't
Oh, Diet Pepsi!
One small calorie
Now you see it
Now you don't.*

**Consumer Television
10 Seconds Campaign**

76 GOLD
ART DIRECTOR
Michael Tesch
WRITER
Patrick Kelly
CLIENT
Federal Express
DIRECTOR
Patrick Kelly
PRODUCTION CO.
Kelly Pictures
AGENCY PRODUCER
Maureen Kearns
AGENCY
Ally & Gargano

76 GOLD

GUY CRYING (OC): I'm sorry, Mr. Dinger, they told me
    they'd get the package there by tomorrow, Mr.
    Dinger
    and I believed them,
    and they made me look bad, Mr. Dinger...
ANNCR (VO): Next time, send it Federal Express.

(SFX: MAN FRANTIC, GOING THROUGH YELLOW PAGES)

ANNCR (VO): If you had a package that *absolutely,
    positively*
    had to be somewhere overnight... who would
    you call?

(SILENT)

SECRETARY: Mr. Lemming, Mr. Lemming, the
package is here.
They used Federal Express.
Wait.

(SFX: TRAFFIC)

ANNCR (VO): Federal Express.
Why fool around with anyone else?

**Public Service
Television Single**

78 GOLD
ART DIRECTOR
Doug Lew
WRITER
Bob Thacker
CLIENT
Minneapolis Institute of Arts
DIRECTOR
Charles Diercks
PRODUCTION CO.
Teleproducers
AGENCY
Chuck Ruhr Advertising/
Minneapolis

79 SILVER
ART DIRECTOR
Wayne Gibson
WRITERS
Kerry Feuerman
Bill Westbrook
CLIENT
Medical College of Virginia
DIRECTOR
Cliff Schwander
PRODUCTION CO.
Thomz Productions
AGENCY PRODUCER
Betsey Barnum
AGENCY
Westbrook/Virginia

78 GOLD

(MUSIC THROUGHOUT)

ANNCR (VO): American Gothic by Grant Wood. No other painting in the world has been so plagiarized.
Now that you've seen all the rip-offs, come see the original.
The Grant Wood Show at the Minneapolis Institute of Arts.

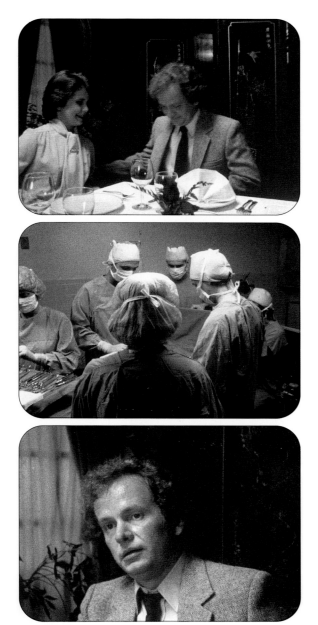

79 SILVER

ANNCR: This man is 20 minutes away from a major heart attack. He's completely unprepared for it. But we've been preparing for this moment for over 20 years. In 1968 doctors at the Medical College of Virginia Hospitals performed America's second heart transplant. In 1979 we learned how to clear blocked arteries without open heart surgery. Now we're teaching this procedure to other doctors at other hospitals.

Last year, MCV was one of the first hospitals in the country to use enzymes to limit the damage of heart attacks.

WOMAN: Are you O.K.?

MAN: Yea... I'll be fine.

ANNCR: And now we're doing research into the cause of heart disease. And how to detect its early warning signs. For information on heart disease call our health line. Don't put off another second.

Presented as a public service by the Medical College of Virginia Foundation.

The Gold Award Winners on The Gold Award Winners

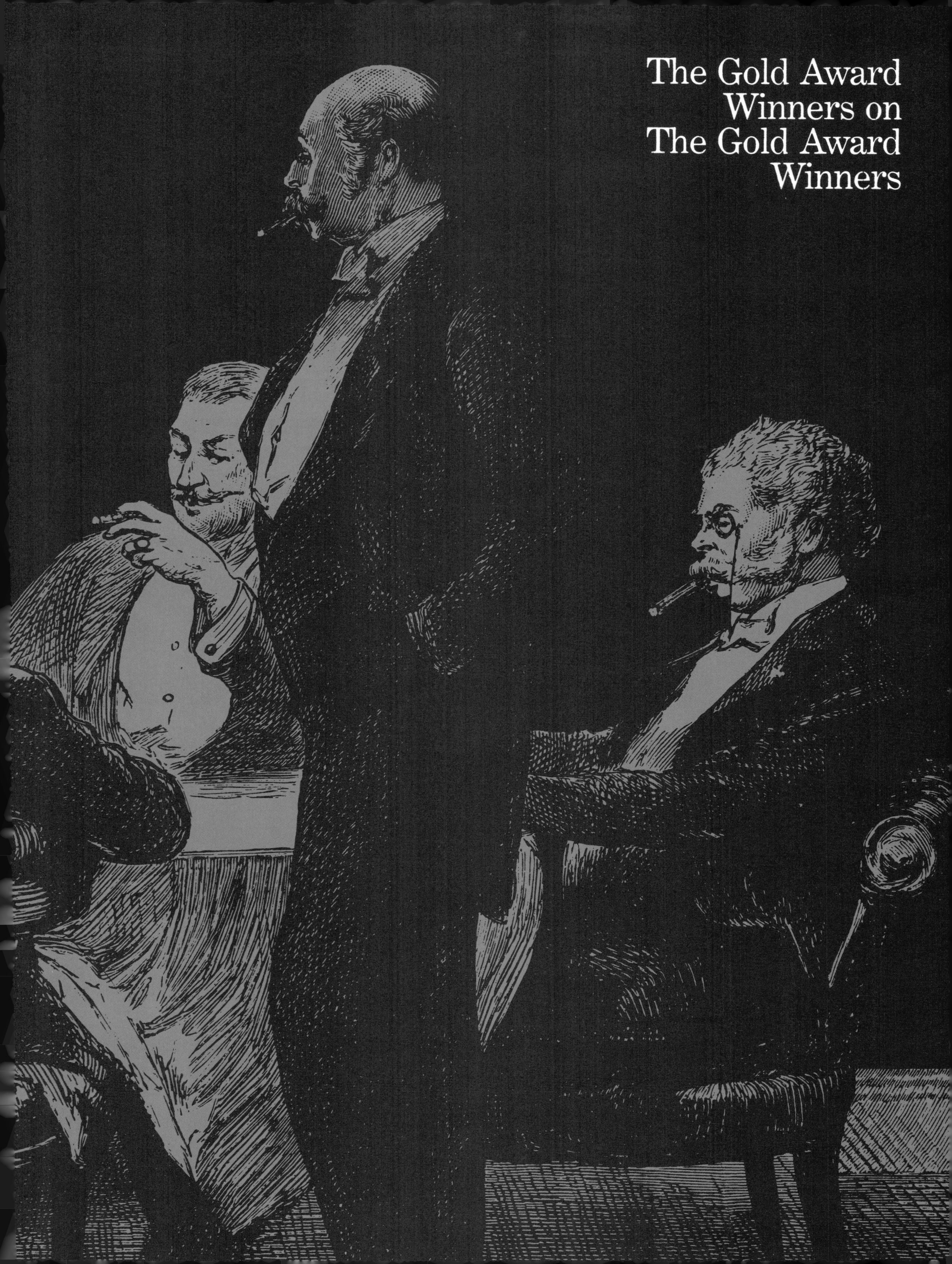

The Gold Award Winners on The Gold Award Winners

AGENCY: Lowe Howard–Spink Campbell-Ewald/ London
CLIENT: Albany Life Assurance

We upholstered the chair on the left in Colefax and Fowler semi–glazed linen, pattern no. 75B/39 (discontinued), with ruched valancing all round.

The chair on the right is a 450V 3-phase model, fully earthed and fitted with a 30-amp fuse. For use in England a separate adaptor is required.

PS. Glad you liked the ad.

Adrian Holmes
Andy Lawson

1 GOLD

In advertising, truth is stronger than fiction.

"Jogger" is Allen Kay's story. "Exercycle" is Lois Korey's story. "Names" is practically everyone's story.

And none of these stories are just stories.

Allen Kay
Lois Korey

How to turn your exercise cycle into something useful.

You told everyone it was the muggers. And the lousy weather. And all that traffic. Of course you wanted to exercise, but New York is not the place to run. Or even to ride.

So you went out and bought an exercise bike and set it up at home. That was the most exercise you ever got from it.

The excuses range from: "I have no time." "It's too much trouble." "I keep forgetting."

The only thing you can't blame are the muggers.

The trouble is you know muscles should be exercised. And the most important muscle to exercise is your heart.

That's where we come in.

We knew what we were doing when we called ourselves Cardio-Fitness. We offer individualized programs for men and women designed to strengthen your heart and lungs.

To reduce your weight and lower your pulse rate and blood pressure. To increase your physical and mental endurance.

A program of safe exercises done under professional guidance. We review your progress constantly, always setting new goals for you. All this takes place in a modern, attractive environment.

Which may be why we boast over 100 chief executive officers. Corporate memberships which include, American Express, Equitable Life, First Boston Corporation, Time Inc., J. Walter Thompson, and Sperry. And many individual members as well.

One reason why over 90% of our members renew is that we make it so easy.

No gym bag to lug around. We supply the fresh shorts, shirts and socks daily. You come at your convenience. There's never a wait. You're in and out in less than an hour.

As for your bike, you could always turn it into a nifty lamp table. A chrome spinning wheel. Or a sculpture labeled simply, "Unused Bicycle, circa 1983."

For more information call:

Cardio-Fitness Center

Midtown: 345 Park Avenue, entrance on 52nd Street, (212) 838-4570.
1221 Avenue of the Americas, McGraw-Hill Bldg. at Rockefeller Center, (212) 840-8240.
Wall Street Area: 79 Maiden Lane, (212) 943-1510.

3 GOLD

MARTY: This ad was the result of a Herculean mental struggle. Here we have a classic case study of two artists triumphing through sheer force of will over adversity.

TIM: To conceive this ad, we dug down deeper into our souls than one would have thought possible.

MARTY: People ridiculed our efforts. They tried to suppress us. We were clearly onto something new and revolutionary, and it frightened them.

TIM: It took five months for me to find a photographer with the necessary boldness and vision to do the job. And the shoot itself took three weeks, working straight through without sleep.

MARTY: I slaved over the body copy for *five and a half months*. You can still see the blood stains on my typewriter keys.

TIM: But it was all worth it.

MARTY: Since winning the Gold Award, Tim and I have each been offered numerous presidencies of major international agencies.

TIM: But we turned them all down. So we could stay here in the trenches—turning out the work—the work schoolchildren will be studying in literature and art classes... CENTURIES from now.

Marty Kaufman
Tim Delaney

"I NEVER CUT CORNERS TO SAVE MONEY ON MY CHICKENS. BUT YOU CAN."

Frank Perdue

SAVE 25¢ ON A FRESH PERDUE WHOLE BROILER.

STORE COUPON

25¢

5 GOLD

**Consumer Newspaper
600 Lines or Less
Campaign**

AGENCY: Posey, Parry & Quest
CLIENT: Reader's Digest

Everybody knows Reader's Digest for its heart-warming stories about loyal pets rescuing families from burning homes. Everybody is half wrong; as one of our favorite rejected headlines said of The Digest, "Just because we publish in Pleasantville doesn't mean everything we publish is pleasant."

This campaign—of six new ads every month—is designed to be as pleasant as cynical and wiseass humor can make it. All to show that The Digest can be enjoyably read even by people as sophisticated as you.

*Jim Parry
Vince Ansaldi*

You can't buy a Congressman for $5000. But you can rent him.

By law, an individual PAC (political action committee) can donate only $5000 to a candidate's primary and general election campaign. But that's plenty. Says Rep. Thomas Downey (D., N.Y.), "You can't buy a Congressman for $5000, but you can buy his vote on a particular issue."

An original article in the July Reader's Digest examines how the millions of PAC dollars *have* influenced particular legislation and how "the best Congress money can buy" could *reform* campaign financing.

For 39 million readers, the best reporting their money can buy is in The Digest."

Reader's Digest

7 GOLD

**Consumer Magazine
Black and White
Page or Spread
Including Magazine
Supplements**

AGENCY: Fallon McElligott Rice
CLIENT: ITT Life

A long photo shoot like this takes a lot out of everybody.

*Dean Hanson
Tom EcElligott*

HOW MUCH WEIGHT DO YOU HAVE TO LOSE BEFORE YOUR INSURANCE COMPANY NOTICES IT?

9 GOLD

**Consumer Magazine
Color Page or Spread
Including Magazine
Supplements**

AGENCY: Chiat/Day-Los Angeles
CLIENT: Apple Computer

We seem to do a lot of headlines and TV ideas for
Apple that have to age in wood for a while before
they're actually used.

This line goes back to 1982, when we really
didn't have the technology to live up to the promise.

But then along came Lisa, the first personal
computer with enough raw power to run a small
multinational conglomerate. And this headline
found a home.

It also reflects another direction we'd been
working in. While everybody was selling computers
on the basis of how many parts numbers they
could remember, we felt there was something
almost sexy about having this much power on your
desk—and that, in today's world, a computer can be
as much of a personal statement as a sports car.

We really thought Porsche would be a better car
to use, but it didn't work with the line. "Think of it
as a Porsche for your pate?"

Mike Moser
Steve Hayden
Brian O'Neill

11 GOLD

**Consumer Magazine
Black and White
Campaign Including
Magazine Supplements**

AGENCY: Grey Advertising
CLIENT: Danskin

Just goes to show you,
some of the best thinking—is done in cabs.
Michael Wolf
Anita Madeira

13 GOLD

The Gold Award Winners on The Gold Award Winners

**Consumer Magazine
Color Campaign
Including Magazine
Supplements**

AGENCY: Ammirati & Puris
CLIENT: BMW of North America

At up to $40,000 each, BMW's obviously aren't for everyone.

It's also obvious that BMW advertising has to position the cars accordingly. The tricky part is doing so without the kind of empty self-

**Consumer Magazine
Less Than One Page
B/W or Color
Single**

AGENCY: Scali, McCabe, Sloves
CLIENT: Mrs. Paul's

Writing this ad was hard. But not nearly as hard as writing an explanation of how we wrote this ad. Before, we were just an ordinary creative team. Now that we're gold award winners, the pressure to come up with a witty and incredibly brilliant

The Gold Award Winners on The Gold Award Winners

**Trade
Less Than One Page
B/W or Color
Single**

CLIENT: Tom McManus

Aren't you tired of hearing that clients ultimately get what they deserve?

This client certainly isn't.

Thank you.

Tom McManus

**Trade
Any Size
B/W or Color
Campaign**

AGENCY: Ally & Gargano
CLIENT: Federal Express

It isn't easy to follow the Fast Talking Man.

Especially in print.

You can't count on Evelyn Wood graduates to read the message.

You can't cut from scene to scene. Or speed up the action.

You pretty much have to tell it straight.

Fortunately, with the right client, straight is enough.

*Susan Picking
Mike Scardino*

I'm Tom McManus and after working hard at Needham, Harper, & Steers Advertising as an art director for more than three years, I'm ready for a deodorant. I would also like to work on a bottle of scotch, sink my teeth into some lipstick or get my hands on some dog food.

So, if you're looking for an art director who can not only use his hands but who can also come up with fresh concepts, call 675-0612 and ask for my portfolio. In it you can see award winning ads for Amtrak, Bacardi, Campbell and Xerox.

I might work up a sweat

working for you, but you could end up smelling like a rose.

MC MANUS
He can make you look good.

25 GOLD

27 GOLD

**Collateral
Brochures
Other than by Mail**

AGENCY: Doyle Dane Bernbach/Australia
CLIENT: Doyle Dane Bernbach/Australia

Who could possibly know better than Bill Bernbach, what DDB stands for?

In a series of exquisitely economical quotes Bill managed to say everything we've ever felt or believed about advertising.

Here in the Sydney office we use his sayings as daily reminders to clients and ourselves, of what we should be doing.

Really, it was Bill who did this brochure.

We just collected the award for him.

*Phil Atkinson
Alan Wooding*

29 GOLD

**Collateral
Sales Kits**

AGENCY: Designframe
CLIENT: Martex-West Point Pepperell

We are pleased that the *Perry Ellis* book has been chosen by The One Club for Art and Copy. Although written copy is not a key part of the book, the story is told through a 48-page leather bound book of color photography. Instead of words, it is the environmental, product and architectural details and a warm sense of lighting that set the mood. The *Perry Ellis* book was a labor of love accomplished by a very special team of client, designers, photographer, printer and binder, and we are very proud of the result.

James A. Sebastian

31 GOLD

The
Gold
Award
Winners on
The Gold
Award
Winners

**Collateral
Direct Mail**

AGENCY: Siddal, Matus & Coughter
CLIENT: Advertising Club of Richmond

Our assignment was to inform Richmond Ad Club members that Mr. McElligott would be speaking at the November meeting. His secretary was kind enough to send us a two pound deposition documenting one remarkable career. We looked through it again and again, trying to come up with a single fact, achievement or ad that immediately "read" Tom McElligott.

Finally, we asked ourselves, "If McElligott had to come to work at 9 o'clock one morning and concept this piece, what would he do?" That was about the time Diane, who fortunately lived in Minneapolis awhile, joked, "I doubt he's in his office by 9. It probably takes him till noon to shovel the snow out of his driveway."

We had our concept.

*Diane Cook Tench
Andy Ellis*

33 GOLD

**Collateral
P.O.P.**

AGENCY: Ammirati & Puris
CLIENT: Sony Corporation

At first we didn't know what to think.

We liked the ad, but why? It did have a certain charm. After all, ducks are inherently cute.

But it also seemed to have a combination of logic and whimsey that was compelling.

Even so, we did our best to ignore it. Since the thing wouldn't go away, we finally presented it, thinking we'd have a dead duck on our hands, so to speak.

We were obviously wrong. Everything went okay. Except for the columnist who claimed we glued the duck to the floor. Which is totally untrue. The duck gave us his complete cooperation, and was a pleasure to work with.

*Richard Pels
Gordon Bennett*

35 GOLD

Outdoor
Single

AGENCY: Fallon McElligot Rice
CLIENT: Vander Zanden

When most people look back on speeches they've given, what they remember is the glory. The applause. The brief taste of celebrity-hood.

In short, the moments after the speech has ended.

What people tend to forget is the abject horror of those few moments before the speech has begun. The sweaty palms. The cotton-mouth. The animal urge to bolt and flee.

All we did was remind them.

Tom McElligott
Dean Hanson

There Are Two Times In Life When You're Totally Alone. Just Before You Die. And Just Before You Make A Speech.

VANDER ZANDEN, INC.
Executive Speechmaking And Storytelling.

37 GOLD

Outdoor
Campaign

AGENCY: McCann-Erickson
CLIENT: Pace University

When I was a kid growing up in New York, Pace was no University.

It was an Institute.

You went there after you graduated high school to learn how to type and take shorthand if you were a girl. And if your were a guy, to learn accounting or drafting or how to pass the various civil service exams the city gave every year.

In other words, you went there to learn how to make a living. Kind of important to many of us in those days because many of our fathers weren't.

Pace has come a long way with the rest of us since.

It is now a University with 5 campuses around the metropolitan area and many of its graduates have gone on to become Captains of Industry or at least to rank high in middle management.

It prepares its students not only for the blue and white collar skills but also in thousands of business and professional disciplines.

But when you come right down to it, what it still prepares you for in New York is to make a living.

A real education for the real world.

Tony and I came from this background and it's what we tried to get across in our subway and outdoor posters.

And if we earned gold for it, we worked for it.

George Adels
Tony LaPetri

YOUR CAREER STARTS THE DAY SCHOOL STARTS.

PACE UNIVERSITY
A REAL EDUCATION FOR THE REAL WORLD.
NEW YORK CITY · WHITE PLAINS · PLEASANTVILLE · BRIARCLIFF

39 GOLD

**Public Service
Newpaper or Magazine
Single**

AGENCY: Fallon McElligott Rice
CLIENT: Projects With Industry

**Public Service
Newpaper or Magazine
Campaign**

AGENCY: Fallon McElligott Rice
CLIENT: The Episcopal Ad Project

**Consumer Television
30 Seconds Single**

AGENCY: BBDO
CLIENT: Pepsico/Diet Pepsi

What is it with this commercial?

We knew it was good, but we weren't prepared for the response we got.

When Pepsi started receiving letters from all over the country, we were amazed. And when we won the One Show Gold Award, we were shocked. People—all kinds of people—truly love this commercial.

So we asked ourselves, "What made this commercial so successful?"

Was it the devilishly clever theme line? (The writer thought so). Was it the beautiful look? (The art director thought so). Was it due to the superlative groundwork laid by our producer, Gene Lofaro? Was it the seductive music written by Peter Cofield? Was it Steve Horn's stylish direction? Was it the seamless editing of Dennis Hayes? Was it the spirited, natural performances of the young actors and actresses? Was it luck?

Of course, all these things contributed to the eventual success of the commercial. But no single one was the key.

In the end, we agreed on what should have been obvious. We believe the reason the commercial was so appealing was because the situation is so human. Everyone can relate to the excitement of getting ready for a date or the anxiety of waiting for one.

We learned the simple truth. If you can somehow tap that common pool of shared human experience, you'll usually end up with a commercial that's well...irresistible.

*Al Merrin
Rich Martel*

**Consumer Television
30 Seconds Campaign**

AGENCY: Dancer-Fitzgerald-Sample
CLIENT: Wendy's

Wendy's had a very competitive story to tell...i.e., Wendy's uses fresh ground beef not frozen as McDonalds and Burger King do...i.e., at Wendy's you can get your hamburger fixed however you want without waiting extra time...i.e., at Wendy's you get special orders at the pick–up window without having to park your car and wait.

The stories were there. We just hadn't hit on a way to tell them. Then the writer came up with a set of short phrases ("Park It," "Step Aside," "Frozen Stiff," "Through the Mill") that seemed to express the experiences customers felt at those "other" hamburger places.

The director took the scripts virtually intact, added his visual magic, and the commercials sold product, got attention and, thank you very much, won awards.

The client liked success. And wanted more built around the fact that Wendy's "single" has more beef than the Whopper and the Big Mac.

First the writer wrote some what seemed like hilarious lines about "big fluffy buns" and a retort, "but where's the beef" and then Donna Weinheim the art director came up with "Home of the Big Bun" and then the director Joe Sedelmaier cast Clara Peller and then the producer Sue Scherl produced it and the rest is history.

*Donna Weinheim
Jean Govoni
Cliff Freeman*

72 GOLD

70 GOLD

**Consumer Television
10 Seconds Single**

AGENCY: Mendelsohn Advertising
CLIENT: Raging Waters Park

When this Raging Waters spot comes on TV the
viewer sees a simple little idea.

What he doesn't see is the 10,000 gallon water
truck pumping water into a 6,000 gallon holding
tank that's hooked up to a giant flumeway.

Nor does the viewer get to see the crew
frantically re-wallpapering the set, take after
take.

Or the actor sitting there trying to remain
perfectly motionless and blasé, knowing he's about
to get smashed with about 2,000 pound of ice–cold
water.

Most of all, he never gets to hear the endless
number of people telling you there's absolutely no
way you can pull off this simple little idea.

Jeff Gorman
Jordin Mendelsohn

74 GOLD

**Consumer Television
10 Seconds Campaign**

AGENCY: Ally & Gargano
CLIENT: Federal Express

We love doing 10 second spots.

There's just enough time to get across the *one*
meaningful thing that gives people a reason to use
Federal Express.

And not enough time to include all the
extraneous bullshit that "Research" always wants
you to stick in.

Mike Tesch
Patrick Kelly

76 GOLD

**Public Service
Television Single**

AGENCY: Chuck Ruhr Advertising
CLIENT: Minneapolis Institute of Arts

**Public Service
Television Campaign**

AGENCY: The Marschalk Company
CLIENT: NYC Department of Transportation

1984 Print Finalists

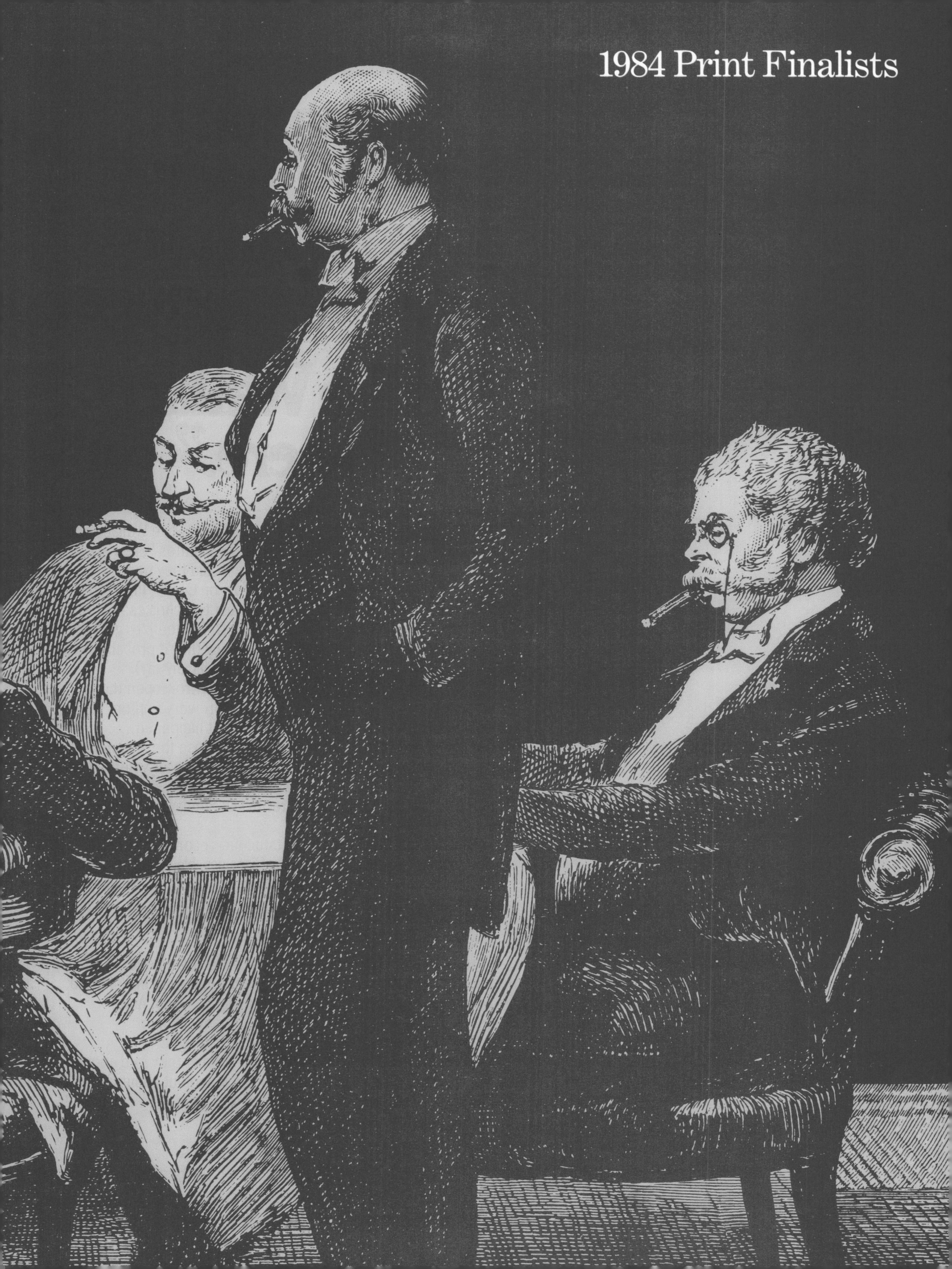

The four most dreaded words in the English language: "Mike Wallace is here."

It was a program that would interest anyone who likes good beer. And the truth.

When Mike Wallace and the "60 Minutes" crew showed up and said they wanted to do a story on Coors, I figured I had just two choices:

1. Tell them to go away (knowing they'd probably do a story on us anyway).

2. Throw open the entire brewery to them (and see what happened).

I chose the second course of action. I told Mike that he was free to go anywhere in our brewery and talk to anybody about anything.

If you saw the "60 Minutes" rerun last Sunday, you saw what happened.

You saw that Coors has an outstanding record for minority employment in many areas—including Hispanics, blacks and women.

You saw that every one of the hundreds of Coors employees polled by Mike Wallace denied the rumor that Coors pries into their personal lives. It's not surprising. We strongly believe in individuals' rights.

You saw that Coors employees enjoy abundant benefits. Because Coors is one of the highest paying employers in Colorado. We offer expansive health and medical programs, too. And programs to help employees continue their educations.

"60 Minutes" helped to set the record straight.

We didn't sponsor it. We had no say in what they said about us. But we think what Mike and his people found out about Coors is of interest to anyone who likes good beer.

And the truth.

**Consumer Newspaper
Over 600 Lines Single**

101
ART DIRECTORS
Ralph Ammirati
Jeff Vogt
WRITER
Tom Thomas
DESIGNERS
Anthony Angotti
Jeff Vogt
PHOTOGRAPHER
Dick James
CLIENT
BMW of North America
AGENCY
Ammirati & Puris

102
ART DIRECTOR
Andy Lawson
WRITER
Adrian Holmes
PHOTOGRAPHER
Jimmy Wormser
CLIENT
Albany Life Assurance
AGENCY
Lowe Howard-Spink
Campbell-Ewald/London

103
ART DIRECTOR
Peter Coutroulis
WRITER
Bill Stenton
PHOTOGRAPHER
Union Bank Library
CLIENT
Union Bank
AGENCY
BBDO/West - Los Angeles

104
ART DIRECTOR
Jordin Mendelsohn
WRITER
Perrin Lam
DESIGNER
Jordin Mendelsohn
ARTIST
John Dearstyne
CLIENT
Raging Waters Theme Park
AGENCY
Mendelsohn Advertising/
Los Angeles

PERHAPS YOUR LUXURY CAR WOULD PERFORM BETTER WITHOUT THE HEAVY BURDEN OF A HOOD ORNAMENT.

Over the years, expensive luxury sedans have been adorned by winged warriors, sylph-like maidens, and various other icons.

None of these have improved the performance of their cars; in fact, the evidence suggests the opposite.

A few ounces of chrome wouldn't seem capable of compromising several thousand pounds of car. But then, the burden isn't physical. It's far more serious than that.

It's philosophical.

THE BMW 733i: A DELIGHTFUL "ECCENTRICITY."

The BMW 733i is built on a belief that, by the standards of the conventional luxury car, verges on eccentricity.

BMW believes that superior performance, not ornamentation, is the only thing that makes an expensive sedan worth the money. It follows that the only architecture worth considering will be found not on the hood but in the inner recesses of engines and suspension systems.

The difference in theory becomes viscerally apparent at the first touch of the gas pedal—a gesture that produces demurral in some cars, but not the 733i. Its fuel-injected engine is designed for the heady response denied other luxury cars by their sheer heft and undernourished technology.

(One reason: Digital Motor Electronics, a microprocessor-based system that constantly analyzes the engine and orders ignition to occur at the precise instant for maximum performance.)

Unlike softly-sprung land yachts that wallow through turns, the 733i rides on a suspension that puts you in mind of racecourses rather than seaways.

That suspension is independent on all four wheels, with design breakthroughs both front and rear. And it provides an agility that left one automotive editor "amazed that we could pull so many G's around the curve with absolutely no lean or suggestion of protest" (Design News).

The 733i is also engineered to take the aiming out of driving. Its finely-calibrated steering system is precise and tactile, never denying the driver the information the road wants you to know.

DRIVING VS. PREENING.

This same philosophical bias, favoring driving over preening, is evident everywhere in the 733i's interior.

Its deep bucket seats, covered in rolls of supple leather, were designed by stylists who value fine upholstery but prize orthopedics; these seats are specially constructed to help reduce driver fatigue.

And since driving is largely a process of making and executing decisions, the 733i provides the information to decide wisely.

An Active Check/Control keeps an account of seven different measures of the car's operational readiness. An onboard computer provides all manner of useful data, including the distance remaining to your destination. There's even a Service Interval Indicator that analyzes how the car has been driven and informs you when routine service is needed.

All this is accompanied by AM/FM stereo, electrically-operated sunroof, and enough other amenities to earn Car and Driver's designation as "the height of refined elegance."

And it is protected accordingly, by BMW's 3-year/36,000-mile limited warranty and 6-year limited warranty against rust perforation.*

The 733i, in other words, does not ask you to spend a small fortune for the privilege of having your senses dulled. Which is why, as one automotive journalist observed, "test-driving the 733i is more a test of the driver than of the car."

If it's been some time since you've measured either your car or yourself, we invite you to visit the standard of comparison at a BMW dealer near you.

THE ULTIMATE DRIVING MACHINE.

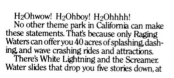

PHOTO COURTESY OF THE NEW YORK HISTORICAL SOCIETY

After spanning the East River for a hundred years the Brooklyn Bridge deserves a little support.

The Brooklyn Bridge is much more than a bridge that spans the East River. It spans too the 19th and 20th centuries. And since 1883 it has crossed between our practical and our aesthetic appreciations.

To celebrate the Bridge's centennial the Brooklyn Museum, sponsored by The Chase Manhattan Bank, has organized The Great East River Bridge Exhibition: a fascinating historical collection of interpretations of the Bridge in paintings, prints, photographs and drawings, which include the original, beautifully drafted engineering plans.

The Brooklyn Bridge's size, beauty and ingenuity made it a source of awe and inspiration in 1883. And it remains so today; an enriching part of New York and America's cultural heritage. So come and see The Great East River Bridge Exhibition at the Brooklyn Museum, which runs through June 19, 1983. A tribute to the Brooklyn Bridge, and mankind's creativity.

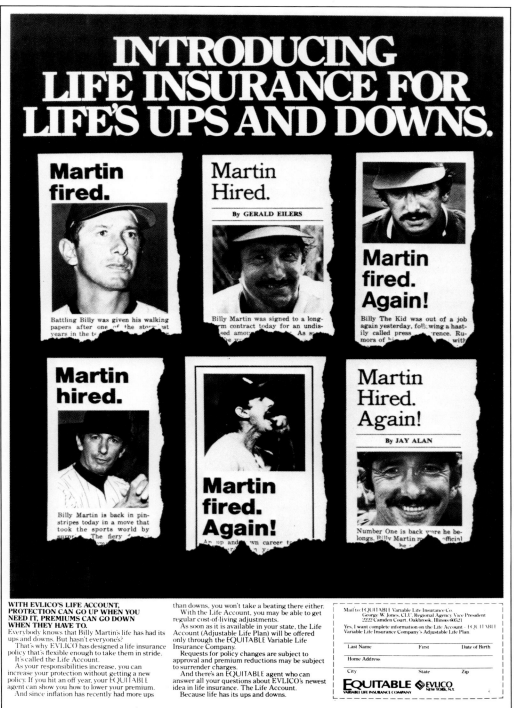

INTRODUCING THE ONLY THEME PARK WITH RIDES GUARANTEED TO MAKE YOU WET YOUR PANTS.

Nobody visits our new 40 acre park and leaves with dry pants. Nobody. Because at Raging Waters Park every ride and attraction is filled with fun and water.

There's White Lightning. The highest, fastest water slide this side of the Rockies. You'll drop an incredible five stories. And reach speeds up to 30 miles per hour.

And, once you've recovered from White Lightning, you're ready for the Screamer. Let's just say somebody riding it gave us the idea for the name.

Then there's Demon's Run, a slide that twists, turns, and snakes its way 430 feet down mountainous terrain before it lets you go. Talk about wetting your pants!

As if that's not enough, there's Wave Cove. A one acre body of fresh water that produces the finest three foot waves in the world. Imagine. The perfect wave every two seconds. Perfect for body surfing. And perfect for rafting.

For the younger kids there's the Lil' Dipper Pool. And for those past the daredevil age, there's pools to rest, relax and swim in.

Raging Waters. There's nothing like it in California. Hours are from 10 AM to 9 PM daily. And one admission price allows you to ride all day and night. Season passes are available.

So, if other rides at other parks leave you with dry pants, you need the excitement of Raging Waters.

Raging Waters
The most fun you can have with your swim suit on.

108

WATCH GOOD TV BY CHOICE. NOT CHANCE.

Until now, trying to find something good to watch on television was like playing a game of chance. Sometimes you did. Most times you didn't.

At The Entertainment Channel, we believe finding something good to watch should be as easy as turning on your TV. That's why we bring you intelligent, quality programming 24 hours a day. Every day.

Turn on The Entertainment Channel at any given time and you might see an exclusive Broadway show. Or an award winning foreign film. Or an original adaptation of a bestselling novel. And that's just for starters. Because we not only bring you great programming, we bring you a great variety of programming.

Like the best from British television, innovative family programming, first rate comedy specials and classic American movies you won't see anywhere else.

What's more, every program on The Entertainment Channel is shown the way it should be shown. Uncut and uninterrupted.

So if you think television could be better than it is, watch The Entertainment Channel. You'll spend less time switching. And more time watching.

THE ENTERTAINMENT CHANNEL

"POLLUTION? WHAT POLLUTION?"

Over ten years ago we declared total war on pollution. Are we winning? Or have we surrendered?

Tonight, Investigative Correspondent Arnold Diaz reports from some environmental danger zones that could be near you. See what pollution is doing to our water. Our land. Our air. And us. See how far we've come. And how much further we have to go.

A five-part Special Report, Monday through Friday.

"BEYOND THE GRAY HORIZON" CHANNEL 2 NEWS AT 6

If it concerns you, it concerns us.

HAVE AMERICANS SWITCHED THEIR POSITION ON SEX?

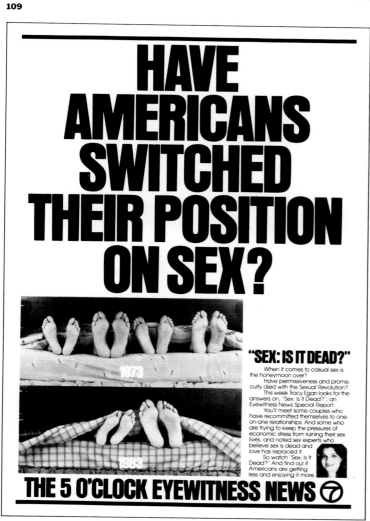

1973

1983

"SEX: IS IT DEAD?"

When it comes to casual sex is the honeymoon over?

Have permissiveness and promiscuity died with the Sexual Revolution? This week Tracy Egan looks for the answers on, "Sex: Is It Dead?", an Eyewitness News Special Report.

You'll meet some couples who have recommitted themselves to one-on-one relationships. And some who are trying to keep the pressures of economic stress from ruining their sex lives, and noted sex experts who believe sex is dead and love has replaced it.

So watch "Sex: Is It Dead?" And find out if Americans are getting less and enjoying it more.

THE 5 O'CLOCK EYEWITNESS NEWS 7

WE INTERRUPT THIS NEWSPAPER TO BRING YOU AN IMPORTANT TV ANNOUNCEMENT.

In the belief that the average television viewer is more intelligent than the average television show, we proudly present The Entertainment Channel.

The first cable network dedicated to bringing you intelligent, quality programming 24 hours a day. Every day.

Turn on The Entertainment Channel at any given time and you might see an exclusive Broadway show. Or an award winning foreign film. Or an original adaptation of a bestselling novel. And that's just for starters. Because we not only bring you great programming, we bring you a great variety of programming.

Like the best from British television, innovative family programming, first rate comedy specials and classic American movies you won't see anywhere else.

What's more, every program on The Entertainment Channel is shown the way it should be shown. Uncut and uninterrupted.

So now that you know about The Entertainment Channel, isn't it time you stopped reading this newspaper and started watching your television.

THE ENTERTAINMENT CHANNEL

113

114

Does Your Bank Give You Toasters When What You Really Need Is Answers?

At Minnesota Federal, we'd rather help you build a small fortune than a collection of small appliances.

And we do so by providing the answers you need to make the right banking decisions at the right time.

What's more, we believe in providing those answers in plain English. As opposed to banks whose explanations need explanations of their own.

That's why we've developed Plain Talk. A program that makes getting the information you need as simple as asking one of our people for it.

As a part of Plain Talk, we've trained our employees not just in money matters, but also in communications.

Which means that they know *how* to tell you about our services as well as *what* to tell you about them.

At the same time, we're rewriting our forms in the same plain English we speak.

So whether you're talking with one of our employees or filling out a loan application, you won't have to decipher any legalese, buzzwords and doubletalk.

We believe getting the services you need is much more profitable over the long term than premiums. And we think once you're our customer, you'll agree.

Because at Minnesota Federal, we're commited to helping you make a lot more than toast.

Minnesota Federal
The Plain Talk Bankers.

116
ART DIRECTOR
Roy Grace
WRITER
Irwin Warren
DESIGNER
Roy Grace
PHOTOGRAPHER
Ken Goldberg
CLIENT
Volkswagen
AGENCY
Doyle Dane Bernbach

117
ART DIRECTOR
Aki Seki
WRITER
Lee Garfinkel
ARTIST
Hank Syversion
CLIENT
The Entertainment Channel
AGENCY
Levine, Huntley, Schmidt
& Beaver

118
ART DIRECTOR
Paul Basile
WRITER
Joe Della Femina
CLIENT
WABC-TV
AGENCY
Della Femina, Travisano
& Partners

1975

Since 1975 we changed a few things on the Rabbit.

If you count every change made on the Rabbit since 1975, you'll arrive at a number just somewhere over 15,000.

Why so many?

Well, not because the Rabbit wasn't a good car to begin with because it was. (It is in fact the most copied car in the world.)

But our habit of starting with a revolutionary design and slowly modifying it toward perfection is a Volkswagen tradition dating back to the Beetle.

So while our competitors were busy playing catch-up, the engineers at Volkswagen were compiling a long list of firsts:

The first transverse mounted automatic transmission.

The first independent rear stabilizer axle.

The first passive restraint system.

The first CIS fuel-injected engine available in a sedan under $8,000.

The first diesel powered small car sold in America.

And so on and so forth.

Still with all the changes you probably noticed a similarity between the 1975 Rabbit in the upper left hand corner of the page and the 1983 Rabbit GTI in the lower right hand corner.

Well, this too is a VW tradition:

The more things change, the more they stay the same.

Nothing else is a Volkswagen.

© 1983 Volkswagen of America

Rabbit GTI. $7990. Mfr's sugg. retail price. Transp., tax, title, dealer prep add'l.

1983

117

118

Is your company small enough for an IBM computer?

If you've been hesitant to call IBM about a computer for your small business, the examples here may be reassuring.

As you can see, not one is a corporate giant.

Yet, surprising as it may seem, they're actually typical IBM customers.

Because, for every large computer we install, we install dozens of small ones to help run companies very much like yours.

Which makes us one of the largest suppliers of small systems in Australia.

You can buy an IBM small business computer for as little as $6,500.

So before you venture into computing, perhaps you should consider the advantages of doing it with us.

Small companies can't afford to get it wrong.

Unless you're experienced with computers, it's a daunting task sorting out what equipment is most appropriate.

You don't want to spend more than necessary.

But then, you don't want to find you've bought less capability than you need either.

The systems engineers at our IBM Customer Support Centres have the experience to analyse your business operation and then recommend an appropriate match of hardware and software for the job.

At the same time they can help you plan to accommodate your future growth.

And perhaps suggest ways a computer could help your business that you hadn't even considered.

Connecting with the Videotex information system for example.

Manufacturing control. Or managing security around your premises. Even reducing energy bills.

Then, when your system is installed, we don't forget you.

If you need help or advice, you can call the IBM Hot Line.

Or come into an IBM Customer Support Centre and work things out with us.

The one system where you shouldn't need any help at all is our smallest, the IBM Personal Computer.

It's designed so simply it can be set up entirely by you. But, just in case, your IBM PC dealer has been intensively trained to provide the advice, assistance and service you need.

More software to choose from.

Business people are now beginning to realise that software is just as important as the computer itself.

And because IBM computers are so widely used,

the amount of software written for our equipment is truly vast.

So whether you're in accountancy or zoology, you'll have a wide range of programs to choose from.

With a big range of sizes, you get a better fit.

IBM makes a wide range of computers that suit small businesses.

And within that range, literally hundreds of variations are possible, with different printers, added storage, and so on.

So we can provide equipment that's a more ideal match for the job.

And less of a compromise.

We answer 90% of service calls in two hours.

When a company is dependent on a computer, it's even more dependent on the company that services that computer.

IBM records show that we respond to 90% of our service calls within two hours of receiving them.

A visit isn't always necessary. We can often solve the problem by telephone.

Here today, here tomorrow.

IBM has been in business now for more than fifty years, and we plan to be in business a lot longer.

Which may be a comforting thought when you're about to make a major investment in your company's future.

If you're seriously considering a small business computer (or thinking of adding small computers to a larger system), please call us.

We'll be very happy to provide more information, or arrange for one of our representatives to call on you.

You'll find our people speak plain English, not 'Computerese'.

And they're interested in all kinds of businesses no matter how small.

Including yours.

For further information on IBM small business systems, please call your local IBM office, on any of the following numbers:

Sydney 234 5678, Melbourne 698 1234, Brisbane 3 8888, Perth 325 6666, Adelaide 274 7299, Canberra 80 8844, Darwin 80 5033, Hobart 23 3999.

IBM Australia Limited. (Inc. in N.S.W.)

THE REASON PEOPLE FIND IT HARD TO LIVE IN MINNESOTA HAS NOTHING TO DO WITH MOSQUITOES OR COLD WEATHER.

If you choose to live in Minnesota, you pay 184% (almost double) the national average in personal income taxes.

Minnesota ranks 18th in personal income per capita. But 4th in state individual income tax collections per capita. If you are a one wage earning family with an income of $15,000 to $50,000, you couldn't find a more expensive state for taxes.

Over the last few years, job growth in Minnesota has been below the national average. Our tax and spending environment is seriously compromising our competitive position in terms of economic growth and jobs. As a result, we are in danger of losing people, business and our stable tax base to other states.

Unlike mosquitos and cold weather, there is something you can do about this. Get out paper and pen. Or pick up your phone.

Ask your legislator to join Governor Perpich and repeal the 10% surtax immediately. Projections show that this surtax will put over 400 million dollars into the state coffers (which already includes a 250 million dollar reserve) that isn't really needed to balance this biennial budget. The state doesn't need it. You shouldn't have to pay it.

Also, insist that your legislator hold the line on additional spending for the current 1983-85 biennium. We believe that our needs can be met through smarter spending instead of higher taxes.

To find out how to contact your legislator, call (612) 296-6013.

END THE SURTAX NOW.

120

GUESS WHO'S COMING TO HARLEM.

Harlem has some of the most sought after real estate in the city.

Who's shopping for this prime property just north of Central Park? And why the sudden interest?

Join Carol Martin for this three-part Special Report. Beginning tonight.

◉2

"HARLEM FOR SALE?" CHANNEL 2 NEWS AT 11
If it concerns you, it concerns us.

121

A BRIEF HISTORY OF THE ALASKAN PACKAGE RUSH

Back in the good old days, if you lived in Anchorage and needed something in a hurry from New York, you might look for it in about a year.

Well, today, Federal Express will deliver important packages, documents and letters to you from virtually any place in the Lower 48 overnight. Or to just about any place down there in two days. Through a network of more than 19,000 locations.

All you have to do is pick up the nearest phone and say, "Hello, Federal". Federal Express will take care of the rest.

Federal Express also has COSMOS℠ tracking that can locate your shipment in seconds. And a 24-hour hot line that can tell you anything else you need to know just as fast.

All with a reputation of reliability that's unbeaten in the air express business.

Our rates are simple. One price anywhere, depending on weight (from 2 oz. to 70 lbs.). (Prices include a small additional charge of $5 on Overnight Letters℠ and COURIER PAK® Envelopes™ to and from Anchorage; $10 on larger packages.) Considering that our discounts accrue against all the Federal Express services you use, we can be very economical in the long run.

For more information, call us at 800-238-3064.

Hurry, please. Thar's gold in them thar packages.

1875 New York to Anchorage: 1 year

1915 Anchorage to New York: 2 months

1934 New York to Anchorage: 4 days

1983 Anchorage to New York: 2 days† New York to Anchorage: overnight*

FEDERAL EXPRESS

HOW MUCH OF YOUR COMPANY'S LONG DISTANCE BUDGET IS BEING USED TO TELL HONEYBUNS THAT HER SNOOKUMS LOVES HER VERY, VERY MUCH?

Love is patient. Love is kind. But when employees use company long-distance lines for personal calls, love is also expensive.

Until now, you couldn't know how expensive. But now there's American Sharecom.

Unlike WATS long-distance service, American Sharecom provides detailed monthly call records. These records make it clear to employees, many of whom believe company long distance is "free," that each call results in a charge.

Once employees understand the real cost of making personal calls on company lines, many companies are able to save an extra 10% or more.

In addition, American Sharecom saves you even more money when you call anywhere in the continental U.S., Puerto Rico and the Virgin Islands. Anywhere. Urban or rural.

And we use Bell-quality lines. So you don't have to put up with echoes, fading or voice cut-offs.

Let us design a money-saving phone service to meet your needs.

There's no installation or monthly minimum required for American Sharecom. And we guarantee to make you happy.

Which, unfortunately, is sometimes more than you can say for love.

For free information, mail the coupon today. Or call us at (414) 278-8005.

Call (414) 278 8005. Or mail coupon to: American Sharecom, Suite 502, 312 East Wisconsin Avenue, Milwaukee, Wisconsin 53202

☐ Please send free information on American Sharecom's money saving long distance service

☐ I've enclosed one of our recent long distance bills. Please let me know how much it would have been with American Sharecom

Name _____ Title _____

Company _____

Address _____

City _____ State ____ Zip ____ Phone _____

AMERICAN SHARECOM

IF YOU THINK MOST OLD PEOPLE ARE SENILE, YOU'RE OFF YOUR ROCKER.

"SENILITY: REMEMBER THERE'S HOPE"

It's unfortunate, but too often people believe, as you grow older, you naturally grow senile.

But that's not true. It's just an old wives' tale. Because senility only affects a very small minority of our elderly.

And tonight, Storm Field helps dispel the myths and misconceptions about senility, and sheds new light on this age old problem.

So watch tonight's Eyewitness News Special Report. Because you're never too old to learn a thing or two.

THE 5 O'CLOCK EYEWITNESS NEWS ⑦

On January 1, your phone won't turn into a monster.

If you're like most people, you've heard that the Bell System is breaking up. And that, after January 1, 1984, you'll have to look to separate sources for local phone service, long-distance phone service, and equipment.

If you're like most people, you're concerned that this will turn your phone service into a monster.

It won't.

New England Telephone will still be your local phone company. We'll still provide you with the same good service New Englanders have counted on for the last 100 years.

Divestiture will mean some changes. For individuals, for business—and for the future.

We think most of the changes will be for the better. And, as they happen, we'll tell you about them. Because the more you know about change, the easier it is to handle.

Some things won't change.

New England Telephone will still provide local phone service. All you have to do is pick up the phone and call. The way you always have.

You've probably heard that the cost of local calling will increase after divestiture. That's because long-distance charges will no longer pay part of the cost of local service. However, the cost of long-distance calling may be reduced. And New England Telephone also offers options—like Measured Service or Unlimited Service—to help you control the cost of local service.

Some things will change.

Among the things that are changing are the ways you obtain equipment and repairs.

New England Telephone will no longer provide home telephone equipment. If you want to buy phones, you can buy them from any number of suppliers. So shop around. Compare prices, features, and service warranties to get the best buys for your money.

If you prefer to lease your phones, simply keep the ones we've provided. But after January 1, you'll automatically be leasing them from AT&T.

Whoever supplies your phones will be responsible for their repair. Of course, New England Telephone will continue to maintain and repair your phone lines.

A short course on long-distance options.

After the break-up, New England Telephone will continue to provide you with long distance service within your area code. And we'll give you access to long-distance service outside your area code. So you can still make and receive long-distance calls.

Your current long-distance service will continue after January 1.

However, if you want to choose a new long-distance company, check your Yellow Pages for a complete listing. Then compare rates and services and make your choice.

What lies ahead?

New England Telephone's been in the forefront of changes in telephone service and technology for the last 100 years. And that's just where we intend to stay.

We're managing today's changes, and we'll continue to offer you new options, all geared to making your phone service the best it can be.

There's been a lot of noise about the Bell System breaking up, but just remember New England Telephone's got it all together.

If you have any questions about the ways these changes will affect you, call our special, toll-free "Let's Talk" number. It's 1 800 555-5000. Monday through Friday from 8:30 a.m. to 5:00 p.m.

New England Telephone

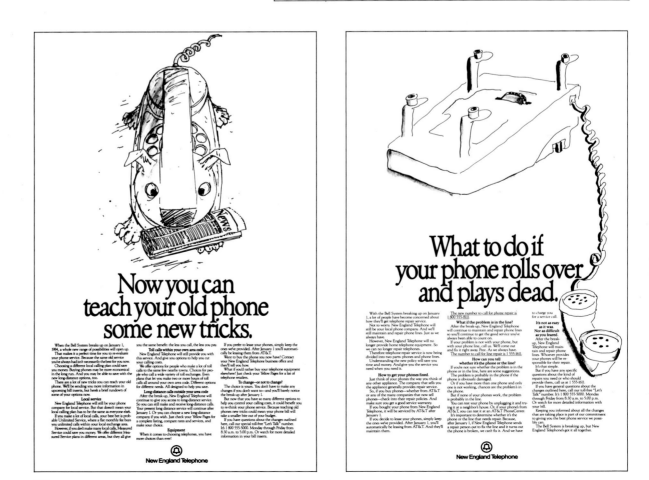

Now you can teach your old phone some new tricks.

When the Bell System breaks up on January 1, 1984, a whole new range of possibilities will open up.

That makes it a perfect time for you to re-evaluate your phone service. Because the same old service you've always had isn't necessarily the best for you now.

Choosing a different local calling plan could save you money. Because buying phones may be more economical in the long run. And you may be able to save with the new long-distance options, too.

There are a lot of new tricks you can teach your old phone. We'll be sending you more information in upcoming bill inserts, but here's a brief rundown of some of your options now.

Local service

New England Telephone will still be your phone company for local service. But that doesn't mean your local calling plan has to be the same as everyone else's.

If you make a lot of local calls, your best bet is probably Unlimited Service, where a flat monthly fee buys you unlimited calls within your local exchange area.

However, if you don't make many local calls, Measured Service could save you money. We offer different Measured Service plans in different areas, but they all give you the same benefit: the less you call, the less you pay.

We offer options for people who make a lot of toll calls to the same few nearby towns. Choices for people who call a wide variety of toll exchanges. Even plans that let you make two or more hours of toll calls all around your own area code. Different options for different needs. All designed to help you save.

Equipment

When it comes to choosing telephones, you have more choices than ever!

Long-distance calls outside your area code

After the break-up, New England Telephone will continue to give you access to long-distance service. So you can still make and receive long-distance calls. Your present long distance service will continue after January 1. Or you can choose a new long-distance company if you wish. Just check your Yellow Pages for a complete listing, compare rates and services, and make your choice.

Toll calls within your own area code

New England Telephone will still provide you with this service. And give you options to help you cut your calling costs.

Want to buy the phone you now have? Contact your New England Telephone business office and they'll tell you how.

What if you'd rather buy your telephone equipment elsewhere? Just check your Yellow Pages for a lot of telephone retailers.

To change—or not to change?

The choice is yours. You don't have to make any changes if you don't want to—and you'll barely notice the break-up after January 1.

But now that you have so many different options to help you control your calling costs, it could benefit you to re-think your phone service. Because teaching old phones new tricks could mean your phone bill will take a smaller bite out of your budget.

If you have questions about the changes outlined here, call our special toll-free "Let's Talk" number. It's 1 800 555-5000. Monday through Friday from 8:30 a.m. to 5:00 p.m. Or watch for more detailed information in your bill inserts.

If you prefer to lease your phones, simply keep the ones we've provided. After January 1 you'll automatically be leasing them from AT&T.

New England Telephone

What to do if your phone rolls over and plays dead.

With the Bell System breaking up on January 1, a lot of people have become concerned about how they'll get telephone repair service.

Not to worry. New England Telephone will continue to maintain and repair phone lines so you'll continue to get the good service you've always been able to count on.

However, New England Telephone will no longer provide home telephone equipment. So we can no longer repair telephones.

Therefore telephone repair service is now being divided into two parts: phones and phone lines. Understanding the new policy will save you time and money. And give you the service you need when you need it.

How to get your phones fixed.

Just think of your phones the way you think of any other appliance. The company that sells you the appliance generally provides repair service.

So, if you buy phones—whether from AT&T or any of the many companies that now sell phones—check into their repair policies. And make sure you get a good service warranty.

If you bought your phone from New England Telephone, it will be serviced by AT&T after January 1.

If you decide to lease your phone, simply keep the ones we've provided. After January 1, you'll automatically be leasing from AT&T. And they'll maintain them.

The new number to call for phone repair is 1 800 555-8111.

What if the problem is in the line?

After the break-up, New England Telephone will continue to maintain and repair phone lines so you'll continue to get the good service you've always been able to count on.

If your problem is not with your phone, but with your phone line, call us. We'll come out and fix it right away. Free. As we always have.

The number to call for line repair is 1 555-1611.

How can you tell whether it's the phone or the line?

If you're not sure whether the problem is in the phone or in the line, here are some suggestions.

The problem is probably in the phone if the phone is obviously damaged.

Or if you have more than one phone and only one is not working, chances are the problem's in the phone.

But if none of your phones work, the problem is probably in the line.

You can test your phone by unplugging it and trying it at a neighbor's house. Or, if your phone's from AT&T, you can test it at an AT&T PhoneCenter.

It's important to determine whether it's the phone or the line that needs repair. Because after January 1, if New England Telephone sends a repair person out to fix the line and it turns out the phone is broken, we can't fix it. And we have to charge you for a service call.

It's not as easy as it was.

Nor as difficult as you feared.

After the break-up, New England Telephone will maintain and repair phone lines. Whoever provides your phones will be responsible for their repair. It's that simple.

But if you have any specific questions about the kind of repairs you need or who should provide them, call us at 1 555-1611.

If you have general questions about the changes outlined here, call our toll-free "Let's Talk" number. It's 1 800 555-5000. Monday through Friday from 8:30 a.m. to 5:00 p.m. Or watch for more detailed information with your bill.

Keeping you informed about all the changes that are taking place is part of our commitment to giving you the best phone service we possibly can.

The Bell System is breaking up, but New England Telephone's got it all together.

New England Telephone

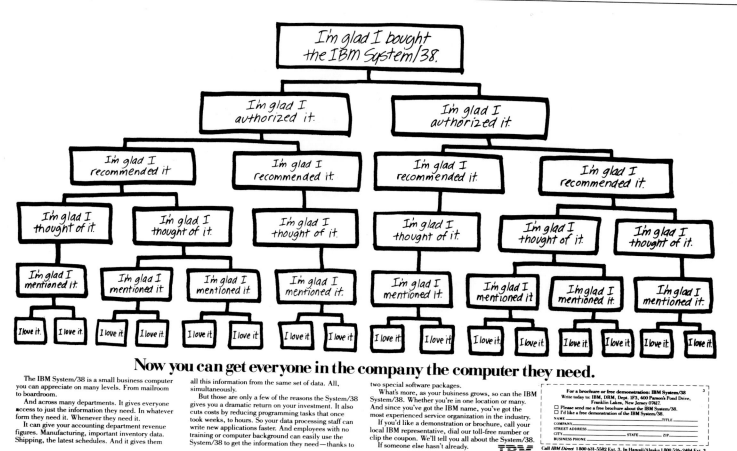

Now you can get everyone in the company the computer they need.

The IBM System/38 is a small business computer you can appreciate on many levels. From mailroom to boardroom.

And across many departments. It gives everyone access to just the information they need. In whatever form they need it. Whenever they need it.

It can give your accounting department revenue figures. Manufacturing, important inventory data. Shipping, the latest schedules. And it gives them all this information from the same set of data. All, simultaneously.

But those are only a few of the reasons the System/38 gives you a dramatic return on your investment. It also cuts costs by reducing programming tasks that once took weeks, to hours. So your data processing staff can write new applications faster. And employees with no training or computer background can easily use the System/38 to get the information they need—thanks to two special software packages.

What's more, as your business grows, so can the IBM System/38. Whether you're in one location or many. And since you've got the IBM name, you've got the most experienced service organization in the industry.

If you'd like a demonstration or brochure, call your local IBM representative, dial our toll-free number or clip the coupon. We'll tell you all about the System/38.

If someone else hasn't already.

No two businesses are alike either.

Your business is unique.
And your problems are unique.
So, if you want to buy a small computer, where can you go to get some understanding and help?
IBM.
We have a range of small computers starting at under $4,000. There's one that can be tailored to fit your unique needs and grow as your business grows.
Thousands of software programs are written for IBM. So whether your business is agriculture or zoology, you can find the right software, right away.
If you ever need help, IBM has the most experienced and widely skilled service organization in the business.
If you didn't think IBM offered so much to solve your unique problems, think of it this way:
We're unique too.
For a free brochure or demonstration of IBM's small computers call your local IBM sales office or our toll-free number below.

IBM

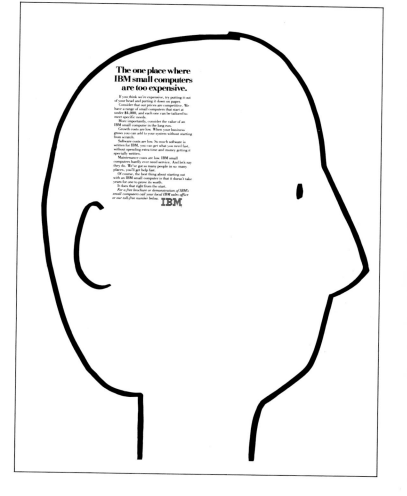

The one place where IBM small computers are too expensive.

If you think we're expensive, try putting it out of your head and putting it down on paper.
Consider that our prices are competitive. We have a range of small computers that start at under $4,000, and each one can be tailored to meet specific needs.
More importantly, consider the value of an IBM small computer in the long run.
Growth costs are low. When your business grows you can add to your system without starting from scratch.
Software costs are low. So much software is written for IBM, you can get what you need fast, without spending extra time and money getting it specially written.
Maintenance costs are low. IBM small computers hardly ever need service. And let's say they do. We've got so many people in so many places, you'll get help fast.
Of course, the best thing about starting out with an IBM small computer is that it doesn't take years for one to prove its worth.
It does that right from the start.
For a free brochure or demonstration of IBM's small computers call your local IBM sales office or our toll-free number below.

IBM

"OK. THAT'S OUR 5TH MEETING; IS EVERYONE CLEAR ON WHAT THEY HAVE TO DO?"

Your people aren't fuzzy thinkers. On the contrary, you've hired some of the sharpest minds around.

So why does it sometimes seem to take so long to get anything done?

Well, consider. The average executive spends roughly two hours a day in meetings. Two hours more on the telephone or handling paper. Another hour and a half tracking down stray bits of information.

In other words, your thinkers are left with precious little time to actually think.

So it's no wonder there's been precious little improvement in white-collar productivity. In fact, since 1977, it's gone up just one measly percent.

These are the problems AIS/American Bell would like to help you solve.

Just call us toll-free at 1-800-AIS-1212, Ext. 22.

We have the products, the know-how, and the systems to help you manage time and move information.

So you, and everyone who works for you, can think smarter, act faster, work happier.

We'll give the best minds in your organization just what they need. Time to focus on the things that are really important.

AT&T

Does the right hand of your company know what the left hand is doing?

Does it sometimes seem that there's a diabolic plan to make your company's best efforts cancel each other out?

Do your people seem to work at cross-purposes, instead of in concert?

Does the right information never seem to get to the right place at the right time?

If so, your company isn't alone.

When it comes to white-collar productivity, slow growth has become a national embarrassment.

Which isn't to say today's office workers are lazy. They're not. They're working harder than ever, just as you are.

But they're bedeviled by too many meetings. Overwhelmed by too much information. They're asked to spend too much time pushing paper, rather than using their brains.

There is an answer—and AIS/American Bell has it.

We have the products, the know-how, and the systems to help your company manage time and move information.

So you and your people can think smarter, act faster, work happier.

Just call us toll-free at 1-800-AIS-1212, Ext. 22.

We'll help you work in harmony.

AT&T

START SMALL. BUT THINK BIG.

Is a basic telephone all your company needs? Or do you also need a system to connect you with information?

Most important: as you grow, will your needs change?

For answers to these and other questions, talk to us. We're American

Bell Advanced Information Systems.

We offer everything from a basic business phone system to one that includes keyboards, printers, data screens, and message centers, all linked by an applications processor.

And we offer something more. Flexibility.

With our range of products, we can tailor a system just for your company.

Start small, and you'll find that our systems can grow as your needs grow.

Everything is modular; obsolescence becomes obsolete.

At any size, our business systems are designed to help your people do their jobs more efficiently. So your company can compete more effectively—and win.

As the deregulated subsidiary of AT&T, we'll bring you the innovative technology of Bell Labs and the product reliability of Western Electric. We have more than 200 sales offices nationwide to meet your business needs.

If you'd like us to put you in touch with an Account Executive trained in your business, just call 1-800-AIS-1212, Ext. 898.

It could be the start of something big.

"Goodbye, Number One."

Special tab on Yaz, Friday, September 30.

For more than two decades the Number 8 has been emblazoned on the back of Carl Yastrzemski.

To the delight of Red Sox fans everywhere, Yaz, the All-Star, has won every award a player can bring home—Golden Glove, Triple Crown, UPI and AP Player of the Year.

To the dismay of fans everywhere, Yaz hangs up his jersey for good after his last game, October 2.

What's a fan to do? How can you hold on to the memory of Yaz forever? Pick up The Boston Globe, September 30. That's where you'll find a special tabloid on Yaz. Twenty-four pages of Yaz, from every angle.

What makes him a hall of famer? How his teammates recall the man. His last road trip. The games he best remembers. Yaz's standing on the all-time lists. And a pictorial album from the start of his career through his final season.

At the newsstand, or by home delivery if you call 929-2222, you can remember Number 8 always if you remember to get The Globe September 30.

The Boston Globe
"The Globe's here!"
For home delivery call 929-2222

On November 20th, we salute a President.

But not with tears.

The Globe remembers John Fitzgerald Kennedy as we knew him. Before—and during—his presidency.

A special edition of The Boston Globe Magazine, two days prior to the twentieth anniversary of his death, will explore the early Kennedy, and the things that made him. And then the events that changed him.

Through the eyes of the Globe's Robert Healy, you'll go back to the ward politics of Boston in 1946. You'll see the Irish wit, the curiosity, and the tough-mindedness. You'll follow Kennedy through the 50's. The race with Henry Cabot Lodge. The nomination of Stevenson and Kefauver in '56.

And, with selections from the Oral History section of the John F. Kennedy Library and 10 pages of photographs, you'll share the feelings of the people who worked with him through the hard realities of his days in office. Bobby Kennedy. George McGovern. Theodore Sorensen.

It's the story of a lifetime.

The Boston Globe
"The Globe's here!"

Coming Sunday, in The Boston Globe Magazine.

"On 2."

The Pro Football Preview, September 2 in Sports Plus.

You'll find facts, figures, stories and predictions. Plus, the new bosses on the sidelines and the new quarterbacks in the field.

What's more, scouting reports, division previews, Patriot's prospectus and sport TV viewing.

Can Denver rookie quarterback John Elway raise the Broncos the way he raised the NFL pay scale?

Did John Robinson find a home in L.A.?

Where does the Patriot's new face Tony Eason stand?

So get into the action before the snap of the '83 season with the special pro football preview in The Boston Globe. It's an instant pre-play you can replay throughout the entire year.

The Boston Globe
"The Globe's here!"
For home delivery call 929-2222

**Consumer Newspaper
Over 600 Lines Campaign**

131
ART DIRECTORS
Bo Zaunders
Glenn McArthur

WRITER & DESIGNER
Jim Johnston

PHOTOGRAPHERS
Sara Smith
Larry Sillen

CLIENT
The Wall Street Journal

AGENCY
Jim Johnston Advertising

KRONE ALONE

In 1950, a 25-year-old designer saw The Art Directors Club annual exhibition dominated by a very new and very small advertising agency. The designer's name: Helmut Krone. The agency: Doyle Dane Bernbach. The rest is history. Here, from a recent conversation, are the singular views of DDB's executive vice president, a creative director, and a member of the Art Directors Hall of Fame, with creative talent so extraordinary the late Bill Bernbach suggested he should be included in this series.

On early ambitions:
I was interested in industrial design and architecture. At 21, I had two interviews scheduled. First, with a designer named Robert Greenwell who was doing freelance ads for a magazine. The second with Raymond Loewy. Greenwell offered me $40 per week. I said, "Gee, that's great." I never interviewed with Loewy. And never looked back. I tell my children, it's not so much what you do but how you do it. Kids today spend half their lives agonizing over their first move, first job. It doesn't matter, it's how you tackle your work. Stop worrying so much and just do *something.*

On advertising:
I was Bauhaus-based. My idol was Paul Rand. Advertising? If you had any respect for design—any self-respect—and you wanted to tell your mother what you were doing, you worked *around* advertising, but *not in it.* So I worked for Greenwell, in pharmaceuticals, in fashion, for publishers—but not for the hard-core advertising agencies. I had to wait for Bernbach to start his agency. I came here in 1954. I was 29, and one of four art directors.

On alternatives:
I have always said there were only two people for whom I could work: Bill Bernbach and myself. Bill did more than start an agency. He made advertising *respectable,* a profession, a high art. We argued a lot. With genuine disagreement but real affection. We could fight like cats and dogs because we *knew we were both after the same thing.*

On television and print:
I'm not crazy about *things that move.* I like things that stand still; that you can study, hold in your hand, look at, contemplate. That's what I hate about television commercials. They're happenings. They go by and you don't even remember the details. In a print ad, you can study them. There's a point to caring about details in print. If you can give a photo just an extra ounce of *caring,* just a touch of inspiration, it shows. While I do my share of TV, I'm known as the print maven around here. I really do like it. After all these years, the idea of the *page* continues to fascinate me.

On work:
Beauty and style are qualities I count as secondary. If they are in the work, they come along for the ride. The only quality I really appreciate is *newness,* to see something no one has ever seen before. New comes at 11 o'clock at night, after you've spent all day hunched over the board. I have worked with a couple of geniuses. I spend long hours making up for not being a genius.

On confidence and clients:
I am very insecure. Nothing I do ever turns out exactly right. It's never what I expected. I like to work with clients. I need their judgment. All I know is that what I'm doing is new. The client can tell me if it's right. I hate presentations: agency

people filing in with a big portfolio, taking out their acetate-wrapped comprehensives and saying, "Here. Make a decision." I like to have clients work with me. I show them scraps of paper. I pull things out of the wastebasket, tissues off the wall. I say "What do *you* think? Should I keep going?" It's not a matter of giving clients what they want. It's a matter of making sure you're on the same wave length.

On working with writers:
I talk with the writer. We come up with a concept. The writer leaves. But I stay. I want to *top* the concept. I want to lay something on top of the concept that's totally unexpected. Most people go home. My work begins *after* we've settled on a headline and picture. The next day, the writer will see the ad. It'll have the headline and the picture we discussed. But it won't look or feel the way they thought it would. And that's unnerving to some writers.

On staying ahead:
I try to have some idea of what I want to do even before I know what has to be done. So before I get an assignment, I know what my attack will be, even before I know the product. You can't explain this to a client. They don't understand the process. But I believe you can bend and twist the idea to fit the problem, and come up with something totally new. Does it sound crazy? Bernbach used to say, "First, you make the revolution. Then you figure out why." Thinking ahead isn't unfair to the client. It gives him a head start.

On ads as information:
I think people want *information.* They don't get it from advertising. Say you're buying a tape deck. Well, you're up against it—especially if you read the ads. You know the formula. A double-entendre headline. Nice photo. But *no real meat* in the ad. Because the people who did the ad don't think you *really* want to know. Advertising people argue that it's good to make it simple. But that's not the point. People want to know. Advertising ought to give them the information they need.

On the page as a package:
The page ought to be a *package* for the product. It should look like the product, smell like the product and the company. If it's a highly technical product—like the Porsche—that's how the page ought to look and feel. I tried to make the Porsche ads look a little like what you see when you raise the hood of the car. It's a *package* for Porsche. Every company, every product needs its own package.

On ideas and making them work:
Good ideas announce themselves. A bell rings. But that's just the start. To stage an idea at the level where I want to work, to do work that's *out at the edge,* you need to know about the tools. Type, photography, illustration, are tools. You need to know how they work, to know nearly as much about them as the people who specialize. For if you can't use the tools, you can't really make a good idea work.

On drawing pads:
Some people begin by drawing layouts. I can't work that way. I begin by *thinking.* I don't want to be influenced by that first scribble. Scribbles can box you in. Think first. I don't want to design *ads.* That's why I've spent my life fighting logos. Logos say "I'm an ad, so turn the page." I don't just leave out the logo. I give the client something better. And it doesn't look like an ad.

On The Wall Street Journal:
Form follows function. That was the Bauhaus revolution. The Journal is Bauhaus. Its form follows its function: information, organized for the reader, gathered for business reasons. I've said you ought to be able to identify your ads if you hang them upside down, forty feet away. The Journal *is* The Journal; there's no mistaking it. I've also said the graphic image ought to reflect reality. The Journal *looks* like business, and it *is* business. Of course, I read The Journal. Of course, I like to see my ads in The Journal. I have had a lifelong fascination with *the page,* and no publication gives me a bigger page than The Journal. As an art director, I am in the business of *staging* ideas for our clients. The Journal does a magnificent job of *staging* advertising.

The Wall Street Journal.
It works.

Norman conquest.

Norman Berry. A sterling British export, he came to America after a career of extraordinary achievement in London. A founder of one of Britain's largest agencies, he was a leader in the resurgence of British creativity—to the point where many believe it superior to the American brand. Since 1978, executive vice president and creative director of Ogilvy & Mather. And a man whose outspoken views may spark controversy and debate—but who won't mince words, on either side of the Atlantic.

On the early days:

My father was creative director for Lever's advertising service. I followed in his footsteps largely because I didn't know what else to do. After school in Dorset and a stint in the Army, I set out to be a painter. My money lasted three months. Facing starvation, I went into advertising. I arrogantly refused to go in on the art side; I didn't want to ruin my art. First two years, I was a rugby-playing layabout pretending to be in advertising. Then I married my boss and found she was making more money than I. So I got to work. Became an account executive. Then I took the copy exam. After Lintas, ten years at Y&R—happiest years of my life—a wonderful company. In 1964, three of us moved to a little industrial agency that had been around for eighty years. We changed the name and did rather good work. People began calling us a hot creative shop. After a few years and a merger we became part of Ogilvy & Mather. That led me here, with no small credit to the late Andrew Kershaw, who kept urging me to come to New York.

On American peculiarities:

Advertising agencies in America are far more *hierarchical* than those in the U.K. You've invented more titles than I've had hot dinners. When I came here, there were 27 titles inside Ogilvy's creative department. Now there are five. Titles aren't important; in fact, they are often counter-productive. What is important is that creative people know the management of the agency believes the creative product is important, and compensates people accordingly. Americans have an inordinate fondness for categorizing everything. I was told one of our writers was a brilliant "cosmetics writer." I thought that absurd, and proceeded to assign the writer a number of accounts outside that field. Not surprisingly, he's proven just as brilliant on *every* assignment. I hate it when people call Ogilvy "a long copy shop," as if our forte were producing words in quantity. Our strength is *selling ideas*, executed with as much taste and charm as we can muster.

On American talent:

Sensationally good. The creative problem isn't with art directors and writers, or with the young kids coming into the business; it's management. Many agency managements ask for great work on Monday. And then on Tuesday they ask for rubbish. Inconsistent standards breed apathy. Writers and art directors conclude excellence doesn't count; it is only a game of giving the client what he asks for. They stop caring. How can you blame them when management doesn't care?

On creative freedom:

In my experience, British agencies are more disciplined than American agencies. Yet there is more freedom. That isn't a contradiction. The difference is that English strategies are very tight, very precise. Satisfy the strategy, and the idea will not be faulted even though it may *appear* to be outrageous. Many U.S. strategies are too vague, too open to interpretation. "The strategy for this product is taste," they'll say. But that is not a strategy. Then, somewhere down at the bottom of the page, there'll be a note concerning tone and manner: "warm and friendly." As if "cold and unfriendly" were an option. English creative groups have grown up with precise strategies so they demand them. They know it's the only way you can get creative freedom. Vague strategies inhibit. Precise strategies liberate.

On hiring:

I look for people with a burning desire to be the best. The best people are the ones who require excellence of themselves. If my job were to walk around with a whip shouting, "YOU'VE GOT TO DO IT BETTER!" I have failed. I want creative people who think of me as a rather backward man who's holding them back. *They* should be pushing *me*. When they present creative work to me, it should be so on strategy that I cannot fault it. Yet it should be so innovative that it makes me break out in perspiration all over.

On creativity and the advertising business:

On a simple law of averages it is likely that even the worst of the major agencies will do good work on one or two accounts. But that is not the test. The test is doing good work for every client, on every assignment. Some agencies label some accounts as "showcase accounts." What about the non-showcase accounts? Are they second-class? As a business practice this borders on the immoral. At Ogilvy, as a matter of personal pride and business honesty, we strive for the best work, the best campaigns, in every category in which we work, from diapers and detergents to perfumes and Peugeots.

On advertising effectiveness:

I am appalled by those who give awards to advertising *exclusively* on the basis of sales. That isn't enough. Of course, advertising must sell. By any definition it is lousy advertising if it doesn't. But if sales are achieved with work which is in bad taste or is intellectual garbage, it shouldn't be applauded no matter how much it sells. Offensive, dull, abrasive, stupid advertising is bad for the entire industry and for business as a whole. It is why the public perception of advertising is going down in this country. Until there is widespread recognition that effective advertising can be intelligent, charming, informative and entertaining, advertising agencies should view themselves as an endangered species.

On the language problem:

Wasn't it Dylan Thomas who said, "We have the barrier of a common language"? When I first came here, I'd tell Americans, "It'll go down like a bomb"—meaning it's great—and they'd say, "Oh, it's not *that* bad." Seriously, there's an incredible amount of ignorance about the U.K. in the U.S.—and vice versa. Yet, on that side, there's an enormous amount of curiosity that bodes well for your European edition.

On helping clients avoid bad work:

I have heard creative people explain bad work by saying, "I didn't want the client to buy *that* ad, but he did." That is nonsense. It is unconscionable to present *anything* unless you want it produced and run. I've told our people if they offer that as an alibi for inferior work, I'll bash them. If you want to do good work, do it—and do nothing else. Don't present anything you're not prepared to produce, run, and publicly call your own. Bad advertising wouldn't exist if someone didn't create it—and then have the hypocrisy to present it as something worth buying.

On print:

Print is the best way for an agency to gain a reputation as "creative" and "hot." Prospective clients know it's the agency that's responsible for great print work, not a brilliant film director or editor, or a talented on-camera person. My objective is for people to recognize Ogilvy & Mather's print advertising as the best in the world. It's how David Ogilvy won his reputation in the first place. That's how we can make that reputation grow.

On The Wall Street Journal:

I've read The Journal on both sides of the Atlantic. In England, I regarded The Journal as one of the very few American newspapers of substance. And I was constantly amazed at the wit as well as the clarity of the writing. Since I've been here, my perception has changed. Now I find it's a newspaper you simply cannot do without. As an advertising medium, The Journal is its own colossus. I believe there's a sense among Americans, and I share it, that if it isn't in The Wall Street Journal, it simply isn't important. As a creative person? A page in The Journal, for a writer or an art director, is the best page you can possibly get. It's where you can do your best work and be proud of it. You can put it on the wall and send it home to mum and dad.

The Wall Street Journal.
It works.

Go, Gargano!

Amil Gargano. President and chief executive of Ally & Gargano. Member of the Art Directors Hall of Fame. Quiet. Reflective. But with a fiery anger incited by the trite and hackneyed. Here, from a recent conversation, are the revealing and provocative views of the man who helps make Ally & Gargano go.

On beginning:

I'm from Detroit. Grew up there; went to Cass Tech High, art school and Wayne University. After serving as a combat infantryman in Korea, I came back, attended Cranbrook Academy of Art and studied to be an illustrator. But I didn't have the portfolio I needed. Advertising? I saw it as a stop-gap measure. I couldn't imagine anyone spending their life in such a trivial business. But Al Scott at Campbell-Ewald talked me into giving it a shot. Carl Ally was with the agency. He went to New York for a vacation, learned Swissair was looking, so he pitched and won the account. Carl served as account manager. Jim Durfee was the writer and I was the art director.

On a new start:

The three of us were a good team. So when the chance presented itself, we started our own agency. Exciting, exhilarating times. We'd work day and night; catch a few winks in sleeping bags on the office floor. We were driven by our anger at the demeaning stuff that passes for advertising—and by our conviction we could do far better.

On overnight success:

This may be the only agency in history that's been an overnight success—over and over again. Our billings would build up to $50 million, $60 million. Then we'd have a setback. The toughest year was 1978 when we lost Pan Am, Fiat and IBM—enough to knock most agencies out for keeps. But we wouldn't give up. We hung in there, sustained by the work we did and the results it generated. After twenty years, we finally topped $100 million in billings. And we've doubled that in little more than a year. If we'd built our shop on nothing more substantial than the idea of growth, we wouldn't have lasted. I think it's proof that you have to begin with a sense of purpose—a desire to change things and a belief in yourself and what you're doing. Then you can weather the setbacks.

On what makes good advertising:

Most advertising is pedestrian at best. The worst—and there's too much of it—is demeaning, trivial, disrespectful of the people for whom it is intended. We believe in advertising that is authentic, informative and useful. That's why we pioneered comparative advertising. It helps people understand a product or service; to see how your product stacks up with all the rest. The purpose of advertising is plain: motivate consumers to buy your product. It should make something happen. That's our strong suit. Nearly all our clients are doing extremely well—even in the recent global recession when other companies were struggling.

On trust:

Trust is the most important factor. That's true in business, politics, marriage and advertising. Cynicism and suspicion abound today—much of it with good reason. That's why advertising won't work unless it is trusted, no matter how clever it might seem. So the one thing we demand is that our advertising works very hard to earn and keep the consumer's trust. And the way to be trusted is to be honest and sensitive to the people you want to reach. Trust and honesty are old-fashioned words. But I guess we're a bit old-fashioned.

On advertising as a creative mirror:

An ad can tell you a great deal about the writer and art director who created it. Your personality shows through in the ads you do. If you're shallow, or dull, or self-indulgent, it shows. The same is true if you're a person who is aware and responsive to people. Don't waste your time in advertising unless you respect people. You can't hide what you are. You're revealed through your work.

On print:

Television is a collaboration: you and fifty other people. In contrast, print is private. If it's bad, it's your fault. If it's good, it's your achievement. And it requires a personal discipline. A flawed idea can be masked by television. Not in print. So you need to have the discipline to dig for an idea that's strong enough to survive without all of the show business of television. I love print—I always have.

On hiring:

Every agency wants to hire winners—but a lot of agencies have trouble identifying them. We look for people with several qualities. First, there's no substitute for talent. Second, a desire to do something *constructive*. Third, a fire inside that drives them to excellence. Hire winners and provide the environment where they can win. We feel good about our people—including those who've left. Look at our alumni list—McCabe, Ammirati & Puris, Altschiller, Raboy—we've helped people grow who've gone on to grow good agencies of their own.

On mergers:

We may be the only agency in the top 50 in the country that's grown over the past twenty years without merger or acquisition. I don't understand why an agency would want to devour other agencies. For what purpose? Why should I acquire a bunch of disparate philosophies and try to assimilate them? Any artist knows that when you mix all of the colors on the palette, the color you end up with is mud. I don't want this agency to turn into that. I want us to continue to stand for something.

On maturity:

We live by the standards we set twenty-one years ago. But with one important change—we have matured. In the early days, we were angry, and perhaps a bit too brash for our own good. We'd present our ideas and if they weren't bought, we'd become belligerent. We've come to realize that a good idea isn't any good unless it runs. And it usually doesn't run until the client can be comfortable with it. If he's not comfortable, it's our job to come up with an idea that's just as good—or even better. That's not compromising our standards. That's raising them. Good ideas should be a comfortable fit—for the agency, for the client, and for the consumer.

On The Wall Street Journal:

As I grew, so did The Journal in importance to me, and my job. I read it every day. I like the brevity; the ability of The Journal to report the news concisely, but without sacrificing information. Good ads get to the point quickly. So does The Journal. And because I value order in my life, I value The Journal. It provides the relevant, the essential news, with a concern for accuracy that earns trust. The Journal has been extremely productive for our clients—in consumer categories as well as for business products and services. That's no surprise. Journal readers are people. They buy clothes, cars, food; take vacations, play as hard as they work. As an agency, we seek to create advertising that is real, that avoids unrealistic promises, that respects readers, that merits trust. If we were a newspaper, I'd hope we'd be a Wall Street Journal!

The Wall Street Journal.
It works.

"What are these buttons for, anyway?"

Contrary to popular belief, these little mysterious buttons that flank the "0" do *not* put you in touch with the planet Neptune.

Nor Mars. (Sorry.)

But what they do put you in touch with is a whole new world of Custom Calling Services now offered by General Telephone.

The " ✳ " button is part of the *Speed Calling* feature which allows you to reach your call in a fraction of the time it took before.

The "#" button is for the *Call Forwarding*

feature. Which means all your calls can be transferred automatically to wherever you go.

In addition, there's *Call Waiting* which enables you to receive calls even if you're on the phone. And with *Three Way Calling* you can actually add a third party to any phone call. (Think of the time you'll save not having to make extra calls.)

So now what can be better than knowing what these little buttons mean? . . . .

Using these little buttons.

General Telephone Custom Calling Services **GTE**

Now cough up 25¢ less for Luden's.

**Consumer Newspaper
600 Lines or Less
Campaign**

135
ART DIRECTOR
Danny Boone
WRITER
Mike Hughes
DESIGNER
Danny Boone
CLIENT
Humphrey's Restaurant
AGENCY
The Martin Agency/Virginia

136
ART DIRECTOR
Jessica Welton
WRITERS
Andy Ellis
Linda Escalera
DESIGNER
Jessica Welton
ARTIST
Jack Williams
CLIENT
Rowletts
AGENCY
Siddall, Matus & Coughter/
Virginia

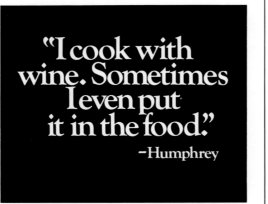

"I cook with wine. Sometimes I even put it in the food."

—Humphrey

Humphrey's Restaurant. Fine dining at the corner of Strawberry & Main. Call 358-8894 for reservations.

"Our steaks make this the best strip joint in town."

—Humphrey

Humphrey's Restaurant. Fine dining at the corner of Strawberry & Main. Call 358-8894 for reservations.

"I serve shrimps. And normal sized people, too."

—Humphrey

Humphrey's Restaurant. Fine dining at the corner of Strawberry & Main. Call 358-8894 for reservations.

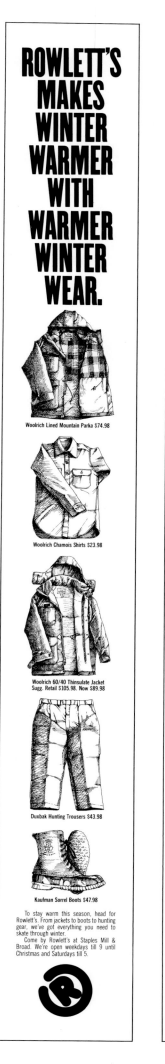
136

**Consumer Newspaper
600 Lines or Less
Campaign**

137
ART DIRECTOR
Pat Burnham
WRITER
Jarl Olsen
DESIGNER
Pat Burnham
ARTIST
Bob Blewett
CLIENT
Minnesota Public Radio
AGENCY
Fallon McElligott Rice/
Minneapolis

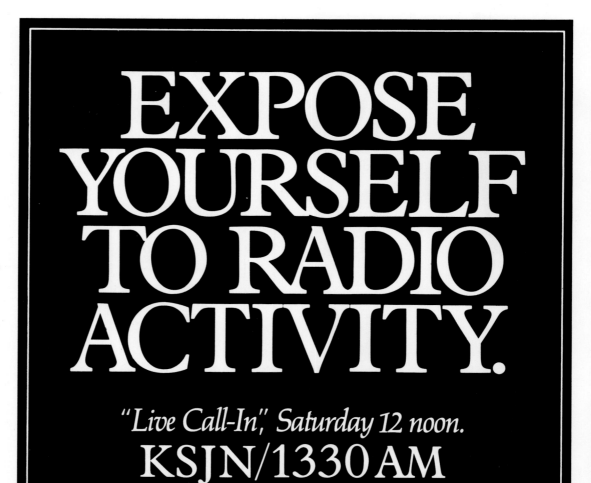

THE
JOY OF SAX.

"The Jazz Image"
with Leigh Kamman, Saturday 10 p.m.
KSJN/1330 AM

"OK. THAT'S OUR 5TH MEETING; IS EVERYONE CLEAR ON WHAT THEY HAVE TO DO?"

Your people aren't fuzzy thinkers. On the contrary, you've hired some of the sharpest minds around.

So why does it sometimes seem to take so long to get anything done?

Well, consider. The average executive spends roughly two hours a day in meetings. Two hours more on the telephone or handling paper. Another hour and a half tracking down stray bits of information.

In other words, your thinkers are left with precious little time to actually think.

So it's no wonder there's been precious little improvement in white-collar productivity. In fact, since 1977, it's gone up just one measly percent.

These are the problems AIS American Bell would like to help you solve.

Just call us toll-free at 1-800-AIS-1212, Extension 22.

We have the products, the know-how, and the systems to help you manage time and move information.

So you, and everyone who works for you, can think smarter, act faster, work happier.

We'll give the best minds in your organization just what they need.

Time to focus on the things that are really important.

 AT&T

142

DO YOU SEE A PRACTICAL CAR OR A PERFORMANCE CAR?

Take a close look at this inkblot.

We'd like to ask you a few questions about what you see.

Do you see power or economy?

A powerful engine and an economical engine are mutually exclusive concepts, right? In the case of Saab, the answer is a definitive "not necessarily."

Consider Saab's APC Turbo. On the one hand, its 0-60 acceleration will leave dust on the windshields of BMWs and many other "performance" cars. Or as the usually reserved *New York Times* put it: "When the [A.P.C.] turbo cuts in, there is a sensation of soaring, of gathering yourself up and flying faster with such a rush of adrenaline and no end in sight."

Yet all this power and exhilaration are achieved with better gas economy than the old fuel-frugal Volkswagen Super Beetle.

Do you see a suspension system designed for racing or for safety?

Over the years, Saab has built up quite an impressive record on the international rally circuit. Their drivers give much of the credit to Saab's double-wishbone suspension and front-wheel drive system, which allow Saab to maneuver and take corners as well as a sports car. (*We* would say better than a sports car, since Saab regularly beats sports cars in such events.)

If you don't happen to have racing in your blood, you might notice the more practical applications of front-wheel drive and taut suspension. Like helping you safely through the first snowfall. Or the last rainfall.

Do you see a car designed for holding the road or for holding luggage?

Before Saab engineers designed cars, they were designing airplanes. So it's not surprising that Saab was one of the first cars to utilize the aerodynamic hatchback design.

To some Saab owners, it's another contributing factor to their cars' superb handling characteristics.

To others, it's been a legitimate excuse to postpone indefinitely the purchase of that unrelentingly utilitarian device – the station wagon. (Saab's hatchback design affords its owners the carrying capacity of a station wagon–56.5 cubic feet of luggage space in the 3-door model.)

1983 SAAB PRICE** LIST	
900 3-door	$9,750
900 4-door	$11,950
900S 3-door	$13,550
900S 4-door	$13,950
900 Turbo 3-door	$16,510
900 Turbo 4-door	$16,910
Automatic transmission $370 additional.	

Back to square one.

If you're still undecided as to whether you see a practical car or a performance car, don't worry.

Saab's version of the Rorschach test is much like the real one. Any answer is correct.

While our version may not reveal your personality traits, instinctual drives, or hidden neuroses, it should reduce any anxieties you might have about buying a Saab.

SAAB
The most intelligent car ever built.

143

A long-winded argument for MCI.

A short-winded argument.

Our argument keeps getting longer and longer.

When we started out a few years ago, we had just one short argument.

Savings. From 15 to 50% over Bell.

That argument was enough to convince over half the Fortune® 500 and nearly 300,000 other companies to join us.

But some companies hung back.

They wondered what they would have to give up. Would they have to learn new habits? Would they be able to call anywhere, anytime?

So we've added more services. And our argument gets longer and longer.

New Advantage Service makes MCI as easy to use as Bell.

With new MCI Advantage Service, you dial every number exactly as you would with Bell. You simply dial the area code and the local number.

You don't do anything differently than you're already doing. And you save on every single call.

You use the same phones you're already using. Either push-button or rotary. And there are absolutely no extra numbers to dial.

Call any other phone in any other state from coast to coast.

Some businesses have wondered if MCI goes everywhere they call.

Now they can stop wondering.

From most major cities, you can now reach any other phone in any other state from coast to coast. Even the most remote phone in the most remote town.

We're also adding service to major business cities throughout Canada.

New MCI WATS service. Bigger savings than ever before.

You might ask how MCI stacks up against Bell's famous WATS line.

We're glad you asked.

MCI now has its own WATS line service. You'll find it's exactly the same as Bell's. But it costs much less.

So now every business can enjoy MCI savings without giving up anything. You can call anywhere from coast to coast, exactly as you did with Bell. And save on every call.

If you would like to know more about MCI, simply fill out the coupon and mail it to us.

Or call your local MCI sales office.

Those are the facts. Now read the figures.

MCI
The nation's long distance phone company.

MCI Telecommunications Corp.
P.O. Box 611
Vienna, VA 22180

Please send me more information about how I can cut my long distance costs.
☐ For Business   ☐ For Home

Name_____
Title_____
Company_____Telephone_____
Address_____
City_____State____Zip____
NE-2

Fortune is a registered trademark of Time, Inc.

LONG DISTANCE CALLS	MINS.	BELL	MCI	SAVINGS
St. Louis to Belleville	1	$ .32	$ .15	53.1%
New York City to Erie	1	.59	.36	39.0
Washington, D.C., to Atlanta	2	1.05	.75	28.6
San Francisco to Denver	3	1.52	1.15	24.3
Dallas to Milwaukee	5	2.34	1.87	20.1
Memphis to Fresno	9	4.16	3.46	16.8
Baltimore to Boston	4	1.85	1.45	21.6
Los Angeles to Chicago	7	3.28	2.69	18.0
Richmond to Baltimore	13	5.26	4.45	15.4
Cincinnati to Louisville	8	3.16	2.62	17.1
Cheyenne to Ft. Wayne	10	4.60	3.84	16.5
Houston to Phoenix	3	1.52	1.15	24.3
Atlanta to Cincinnati	6	2.69	2.18	19.0
Boston to Providence	1	.48	.27	43.8
Chicago to Cleveland	11	4.79	4.00	16.5
Knoxville to St. Louis	4	1.85	1.45	21.6
Jackson, MS, to Greensboro	12	5.35	4.49	16.1
Austin to Miami	8	3.72	3.07	17.5

Rates show comparative pricing between Bell's business day rate and MCI's business day rate. Final rate authorities on all tariffed services are MCI Tariff FCC 1 and AT&T Tariff FCC 263.

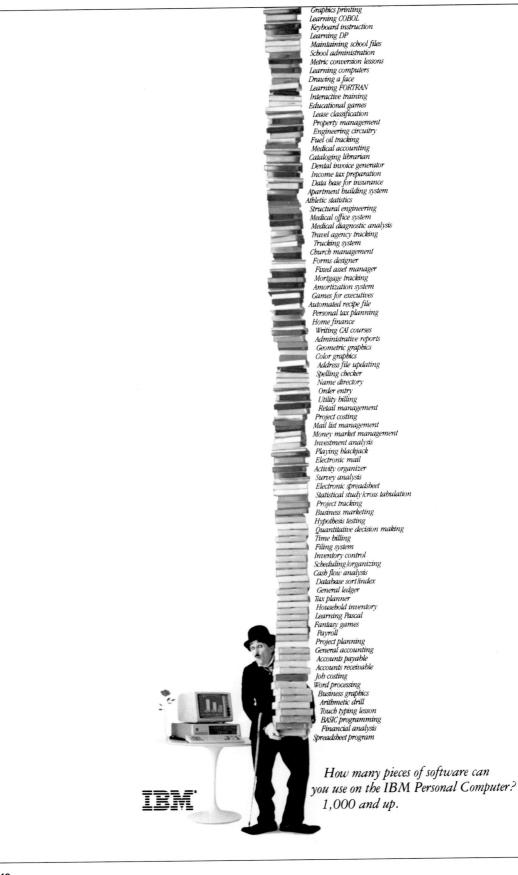

How many pieces of software can
you use on the IBM Personal Computer?
1,000 and up.

149

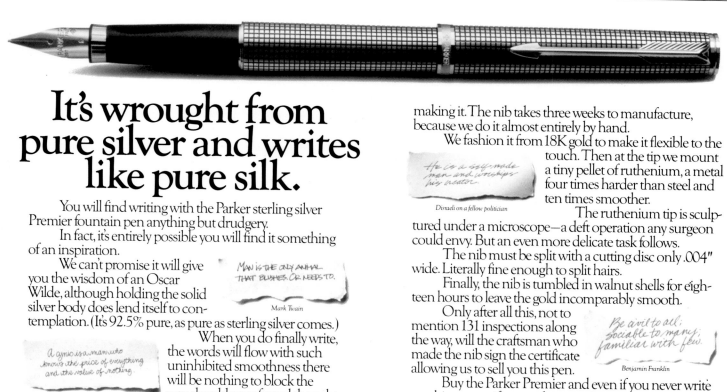

It's wrought from pure silver and writes like pure silk.

You will find writing with the Parker sterling silver Premier fountain pen anything but drudgery.

In fact, it's entirely possible you will find it something of an inspiration.

We can't promise it will give you the wisdom of an Oscar Wilde, although holding the solid silver body does lend itself to contemplation. (It's 92.5% pure, as pure as sterling silver comes.)

MAN IS THE ONLY ANIMAL THAT BLUSHES. OR NEEDS TO.
Mark Twain

When you do finally write, the words will flow with such uninhibited smoothness there will be nothing to block the way should a profound thought happen to wander along.

A cynic is a man who knows the price of everything and the value of nothing.
Oscar Wilde

Thank the nib for that. And the extremes we go to making it. The nib takes three weeks to manufacture, because we do it almost entirely by hand.

We fashion it from 18K gold to make it flexible to the touch. Then at the tip we mount a tiny pellet of ruthenium, a metal four times harder than steel and ten times smoother.

He is a self-made man and worships his creator.
Disraeli on a fellow politician

The ruthenium tip is sculptured under a microscope—a deft operation any surgeon could envy. But an even more delicate task follows.

The nib must be split with a cutting disc only .004" wide. Literally fine enough to split hairs.

Finally, the nib is tumbled in walnut shells for eighteen hours to leave the gold incomparably smooth.

Only after all this, not to mention 131 inspections along the way, will the craftsman who made the nib sign the certificate allowing us to sell you this pen.

Be civil to all; sociable to many; familiar with few.
Benjamin Franklin

Buy the Parker Premier and even if you never write anything magnificent, at least you will never write anything but magnificently.

✦ **PARKER**

For the stores near you which carry Parker Premier pens, call toll-free 1-800-356-7007. Or write The Parker Pen Company, P.O. Box 5100, Dept. P, Janesville, WI 53547. ©1983 TPPC.

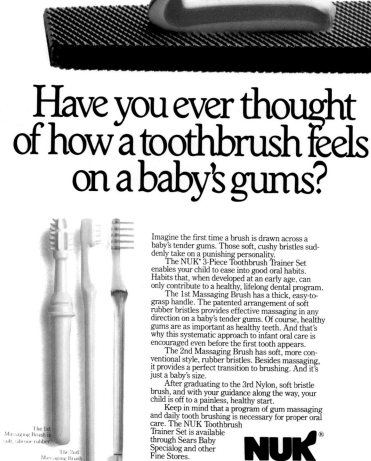

Have you ever thought of how a toothbrush feels on a baby's gums?

Imagine the first time a brush is drawn across a baby's tender gums. Those soft, cushy bristles suddenly take on a punishing personality.

The NUK* 3-Piece Toothbrush Trainer Set enables your child to ease into good oral habits. Habits that, when developed at an early age, can only contribute to a healthy, lifelong dental program.

The 1st Massaging Brush has a thick, easy-to-grasp handle. The patented arrangement of soft rubber bristles provides effective massaging in any direction on a baby's tender gums. Of course, healthy gums are as important as healthy teeth. And that's why this systematic approach to infant oral care is encouraged even before the first tooth appears.

The 2nd Massaging Brush has soft, more conventional style, rubber bristles. Besides massaging, it provides a perfect transition to brushing. And it's just a baby's size.

After graduating to the 3rd Nylon, soft bristle brush, and with your guidance along the way, your child is off to a painless, healthy start.

Keep in mind that a program of gum massaging and daily tooth brushing is necessary for proper oral care. The NUK Toothbrush Trainer Set is available through Sears Baby Specialog and other Fine Stores.

The 1st Massaging Brush is soft, silicone rubber.

The 2nd Massaging Brush has soft rubber bristles.

The 3rd brush is "child sized" with nylon bristles.

NUK®

Reliance Products Corporation
108 Mason Street, Woonsocket, RI 02895
A subsidiary of Gerber Products Company.

152

If you can work these, you can work this.

Computers aren't complex mysteries, they're blindingly simple.

And Apple, the personal computer company, would like to be the first to tell you so.

These daunting machines can be broken down into embarrassingly ordinary parts.

Take the monitor, for a start.

No more than a simplified TV set, it comprises a screen, a contrast knob and an on/off switch.

It's so basic, it can't even pick up Get Smart repeats.

Then there's the keyboard.

Not a million miles from an office typewriter, really.

Except a computer keyboard is a bit more versatile, and easier to use.

(Sure, it has a handful of microcircuits inside, but so does your radio.

(And since when did you have to understand those to get the cricket scores?)

This basically leaves one final item of equipment to come to grips with.

The disk drive.

Carrying the parallels just a little further, the disk drive is in many ways no more than a miniature record player.

Now you know just about all there is to know (or need to know) about hardware.

Which brings us, neatly, to the subject of software.

Do you have any idea of how simple that is? (You'll laugh when we tell you this.)

Software is essentially information (or the programme) stored on something like a scaled-down record album. Except the disk is soft and pliable. (Hence, the incredibly technical term, floppy disk.)

So there you have it.

A TV set, sitting on top of a typewriter with a record player plugged into one side.

Dazzling stuff.

And anyone who can run these, can run a computer.

Even if you can only type with one finger.

Even if you're so un-technical you can't work a coffee percolator or the office copier.

And if you don't believe us, we'll prove it to you.

Go along to your nearest Apple dealer, and ask to play with the new Apple //e.

Ask if you can use the new self-teaching programme; "Apple presents Apple".

This remarkable creation, recently introduced by Apple, takes the worry out of learning to use a computer.

Mainly because the computer itself teaches you.

Yes, the computer.

That infinitely patient, polite, helpful machine will take you through all the basic steps of computer use.

Enough to enable you to start on any one of the 2,000 or so programmes ready-to-run on your Apple.

And give you access to the tools that will make your working life so much more productive; Apple's Business programmes.

Just slot in the self-teaching disk, and away you go.

You'll be led by the hand through the keyboard.

You'll uncover such deep mysteries as the menu (no more than an index), as well as capitals, characters, buttons, keys, escapes, and moving cursors (like a video game, only practical). And much more.

You'll even have the computer showing you how to fix things when you make (gasp) mistakes.

But, most of all, it'll show you how to relax and have fun with computers.

As well as your job.

For more information write to: "Freepost 9", Apple Australia Pty. Ltd., P.O. Box 812, Chatswood 2067. (No stamp needed.) Or CED Distributors Ltd., 86 Wairau Road, Takapuna 9, New Zealand.

🍎 apple
The personal computer.

153

Once you decide which of these two pages is easier to read, you'll have decided which word processor is easier to work with.

The words on both pages are identical.

Only the colors are different—and for good reason.

The green-on-black page resembles the standard display screen you'll find on most word processors. Including IBM and Lanier.

But the black-on-white page is like the unique black-on-white screen of a CPT word processor.

The green-on-black side claims that they're easier on the eyes.

But which side did *your* eyes naturally turn to?

COULD YOUR EYES TAKE IT?

The eyes of a word processor operator travel back and forth between screen and paper up to 12,000 times a day.

Typing from white paper onto a black screen is like bouncing back and forth between the pages of this ad for eight hours at a stretch—enough to give you quite a headache.

Imagine how much easier it would be to type from a black-on-white sheet of paper onto a black-on-white "electronic paper" CPT screen.

50,000 HAVE ALREADY DECIDED ON CPT

The Office Products Analyst called CPT's screen "the best display in the industry."

And buyers in 60 countries have purchased over 50,000 CPT word processors with this one-of-a-kind black-on-white screen.

In many cases, they chose CPT over models with green-on-black screens.

But that's not surprising when you keep in mind that the easier a word processor is to work with, the more work you get out of it.

That's called making a smart business decision.

STILL NOT PERSUADED?

Let us show you how

CPT's word processors can improve upon your current way of typing.

While we're at it, we'll demonstrate how CPT word processors can help you automate your entire office, with CPT's planned Office Dialog Link™ network.

Our latest booklet explains it all in plain English.

For your free copy, simply mail the coupon below.

The *black-on-white* coupon.

FREE 28-PAGE BOOKLET

Word Processing—A Step At A Time explains everything from the basics to office automation. Packed with useful advice.

Mail to: CPT Information Services P.O. Box 4600 Peoria, Illinois 61614. Or call 800-447-4700 (In Alaska 907-277-3577, In Hawaii 808-498-7291.)

Name
Company
Address
City
State
Phone

CPT

The easy way to automate your office.

Once you decide which of these two pages is easier to read, you'll have decided which word processor is easier to work with.

The words on both pages are identical.

Only the colors are different—and for good reason.

The green-on-black page resembles the standard display screen you'll find on most word processors. Including IBM and Lanier.

But the black-on-white page is like the unique black-on-white screen of a CPT word processor.

The green-on-black side claims that they're easier on the eyes.

But which side did *your* eyes naturally turn to?

COULD YOUR EYES TAKE IT?

The eyes of a word processor operator travel back and forth between screen and paper up to 12,000 times a day.

Typing from white paper onto a black screen is like bouncing back and forth between the pages of this ad for eight hours at a stretch—enough to give you quite a headache.

Imagine how much easier it would be to type from a black-on-white sheet of paper onto a black-on-white "electronic paper" CPT screen.

50,000 HAVE ALREADY DECIDED ON CPT

The Office Products Analyst called CPT's screen "the best display in the industry."

And buyers in 60 countries have purchased over 50,000 CPT word processors with this one-of-a-kind black-on-white screen.

In many cases, they chose CPT over models with green-on-black screens.

But that's not surprising when you keep in mind that the easier a word processor is to work with, the more work you get out of it.

That's called making a smart business decision.

STILL NOT PERSUADED?

Let us show you how

CPT's word processors can improve upon your current way of typing.

While we're at it, we'll demonstrate how CPT word processors can help you automate your entire office, with CPT's planned Office Dialog Link™ network.

Our latest booklet explains it all in plain English.

For your free copy, simply mail the coupon below.

The *black-on-white* coupon.

FREE 28-PAGE BOOKLET

Word Processing—A Step At A Time explains everything from the basics to office automation. Packed with useful advice.

Mail to: CPT Information Services P.O. Box 4600 Peoria, Illinois 61614. Or call 800-447-4700 (In Alaska 907-277-3577, In Hawaii 808-498-7291.)

Name
Company
Address
City
State
Phone

CPT

The easy way to automate your office.

$10,945. Mfr's sugg. retail price includes a 12-month unlimited mileage, limited warranty. Transp., tax, license, dealer prep add'l.

Pictured: The Wolfsburg Limited Edition model. Special white seats, white alloy wheels, white convertible top all standard.

It's a marvel of German engineering.

Who cares?

Starting at the top:

The top of a Volkswagen Rabbit Convertible is a symphony of old fashioned hand fitting and space age weather resistant padding, virtually eliminating wind noise and moisture.

It even has a proper glass rear window that's electrically heated.

The body is made at the Karmann Coachworks in Osnabrück, West Germany where human hands still outnumber machines.

Examine it closely: body panels fit. Doors close flush. And you can see your face in the bright enamel finish.

Its engine? A temple of efficiency: 1.7 liters. Fuel injected.

Steering: Rack-and-pinion. Front suspension: MacPherson strut.

So as you can see, the Volkswagen is really the most technologically sophisticated 4 passenger German convertible you can buy.

But then again...

Nothing else is a Volkswagen

VW

If you can find the trash can, you can run a computer.

You don't have to know it's the world's most powerful personal computer.

You don't have to appreciate its unique 32-bit architecture. Or get weak in the knees when we tell you it has a million bytes of internal memory.

All you really have to know is that it's the only computer you can learn to use in under 30 minutes.

Because it's Lisa.™ From Apple.

Lisa replaces complex computer commands with simple "icons," pictures of objects familiar to anyone who's ever worked at a desk.

File folders look like file folders. Memos like memos.

There's even a calculator and a clipboard.

To tell Lisa what you want, just point to the appropriate icon using a palm-sized device called a "mouse." As you move the mouse on your desk, the pointer moves on Lisa's screen.

So you work intuitively, right from the start.

And every Lisa program works the same way. Once you've learned one, you'll learn the next even faster.

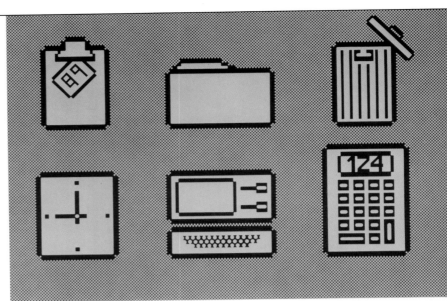

That's the difference between Lisa and every other computer in the world.

It lets you concentrate on what you want done.

Not on how to get a computer to do it.

Soon there'll be just two kinds of people. Those who use computers and 🍎 those who use Apples.

For literature or information on our National Account Program, call **(800) 538-9696**. Or write Apple Computer Inc., Dept. L, 20525 Mariani Avenue, Cupertino, CA 95014. In Canada call. **(800) 268-7796** or **(800) 268-7637**. © 1983 Apple Computer Inc.

156

Why it's smart to make babies work for their meals.

The hole aims up during feeding, so milk won't simply squirt down the baby's throat.

The soft, flat, slender neck helps keep baby's lips closed, encouraging nasal breathing.

The flat side of the Nipple is designed to be a natural tongue rest for proper positioning.

In order to extract milk, the baby must exercise his bottom jaw to actually strip the liquid out.

When an infant takes milk from a mother's breast there's a lot that goes on beyond just satisfying a little hunger.

There's the natural sucking action. The contraction and release of certain muscles. The movement of the bottom jaw. The strategic positioning of the tongue.

Milk doesn't simply pour out of the breast. It has to be systematically, almost mechanically pumped away. An instinctive routine that enables a baby to feed while exercising and developing the important muscles.

And if mothers were to tell us that a well-fed, well-exercised baby has a better temperament and sleeps better, we wouldn't be surprised.

The NUK® Orthodontic Nipple was designed to perform like a mother's breast.

This unusual shape is designed to simulate the configuration of a breast during feeding. Every contour has a purpose. In fact, the NUK Nipple is the original orthodontic shape. And the American Academy of Pedodontics suggests the use of a nipple closely resembling a mother's breast.

When the NUK Nipple is positioned for feeding, the hole is on the top so milk hits the roof of the mouth mixing with saliva for easy digestion.

Plus, the hole is smaller than most

The NUK Nipple shape is designed to simulate a mother's breast during feeding. (Playtex® version shown.)

conventional rubber nipples so your baby gets a work out similar to breast feeding.

And the simple flat tongue rest provides the solid foundation for good, hard sucking.

As you can see NUK Nipples are available to fit all major brands of disposable and reusable nursers. So you only have to change nipples to give your baby all the NUK advantages.

The NUK Nipple is part of a complete family of NUK® products all designed to help your baby's oral development. We also supply pacifier-teethers, pacifier-exercisers, nursers, teething gel and other fine products.

There's a NUK Nipple for the Evenflo® nurser.

There's a NUK Nipple for the Playtex® nurser.

There's a NUK Nipple for the Gerber® nurser.

Reliance Products Corp., 108 Mason St., P.O. Box 1220, Woonsocket, RI 02895. A subsidiary of Gerber Products Company.

NUK is a licensed trademark owned by Mapa GmbH, Gummi-und Plastikwerke, Zeven, Federal Republic of Germany.
©1983 Gerber Products Company.

157

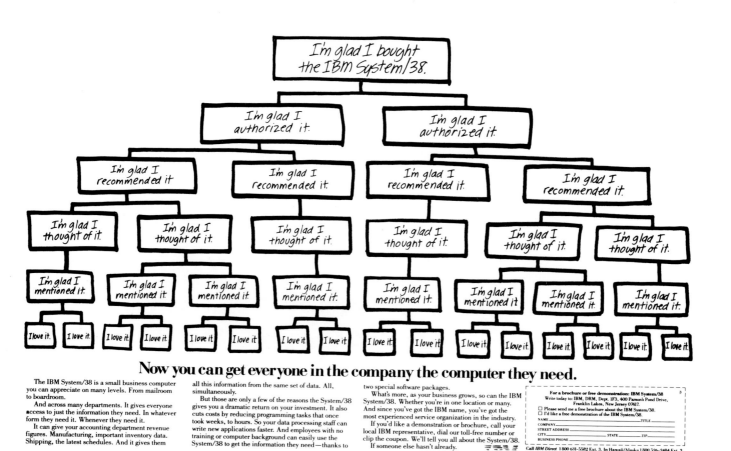

Now you can get everyone in the company the computer they need.

The IBM System/38 is a small business computer you can appreciate on many levels. From mailroom to boardroom.

And across many departments. It gives everyone access to just the information they need. In whatever form they need it. Whenever they need it.

It can give your accounting department revenue figures. Manufacturing, important inventory data. Shipping, the latest schedules. And it gives them all this information from the same set of data. All, simultaneously.

But those are only a few of the reasons the System/38 gives you a dramatic return on your investment. It also cuts costs by reducing programming tasks that once took weeks, to hours. So your data processing staff can write new applications faster. And employees with no training or computer background can easily use the System/38 to get the information they need—thanks to two special software packages.

What's more, as your business grows, so can the IBM System/38. Whether you're in one location or many. And since you've got the IBM name, you've got the most experienced service organization in the industry.

If you'd like a demonstration or brochure, call your local IBM representative, dial our toll-free number or clip the coupon. We'll tell you all about the System/38. If someone else hasn't already.

IBM

FOR THOSE TOO LAZY TO WOK.

In the last year, the wok has burst like a Chinese firecracker upon the British cookery scene.

Nothing, say its fans, leaves food so crisp outside yet so tender inside.

It's worth the hours you have to spend scrubbing, scouring and oiling the rusty thing. (No wonder a woman's wok is never done.)

But there is an easier way to achieve the results which made the wok famous.

To stir-fry vegetables, steam rice and prawns, throw together a quick crab and corn soup.

It's called a Philips 8930 Cooktronic microwave oven.

PHILIPS GIVES YOU STIR-FRYING WITHOUT FRYING.

Stir-frying at high temperatures instantly crisps foods, sealing in their juices. They crunch when you bite them, but are meltingly tender and full of flavour.

The Philips 8930 does not fry foods, so here's how you get that delectable stir-fried effect.

Chop your vegetables finely, slicing along stems and roots to produce long oval shapes. Cut your meat into paper thin slices (it's fairly easy if the meat is partly frozen).

Sparingly brush sliced meat and vegetables with oil, mix up in a dish and pop into the oven.

Open the door once or twice during cooking and stir vigorously.

PHILIPS GIVES YOU CRUNCHIER VEGETABLES

Don't boil vegetables. When you do their flavour and vitamins drain out into the water which then gets poured down the sink.

Steam them instead in your Philips 8930. Here's how.

Do any chopping (for instance topping and tailing runner beans) before you wash them.

Rinse them briefly under the cold tap, then give them a good shake, but don't dry them.

Put the still wet vegetables in a polythene bag or in a covered dish and place in the oven.

They're ready almost at once. And they taste fresher and crunchier, look better and keep their vitamins.

PHILIPS MAKES THE TASTIEST SOUPS IN CHINA.

Those lovely thick Chinese soups like crab and sweetcorn or black bean broth would be spoiled by boiling.

So the Philips 8930 makes sure they don't boil.

A slim metal probe monitors the temperature at the heart of the tureen and switches off the oven when the soup reaches the right heat.

The oven informs you with a bleep, then holds the soup simmering until you're ready to serve.

You can also use the temperature probe for roasts.

Simply slide the probe into the centre of the joint and decide how well you want the meat cooked.

The Philips 8930 does the rest.

PHILIPS LEAVES THE TURNTABLE SIMPLY YEARS BEHIND.

Most microwave ovens have bulky turntables, without which they could not cook food evenly.

Philips Cooktronic ovens do not need turntables. A hidden antenna rotating beneath the oven floor guides the microwaves evenly around the oven.

No turntable means no turntable to clean under, around and behind. Philips ovens simply wipe clean.

But the great benefit is being able to cook things in the Philips oven that wouldn't fit on a turntable.

Things like a 14 inch sea trout. Or a 12 pound Christmas turkey.

THE SECRET LIFE OF PHILIPS OWNERS.

When you buy a Philips microwave oven, you automatically become a member of the Philips Microwave Club.

Its newsletter keeps you abreast of all the latest recipes and discoveries.

There are plenty of new recipes because Philips owners tend to be adventurous cooks. And each newsletter seems to bring another exciting discovery.

One club member taught us to dry fresh garden herbs in the microwave.

Another told us how a few seconds in a Cooktronic does wonders for the bouquet of red wine.

For more information about Philips Cooktronic microwave ovens please post this coupon to Julie Castello, Philips Electronics, Lightcliffe, Halifax HX3 8DE.

NAME _____

ADDRESS _____

PHILIPS OUR MICROWAVE OVENS LEAVE THE TURNTABLE SIMPLY YEARS BEHIND.

LAST OFF THE MOUNTAIN

The weather's closing in; the temperature's dropping; the others are back at the lodge on their second round.

Still, you're out there. Just you and the mountain.

And you need a ski that'll help you stay out there. A ski that can handle anything.

And that's the kind of ski the STS is. A descendant of the famous ST Comp. And the most popular high performance ski in North America today.

Now there's the all-new Falcon. A sophisticated fusion of fiberglass and metal. Engineered for a slalom ski's quickness, a cruising ski's control.

And for cruising at more moderate speeds, there's the versatile Eagle. With softer flex and a racing sidecut for superb, wide-ranging performance.

STS. Falcon. Eagle. The Rossignol *Sport* skis. For the advanced, athletic skier. All made to do whatever you want them to do. On any terrain, on any snow, in any weather...and that's good to know, when you're last off the mountain.

ROSSIGNOL
Let others compromise®

We started taking people to the state of Alaska 12 years before it was a state.

Find the cooker.

A gas cooker doesn't have to be built-in to blend in. New World's Option 3, for instance, combines oven, grill and hotplate   in one movable unit that fits flush with your kitchen furniture. The only thing that stands out is the cooking.

SUNDAY SHOULD BE A DAY OF REST.

PHILIPS OUR MICROWAVE OVENS LEAVE THE TURNTABLE SIMPLY YEARS BEHIND.

163

WHEN YOU HAVE TEN YEARS TO BUILD A NEW CAR, YOUR MISTAKES END UP IN THE WASTEBASKET. NOT IN SOMEBODY'S GARAGE.

When many companies design a new car, the pressures to get that car out into the marketplace are often so intense, the car gets churned out overnight.

And all too frequently, car buyers pay the price. They can end up with cars that are totally unimaginative, or poorly thought out, or inadequately tested.

In designing the new Volvo 760 GLE, one thing we gave ourselves plenty of was time. Ten long years. Time to challenge accepted notions about building automobiles. Time to try off-the-wall ideas. Time to make mistakes, then correct them. And above all, time to test, test, test.

What emerged from this process is a car that's remarkable indeed.

The Volvo 760 GLE is more aerodynamic than a Porsche 928, yet holds five adults. It has traveled through a high-speed slalom course faster than a Jaguar or Audi.

It has a climate control system so advanced, it can change the interior air five times a minute.

Prototypes of the 760 GLE were test driven a total of two million torturous miles. This testing led to hundreds of design improvements. And after we'd made the improvements, we tested again. And improved on the improvements.

So when the new Volvo 760 GLE is sitting in your garage, you'll own one of the most patiently-built cars in history.

And as everyone knows, patience has its rewards.

THE VOLVO 760 GLE
The closest thing yet to a perfect car.

167

168

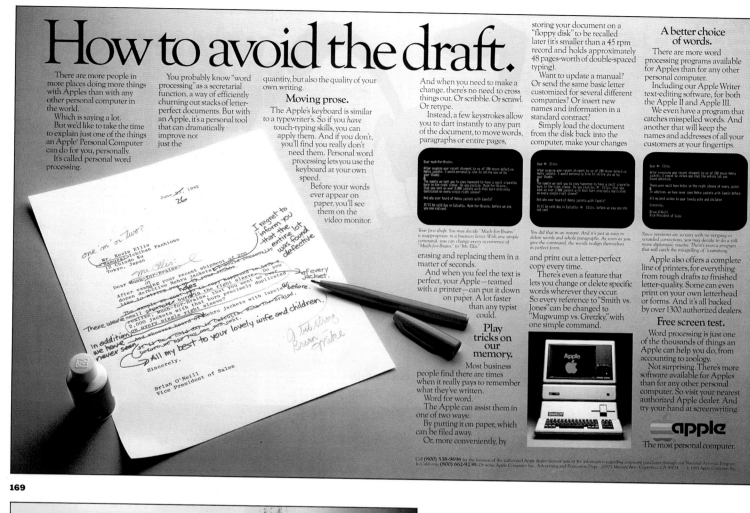

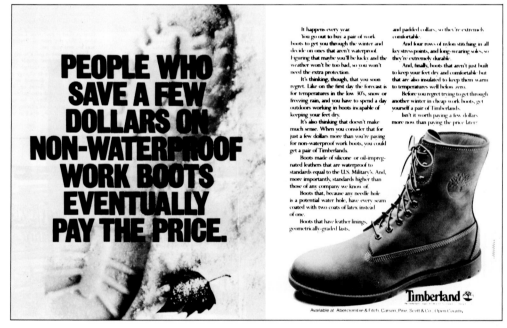

HOW MUCH WEIGHT DO YOU HAVE TO LOSE BEFORE YOUR INSURANCE COMPANY NOTICES IT?

Anyone who's ever tried knows that losing weight can be a real struggle. You go to bed hungry. You wake up hungry. You learn to despise lettuce. You exercise until you ache.

The good news is that according to recent studies, people who stay trim and exercise regularly live longer and are better life insurance risks. So now, ITT Life has come up with a Good Health Bonus* for non-smokers and people who are trim and

fit. Which means that if you don't smoke, you could earn a 65% insurance bonus. *With no increase in your insurance premiums.*

If you stay trim and don't smoke, you could get a 100% life insurance bonus. And over half of the non-smokers who apply meet the special underwriting criteria for the Good Health Bonus.

Look. You work very hard to keep your body trim. Isn't it about time you got the trimmer life insurance premiums you deserve?

For more details call free: **1-800-328-2193** and ask for operator 901. In Minnesota call us at 612-545-2100. Or mail the coupon to us today.

ITT Life Insurance Corporation ITT

SOMETHING IS WRONG WHEN A SIZE 34 WAIST PAYS THE SAME INSURANCE AS A SIZE 48 WAIST.

It's a sad fact of life. After about age 30, it gets harder and harder to keep your stomach from dominating your body. Most people can't do it without regular exercise.

But studies show that people who *do* exercise regularly and who *don't* smoke are better life insurance risks. Ironically, however, few insurance companies give genuine rewards to physically fit non-smokers. And while some companies offer non-smoker's

discounts, ITT Life offers a Good Health Bonus* that rewards both non-smokers and regular exercisers with bonus insurance coverage. With the ITT Life plan, if you don't smoke you could earn a 65% life insurance bonus.

For example, ie, your $50,000 policy could be increased to $82,500. *With no increase in premiums.*

If you exercise regularly and don't smoke, you could receive a 100% life insurance bonus.

Over half of the non-smokers applying meet the special underwriting criteria for the ITT Life Good Health Bonus. So if you've been able to defy cigarettes and gravity, why not collect the reward you deserve on your life insurance? For details call free: **1-800-328-2193**. Ask for operator 981. In Minnesota call 612-545-2100. Or mail this coupon.

ITT Life Insurance Corporation ITT

ITT LIFE BELIEVES A BEAUTIFUL BODY SHOULD BE WORTH MORE THAN A FEW WHISTLES AT THE BEACH.

When you're young, a beautiful body may be something you take for granted. As you grow older, however, keeping your body beautiful takes work.

For those of you who haven't given in to rich foods, cigarettes, and gravity, however, ITT Life has good news: the ITT Life Good Health Bonus.* This is a life insurance plan which truly recognizes that people who exercise regularly and don't smoke live longer on the average and, therefore, are better life insurance risks.

ITT Life rewards them for those good habits.

If you don't smoke, the Good Health Bonus could be worth a 65% insurance bonus to you. For example, your $50,000 policy would be increased to $82,500. *With no increase in premiums.*

If you don't smoke and you also exercise regularly, you could earn a 100% life insurance bonus — *double the protection without any increase in premiums.* And over half of the non-smokers who apply are meeting the special underwriting criteria for the Good Health Bonus.

Isn't it time you began getting the beautiful insurance rates your beautiful body deserves?

For details call free **1-800-328-2193** and ask for operator 599. In Minnesota: 612-545-2100. Or mail the coupon.

ITT Life Insurance Corporation

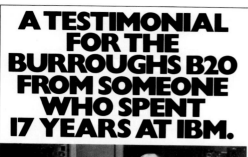

185

186

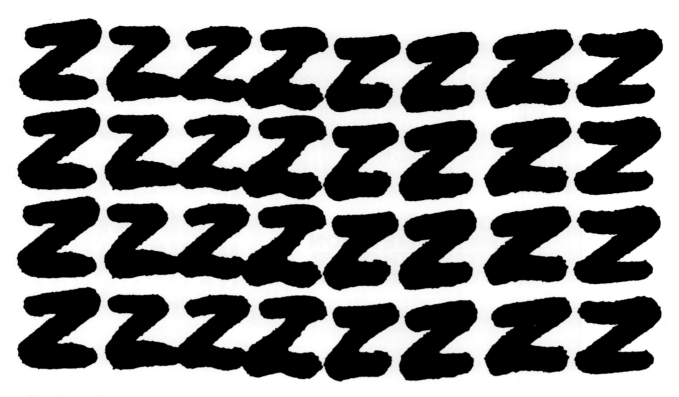

THERE IS A DIFFERENCE BETWEEN JOHNNY CARSON AND ALAN THICKE.

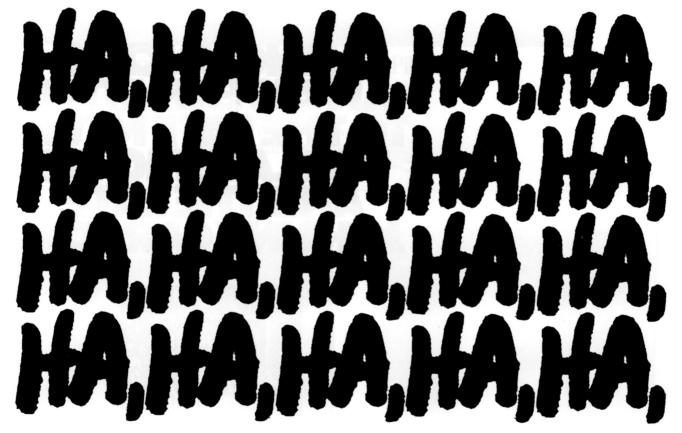

TURN ON *THICKE OF THE NIGHT* WEEKNIGHTS AT 10:30.

32
WFLD TV
METROMEDIA CHICAGO

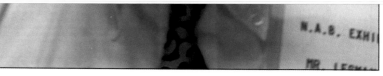

Genital herpes viruses may live on towels for 72 hours and on toilet seats for four hours. Choose your bathrooms carefully.

The latest news about genital herpes isn't exactly encouraging. The January Reader's Digest reports that this incurable disease doesn't even depend on genital intercourse for transmission: Contact with an infected finger, mouth, towel or toilet seat may be sufficient.

And once someone gets genital herpes, a recurrence can be triggered simply by the stress of *worrying* about it.

This kind of news makes casual sex less attractive. But this kind of reporting helps The Digest® attract 39 million readers.

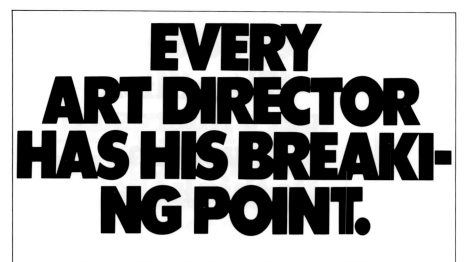

213

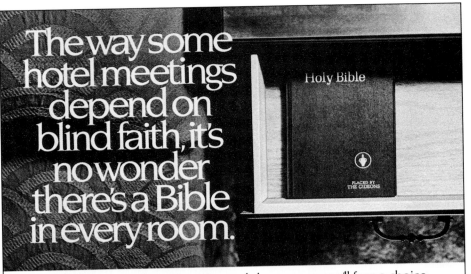

The way some hotel meetings depend on blind faith, it's no wonder there's a Bible in every room.

Book an ordinary meeting and chances are you'll face a choice: Should you worry about all those details yourself? Or should you pray that the hotel staff will cover them?

Book a Radisson Assured Meeting and nothing is left to chance. We'll work with you and help plan your meeting a detail at a time.

You'll deal with the key people on our hotel staff, starting with the General Manager. You'll be provided a Meeting Coordinator whose sole responsibility is making sure your meeting goes right. You'll also get a list of staff names and telephone numbers and a VIP lapel pin that identifies you as someone very special. Wear it and watch things happen.

We've just spent $300 million for new hotels and meeting facilities in some of America's fastest growing business centers.

But we're not going to sit back and wait for them to fill themselves. We're going to fill them by giving meeting planners exactly what they need: Hotels that take more of the worries and less of the credit.

For complete details and specifications on any of the Radissons listed below, just call toll free **1-800-228-9822.**

ℙ The Radisson Hotels Assured Meeting™

Radisson Hotels are located in: Scottsdale, AZ; Wilmington, DE; Atlanta, GA; Lexington, KY; Boston (Danvers), MA; Saginaw, MI; Alexandria, MN; Duluth, MN; Minneapolis, MN (2); St. Paul, MN (2); Kansas City, MO; St. Louis, MO; Charlotte, NC; Raleigh, NC; Nashville, TN; Dallas, TX; Burlington, VT; LaCrosse, WI; Superior, WI; Kenora (Minaki), Ontario; Cairo, Egypt.

We do more for your meeting than just wish you good luck.

Some hotels appear to think that all a meeting planner needs is a room key and a good-luck handshake.

Not Radisson. Consider our Assured Meeting. There isn't a smarter, more trouble-proof buy in the industry.

Book one and you'll deal with the key people on our staff, starting with the General Manager. You'll have a Meeting Coordinator whose sole responsibility is making sure your meeting goes right. You'll also get a list of staff names and telephone numbers and a VIP lapel pin that identifies you as someone very special. Every member of the staff will honor it.

We've just spent $300 million for new hotels and meeting facilities. We're not going to sit back and wait for them to fill themselves.

We're going to fill them by doing even more for meeting planners just like you: by leaving absolutely nothing to chance.

With a Radisson Assured Meeting, your meeting will be a stroke of genius, not just a matter of luck.

For complete details and specifications on any of the Radissons listed below, just call toll free **1-800-228-9822.**

ℙ The Radisson Hotels Assured Meeting™

Radisson Hotels are located in: Scottsdale, AZ; Wilmington, DE; Atlanta, GA; Lexington, KY; Boston (Danvers), MA; Saginaw, MI; Alexandria, MN; Duluth, MN; Minneapolis, MN (2); St. Paul, MN (2); Kansas City, MO; St. Louis, MO; Charlotte, NC; Raleigh, NC; Nashville, TN; Dallas, TX; Burlington, VT; LaCrosse, WI; Superior, WI; Kenora (Minaki), Ontario; Cairo, Egypt.

You know you've booked the wrong hotel when the "Do Not Disturb" signs are hung on the staff.

There is no room for apathy at a Radisson Hotel.

We've just spent $300 million for new hotels and meeting facilities in some of America's fastest growing business centers.

And we have the Radisson Assured Meeting. There isn't a smarter, more trouble-proof buy in the industry.

Book one and you'll deal with the key people on our staff, starting with the General Manager. You'll have a Meeting Coordinator whose sole responsibility is making sure your meeting goes right. You'll also get a list of staff names and telephone numbers and a VIP lapel pin that identifies you as someone very special. Wear it and watch things happen.

With a product like this, The Radisson Hotels are going to be an even greater factor in the meeting and convention industry. We're going to build our business by earning your business.

And we're going to earn your business by making sure all of us here at Radisson stay on our toes. And off our duffs.

For complete details and specifications on any of the Radissons listed below, just call toll free **1-800-228-9822.**

ℙ The Radisson Hotels Assured Meeting™

Radisson Hotels are located in: Scottsdale, AZ; Wilmington, DE; Atlanta, GA; Lexington, KY; Boston (Danvers), MA; Saginaw, MI; Alexandria, MN; Duluth, MN; Minneapolis, MN (2); St. Paul, MN (2); Kansas City, MO; St. Louis, MO; Charlotte, NC; Raleigh, NC; Nashville, TN; Dallas, TX; Burlington, VT; LaCrosse, WI; Superior, WI; Kenora (Minaki), Ontario; Cairo, Egypt.

As a group, ministers have a lower mortality rate than most mortals.

But a long life puts special demands on your life insurance and retirement programs. Demands that most insurance companies can't live up to.

At Ministers Life, we see your longevity as a virtue. Because we insure *only* religious professionals, we can offer you the kind of comprehensive and affordable coverage your longevity should command.

Furthermore, we're as well-acquainted with your life style as we are your life expectancy. Our representatives are familiar with all the special requirements and complexities of your profession, including your unique tax status and housing situations. And they use what they know to shepherd your assets wisely.

Find out if your insurance and retirement programs live up to your special needs. Call us for a free financial review. There's no obligation so call us today at **1-800-328-6124**, ext. 246 (In Minnesota, call 612-927-7131.)

ML Ministers Life
a mutual life insurance company
Ministers Life Building, Minneapolis, Minnesota 55416
© 1983 Ministers Life

Ministers go to heaven 23% slower.

As a minister, you are one of a handful of people who qualify to invest in both a Tax-Deferred Annuity (TDA) as well as in an Individual Retirement Account (IRA). And while we offer both of these tax-advantaged retirement plans, there are important differences you should know about before you invest.

With a TDA, contributions are taken out of your checks before you get them. So they're not subject to Social Security taxes the way IRA contributions are. (With next year's huge increase in Social Security taxes for ministers, that's no small consideration.) And you can defer up to 1/6th of your income this way, usually more than the $2,000 ceiling on IRAs.

Since IRA contributions are deducted from your income when you file your return, any deposit you or your spouse make between now and April 15th could mean a substantial reduction on last year's taxes.

Each plan has its own advantages and making the right choice calls for a careful analysis of your financial needs.

And at Ministers Life, we are uniquely qualified to help you do this. Call us toll-free at **1-800-328-6124**, ext. 246 (in Minnesota, call collect 612-927-7131).

ML Ministers Life
a mutual life insurance company
Ministers Life Building, Minneapolis, Minnesota 55416
© 1983 Ministers Life

Ministers now have two ways to reduce their annual offering.

Internal Revenue Service Center
Ogden, UT 84201

Almost all ministers live in parsonages owned by the church, or in their own homes with the benefit of a housing allowance.

Yet the importance of this fact is lost on almost all the insurance industry. Few agents realize that the parsonage or housing allowance is a large part of a minister's compensation package. And that to provide complete protection, this "invisible income" must be insured against loss.

At Ministers Life, our representatives know how to insure your income completely. They can also help insure that your family will always have a roof over its head, even in the event of your retirement, disability, or death.

But our representatives understand more than just your housing situation. They're at home with all the complexities of your profession, including your unique tax status and denominational benefits.

And because Ministers Life insures only religious professionals, we can offer you the kind of comprehensive and affordable coverage your life style requires.

To find out just how much your Ministers Life representative knows about a minister's life, call **1-800-328-6124**, ext. 246. (In Minnesota, 612-927-7131.)

ML Ministers Life
a mutual life insurance company
Ministers Life Building, Minneapolis, Minnesota 55416
© 1983 Ministers Life

Does your insurance agent realize who your landlord is?

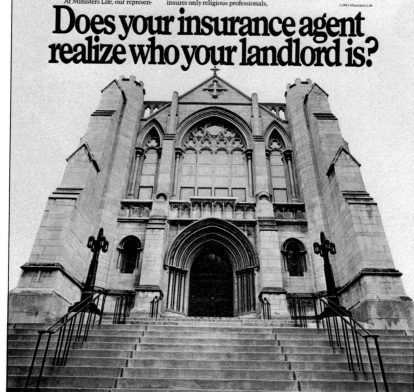

228

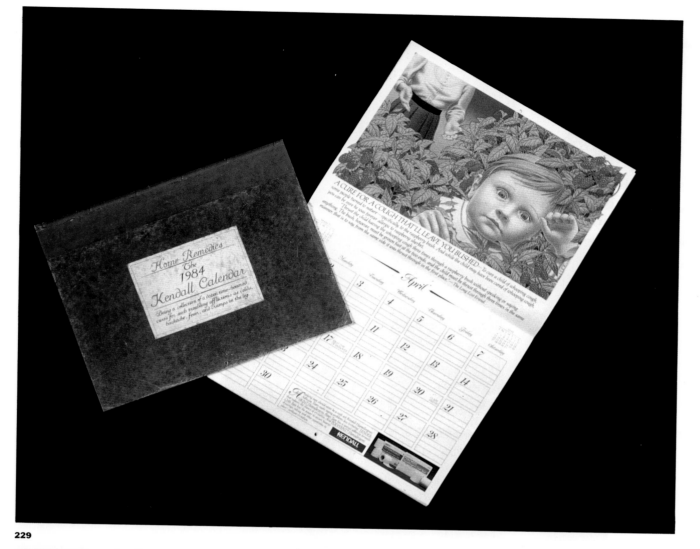

229

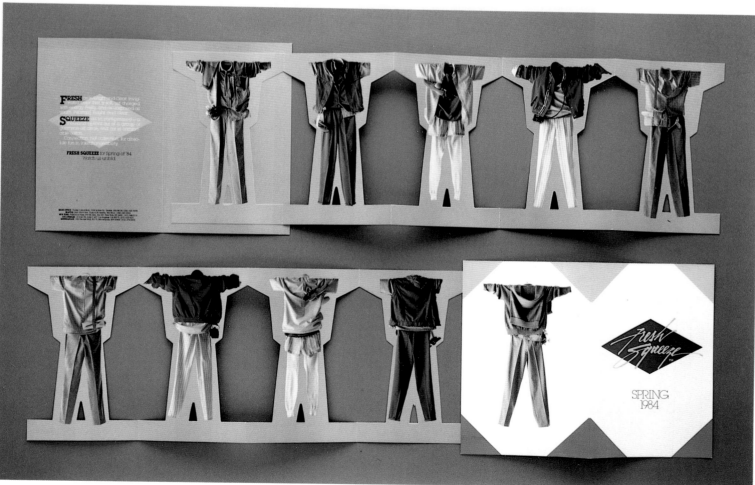

230

250
ART DIRECTOR
Hal Tench
WRITER
Barbara Ford
DESIGNER
Hal Tench
PHOTOGRAPHER
Dean Hawthorn
CLIENT
Mobil
AGENCY
The Martin Agency/Virginia

251
ART DIRECTORS
Gayl Ware
Chuck Carlberg
WRITERS
Gayl Ware
Amy Vanderbilt
DESIGNER & ARTIST
Gayl Ware
CLIENT
Chuck & Gayl Carlberg
AGENCY
Rives Smith Baldwin Carlberg
+ Y&R/Houston

252
ART DIRECTOR
Bernie Horton
WRITER
Don Jeffries
CLIENT
Wray/Ward Advertising
AGENCY
Wray/Ward Advertising/
North Carolina

250

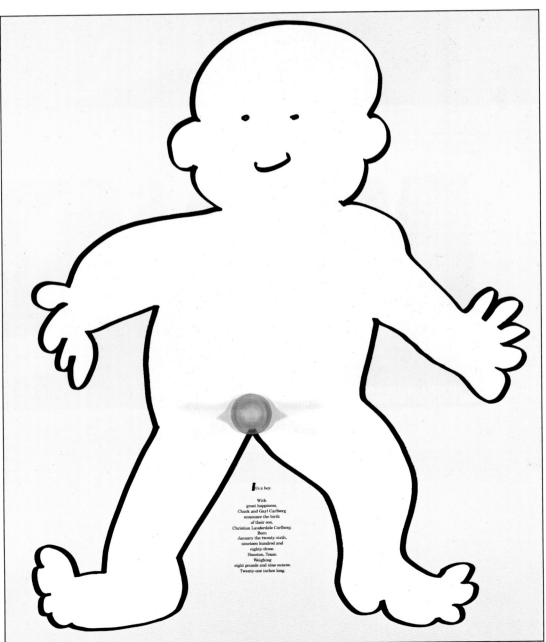

251

257
ART DIRECTOR
Hal Tench
WRITER
Mike Hughes
DESIGNER
Hal Tench
PHOTOGRAPHER
Richard Foster
CLIENT
General Motors,
Electro-Motive Division
AGENCY
The Martin Agency/Virginia

258
ART DIRECTOR
Ron Vareltlis
WRITER
Pat Blagden
DESIGNER
Ron Vareltlis
PHOTOGRAPHERS
Mel Small
Gallucci
CLIENT
Geigy Pharmaceuticals
AGENCY
C & G Advertising/
New Jersey

259
ART DIRECTOR
Nancy Rice
WRITER
Tom McElligott
DESIGNER
Nancy Rice
ARTIST
Edward Munch
CLIENT
The Show
AGENCY
Fallon McElligott Rice/
Minneapolis

260
ART DIRECTOR
Raymond Nichols
WRITER
DEsigners
DESIGNERS
Michael Dodson
DEsigners
ARTIST
DEsigners
CLIENT
Visual Communications Group/
University of Delaware
ENTRANT
University of Delaware/
Department of Art

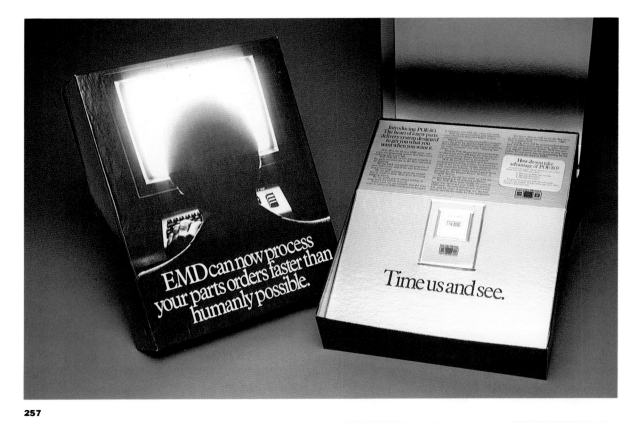

257

258

EDVARD MUNCH. *The Scream*, 1893.

259

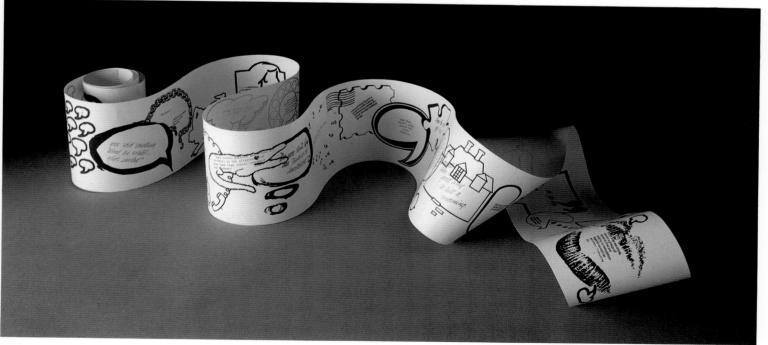

260

Unfortunately, this is how 14 million Americans deal with their hearing problems.

Starkey
Your hearing is our concern.

261

**HURT PENGUIN BOOKS
AT REDUCED PRICES.**

B. Dalton
BOOKSELLER

262

263

264

**Collateral
P.O.P.**

265
ART DIRECTOR
John Byrnes
WRITER
Susan McFeatters
PHOTOGRAPHER
Peter Vaeth
CLIENT
The United States Army
AGENCY
NW Ayer

266
ART DIRECTOR
Lee Stewart
WRITER
Bill Teitelbaum
ARTIST
Paul Blakey
CLIENT
W.R. Grace
AGENCY
Howard, Merrell & Partners/
North Carolina

267
ART DIRECTORS
John Doyle
Sue Snitzer
WRITER
Ted Charron
PHOTOGRAPHER
Bob Oliviera
CLIENT
Tretorn
AGENCY
Impecunious/Massachusetts

268
ART DIRECTOR
Mike Murray
WRITER
Bill Miller
PHOTOGRAPHER
Marvy
CLIENT
International Multifoods
AGENCY
Chuck Ruhr Advertising/
Minneapolis

HOW TO DECODE
A SOLDIER.

When you know how to read it, a soldier's uniform is actually a wealth of information about the person wearing it. It not only tells you who he is. It also tells you what he does. Even how well he does it. The insignia, emblems and badges also reflect the many choices and options the Army offers.

In the Army, you wear success on your sleeve. If there is no grade insignia, it means the soldier is a new recruit. Stripes come quickly, though, as you master your skill.

The branch insignia (in this case, Air Defense Artillery) reflects personal choices and decisions a soldier makes at enlistment. The U.S. insignia reflects the Army tradition of duty, honor, country.

YOUR NAME

Putting on a uniform doesn't mean you'll lose your own identity.

In the Army, when you're good, everybody knows it. These medals are for marksmanship. During basic training, you'll compete for marksman, sharpshooter or expert.

LOYALTY

Crests like this tell you what outfit the soldier belongs to. Army outfits resemble NFL teams—each has its own character, traditions and emblems. (Each one also thinks it's the best.)

Jump wings mean the soldier has graduated from airborne school. As you might guess, it's no ordinary school. The final exam is given at 1,250 feet.

Ribbons and medals usually recognize a soldier's achievements. This is a Good Conduct ribbon. It recognizes a soldier's character.

This distinctive patch identifies a special breed of soldier. Airborne qualified, rigorously trained. Rangers can also be easily identified by their black berets and unmistakable aura of pride.

The Army is made up of many different kinds of units, including brigades, divisions, corps, regiments and groups. Like the crest, this patch tells you where the soldier belongs. In this case, Army Communications Command.

ARMY.
BE ALL YOU CAN BE.

This tells you the soldier welcomes challenges. To earn the Expert Infantryman badge, you have to pass a battery of tests that are both physically and mentally challenging. Not many do.

265

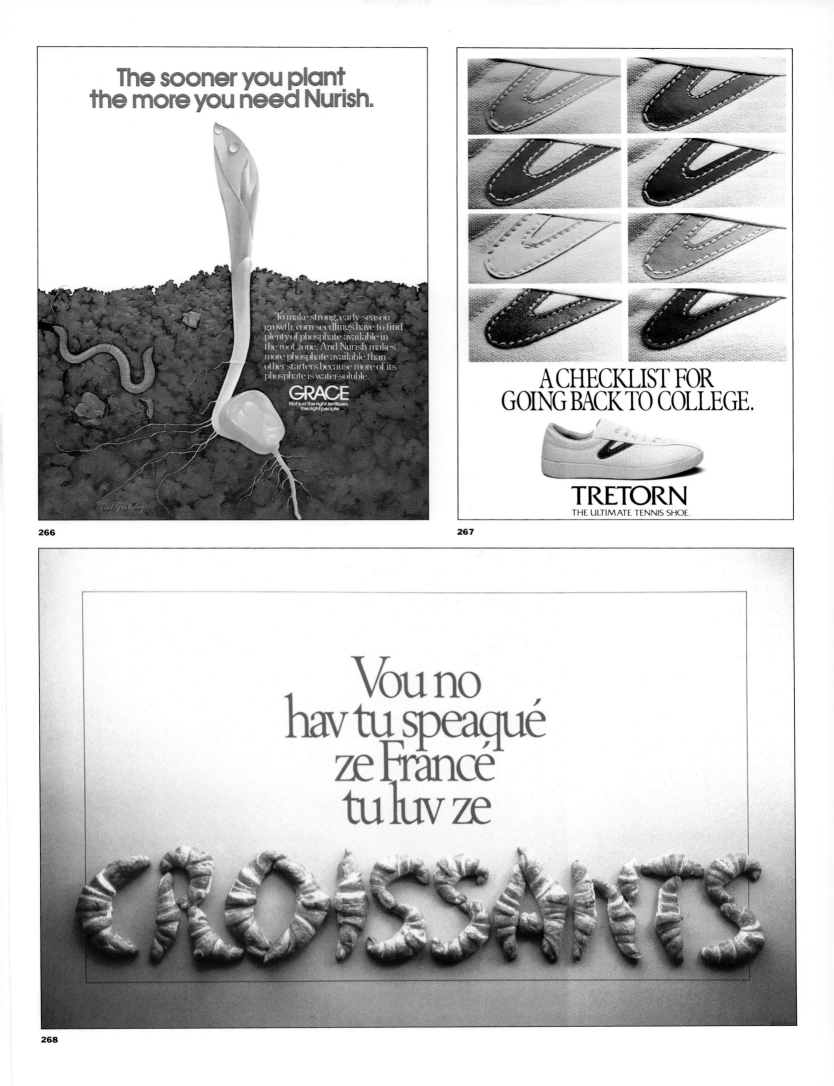

The sooner you plant the more you need Nurish.

To make strong, early-season growth, corn seedlings have to find plenty of phosphate available in the root zone. And Nurish makes more phosphate available than other starters because more of its phosphate is water-soluble.

GRACE
Not just the right fertilizer.
The right people.

266

A CHECKLIST FOR GOING BACK TO COLLEGE.

TRETORN
THE ULTIMATE TENNIS SHOE.

267

Vou no
hav tu speaqué
ze Francé
tu luv ze

CROISSANTS

268

271

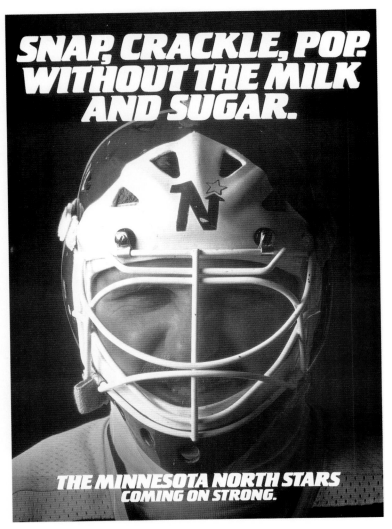

272

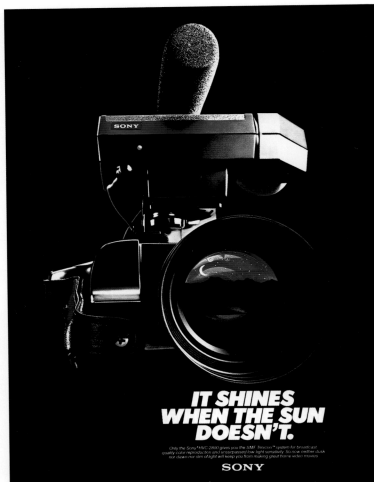

273

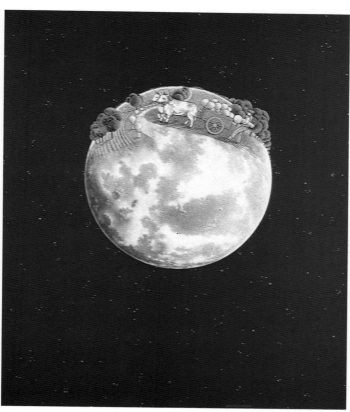

276

277

BEGIN YOUR CAREER AT ANY ONE OF OUR BRANCH OFFICES.

NAVY OFFICERS GET RESPONSIBILITY FAST.

278

Over a million copies sold.

Based on 1981-1983
worldwide sales and production figures.

Ford Escort FORD

279

292

293

294
ART DIRECTOR
John Knight
WRITER
Chris Martin
DESIGNER
Geoff Halpin
ARTISTS
Colin Elgie
Richard Manning
Geoff Halpin
CLIENT
Wolverhampton &
Dudley Breweries
AGENCY
TBWA/London

**Public Service
Newspaper or Magazine
Campaign**

295
ART DIRECTOR
Mickey Tender
WRITER
Susan McFeatters
PHOTOGRAPHER
Anthony Edgeworth
CLIENT
The United States Army
AGENCY
NW Ayer

11 BRAVO
INFANTRY

In today's Army, you can stretch your muscles and your mind. "11 Bravo" is Army shorthand for a soldier who can handle both sophisticated tactics and modern weapons. We have over 300 career training areas, from high adventure to high technology. Qualify, and we'll guarantee your choice of training. Which means you can serve your country in the way that best suits your talents.

So if it's not 11 Bravo, it might be 35 Kilo.*

ARMY.
BE ALL YOU CAN BE.

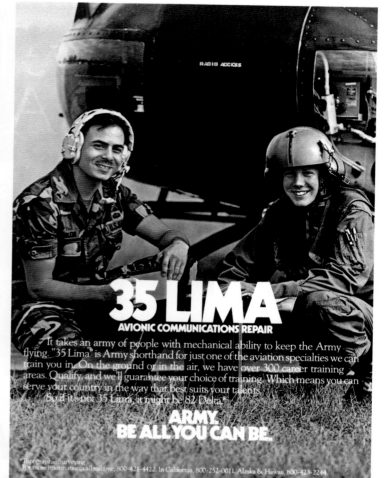

35 LIMA
AVIONIC COMMUNICATIONS REPAIR

It takes an army of people with mechanical ability to keep the Army flying. "35 Lima" is Army shorthand for just one of the aviation specialties we can train you in. On the ground or in the air, we have over 300 career training areas. Qualify, and we'll guarantee your choice of training. Which means you can serve your country in the way that best suits your talents.

So if it's not 35 Lima, it might be 82 Delta.*

ARMY.
BE ALL YOU CAN BE.

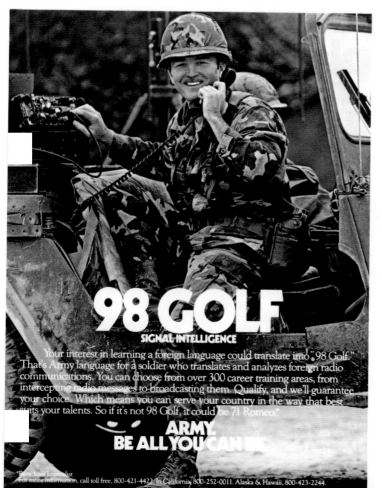

98 GOLF
SIGNAL INTELLIGENCE

Your interest in learning a foreign language could translate into "98 Golf." That's Army language for a soldier who translates and analyzes foreign radio communications. You can choose from over 300 career training areas, from intercepting radio messages to broadcasting them. Qualify, and we'll guarantee your choice. Which means you can serve your country in the way that best suits your talents. So if it's not 98 Golf, it could be 71 Romeo.*

ARMY.
BE ALL YOU CAN BE.

304

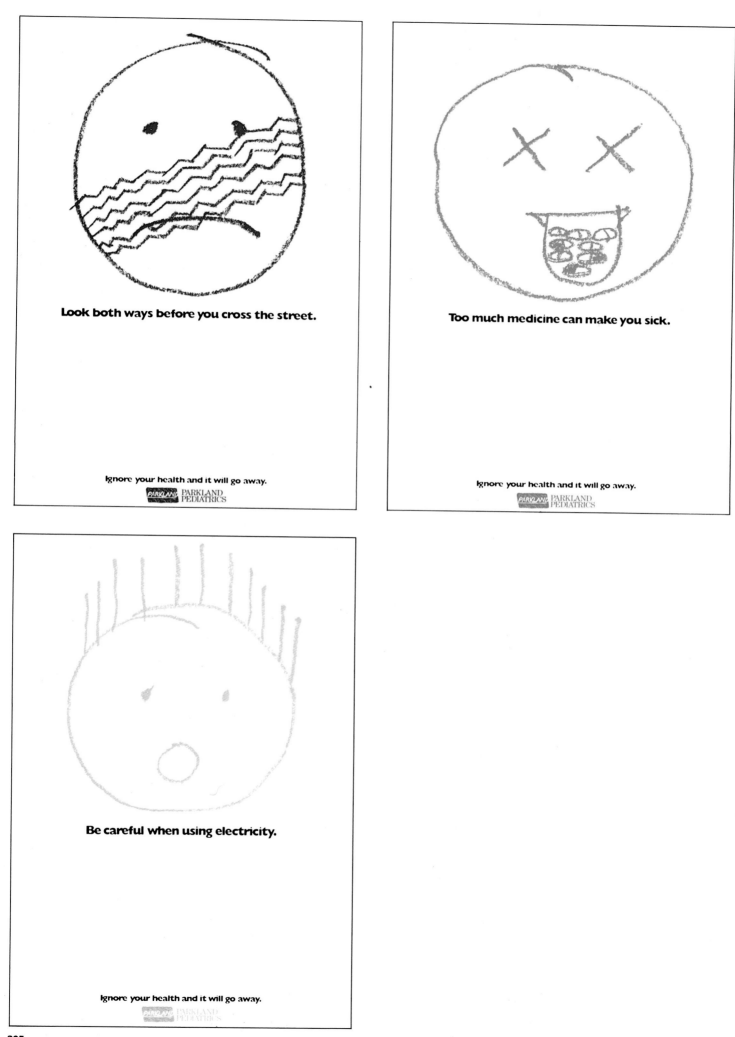

Look both ways before you cross the street.

Ignore your health and it will go away.

PARKLAND PEDIATRICS

Too much medicine can make you sick.

Ignore your health and it will go away.

PARKLAND PEDIATRICS

Be careful when using electricity.

Ignore your health and it will go away.

PARKLAND PEDIATRICS

**Public Service
Outdoor Campaign**

306
ART DIRECTOR
Kathleen Bauer
WRITER
Erik Perera
DESIGNERS
Kathleen Bauer
Terry Schneider
CLIENT
United Way of the
Columbia-Willamette
AGENCY
Gerber Advertising/
Oregon

307
ART DIRECTOR
Nancy Rice
WRITER
Tom McElligott
DESIGNER
Nancy Rice
CLIENT
The Episcopal Ad Project
AGENCY
Fallon McElligott Rice/
Minneapolis

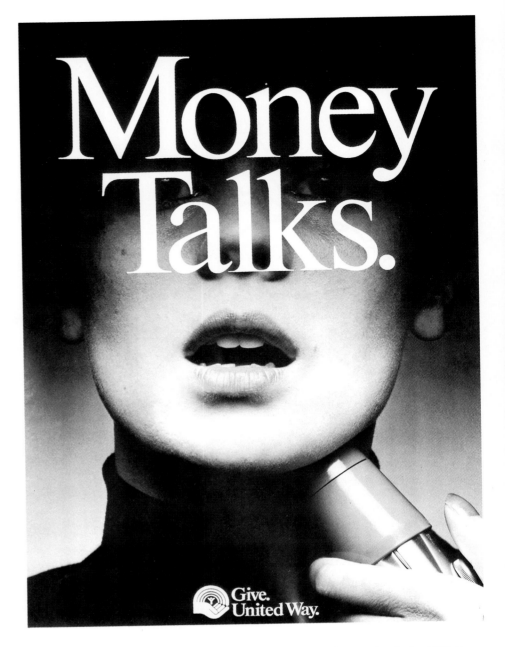

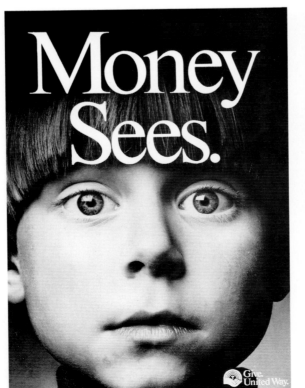

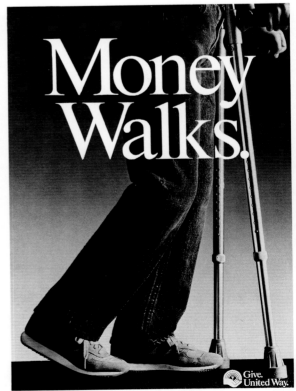

306

Considering the fact that Jesus had his doubts, why can't you?

The Episcopal Church

If you think being a Christian is inconvenient today, just look back 1500 years.

The Episcopal Church

Whose birthday is it, anyway?

The Episcopal Church

307

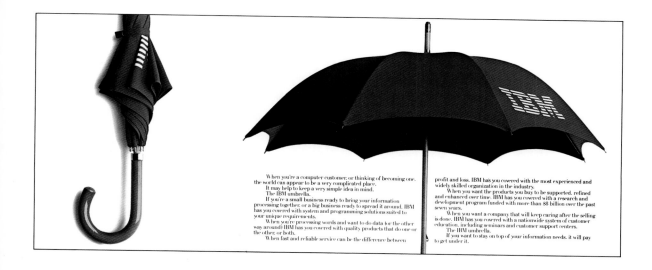

When you're a computer customer, or thinking of becoming one, the world can appear to be a very complicated place.

It may help to keep a very simple idea in mind.

The IBM umbrella.

If you're a small business ready to bring your information processing together, or a big business ready to spread it around, IBM has you covered with system and programming solutions suited to your unique requirements.

When you're processing words and want to do data (or the other way around) IBM has you covered with quality products that do one or the other, or both.

When fast and reliable service can be the difference between profit and loss, IBM has you covered with the most experienced and widely skilled organization in the industry.

When you want the products you buy to be supported, refined and enhanced over time, IBM has you covered with a research and development program funded with more than $8 billion over the past seven years.

When you want a company that will keep caring after the selling is done, IBM has you covered with a nationwide system of customer education, including seminars and customer support centers.

The IBM umbrella.

If you want to stay on top of your information needs, it will pay to get under it.

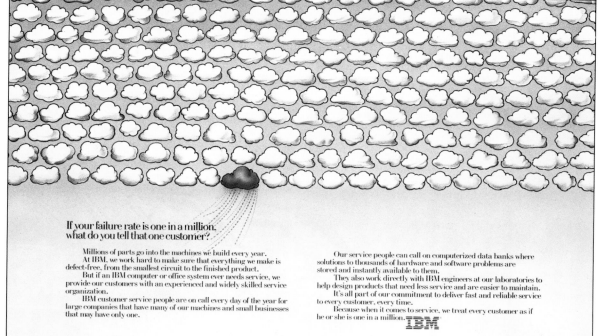

If your failure rate is one in a million, what do you tell that one customer?

Millions of parts go into the machines we build every year.

At IBM, we work hard to make sure that everything we make is defect-free, from the smallest circuit to the finished product.

But if an IBM computer or office system ever needs service, we provide our customers with an experienced and widely skilled service organization.

IBM customer service people are on call every day of the year for large companies that have many of our machines and small businesses that may have only one.

Our service people can call on computerized data banks where solutions to thousands of hardware and software problems are stored and instantly available to them.

They also work directly with IBM engineers at our laboratories to help design products that need less service and are easier to maintain.

It's all part of our commitment to deliver fast and reliable service to every customer, every time.

Because when it comes to service, we treat every customer as if he or she is one in a million. IBM

What most people want from a computer company is a good night's sleep.

We want you to rest easy about buying a computer.

If you're a small business that's ready to bring your information processing together, or a big business ready to spread it around, IBM will make you feel secure with system and programming solutions suited to your unique requirements.

Whether you want to process words or process data (or both), IBM will make you feel secure with a full line of quality products—from office systems to large computers—that can help you manage your own growth processes.

When fast and reliable service can be the difference between profit and loss, IBM will make you feel secure with a broad range of service options from the most experienced and widely skilled people in the industry. You'll rest easy knowing your call brings responsive service quickly, if you need it.

When you want to design and develop new applications to help make the most of your equipment, IBM has experienced people who can work with you. And when you want a company that will keep caring after the selling is done, IBM will make you feel secure with a nationwide system of customer education, including seminars and customer support centers.

It's all part of the IBM difference. And it can make a difference for you or your business.

315
ART DIRECTOR
Cathie Campbell
WRITER
Bob Nadler
PHOTOGRAPHER
David Langley
CLIENT
Volvo
AGENCY
Scali, McCabe, Sloves

IN 28 YEARS WE'VE ONLY SOLD SEVEN CARS.

Volvo is the leading importer of European cars in the U.S. today.

Perhaps that's because over the past 28 years, we've only made seven different models.

You see, as a company whose reputation is built around giving people something they can hold on to, we're interested in taking a good car from one year and making it better the next.

This affords us the time to build the kind of intelligent, well-constructed car people don't feel the need to part company with every few years.

The same kind of thinking also goes into other things we make like buses, trucks and marine engines.

Of course, this hasn't won us many friends among those interested in the latest fads and gadgets. But it has won us a lot of loyal followers among people interested in something that never goes out of style.

Quality.

VOLVO NORTH AMERICA CORPORATION

© 1983 Volvo North America Corporation.

315

THIS LADY IS BEING PULLED BY HER VOLVO.

A lot of people who depend on Volvos have never driven our cars.

Maybe that's because many Volvos are built for America's waterways. Not its highways. You see, Volvo is one of the leading manufacturers of marine engines in the U.S. today.

But we still believe that on terra firma there's great potential for growth. That's why we're involved in the manufacture and servicing of trucks through the Volvo White Truck Corporation.

And although you've probably never seen a Volvo bus, you'll probably be seeing a lot of them in the near future. Because this year, we're starting up full scale production in our Chesapeake, Va. plant.

So if you think Volvo only makes cars, you're missing the boat. And the bus. And the truck.

VOLVO NORTH AMERICA CORPORATION

ALL THESE PEOPLE COULD HAVE FIT IN ONE VOLVO.

There's a Volvo with enough legroom for 73 passengers, enough headroom for a 7-footer and enough elbow room for all these passengers to stretch out.

That's because this Volvo isn't a car. It's a bus.

Even though you've probably never seen one, Volvo is one of the leading manufacturers of buses in the world. And this year, we started up full-scale production in our Chesapeake, Va. plant.

What's more, Volvo is no slouch in the trucking industry. The Volvo White Truck Corporation is  rapidly accelerating its production schedule. And we're also one of the leading manufacturers of marine engines in the U.S. today.

So if you think of a Volvo as the perfect vehicle for lugging around kids, making trips to the supermarket, or taking the family out for a Sunday drive, you're right. It is. Even if you include all your aunts, your uncles, your cousins, your neighbors…

VOLVO NORTH AMERICA CORPORATION

**Student Competition
College**

324
ART DIRECTOR & WRITER
Rich Croland
CLIENT
Manufacturer of
Running Shoes
SCHOOL
School of Visual Arts

325
ART DIRECTOR
Diane Baver
WRITER
Jane Brody
CLIENT
Manufacturer of
Running Shoes
SCHOOL
School of Visual Arts

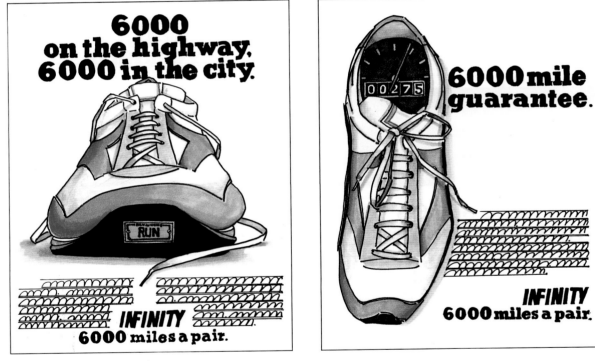

324

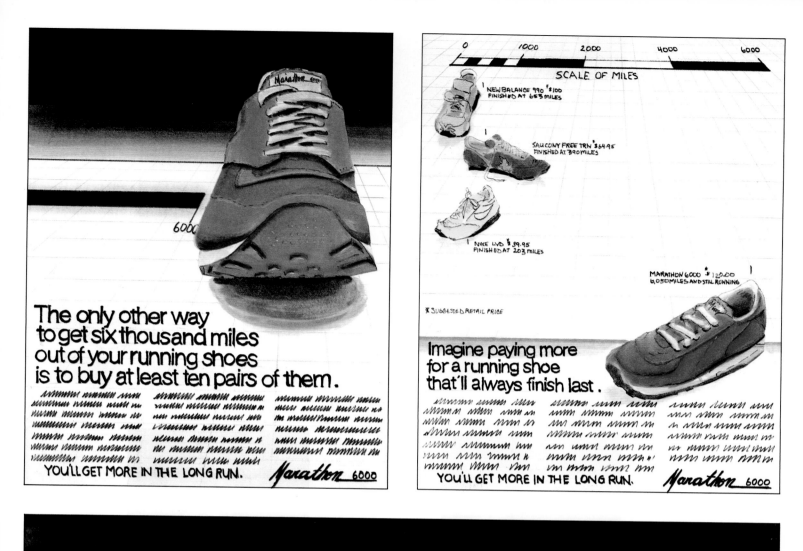

The only other way
to get six thousand miles
out of your running shoes
is to buy at least ten pairs of them.

YOU'LL GET MORE IN THE LONG RUN. *Marathon* 6000

SCALE OF MILES

NEW BALANCE 990 $100
FINISHED AT 653 MILES

SAUCONY FREE TRN $64.95
FINISHED AT 390 MILES

NIKE LVD $39.95
FINISHED AT 203 MILES

MARATHON 6000 $120.00
6,050 MILES AND STILL RUNNING

✱ SUGGESTED RETAIL PRICE

Imagine paying more
for a running shoe
that'll always finish last.

YOU'LL GET MORE IN THE LONG RUN. *Marathon* 6000

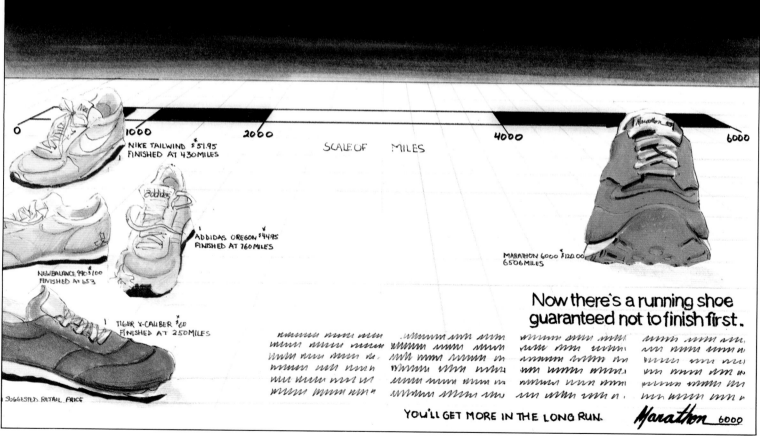

SCALE OF MILES

NIKE TAILWIND $51.95
FINISHED AT 430 MILES

ADDIDAS OREGON $44.95
FINISHED AT 760 MILES

NEW BALANCE 990 $100
FINISHED AT 653

TIGER X-CALIBER $60
FINISHED AT 250 MILES

SUGGESTED RETAIL PRICE

MARATHON 6000 $120.00
6506 MILES

Now there's a running shoe
guaranteed not to finish first.

YOU'LL GET MORE IN THE LONG RUN. *Marathon* 6000

325

Radio Finalists

Consumer Radio Single

328
WRITER
Martin Solow
CLIENT
Vita Food Products
AGENCY PRODUCER
Martin Solow
AGENCY
Durfee & Solow

329
WRITER
Richard L. Fish
CLIENT
The Herald-Telephone
AGENCY PRODUCERS
Rexford C. Hunt Jr.
Rick Heinsohn
AGENCY
LodesTone Productions/
Indiana

330
WRITER
Jane Hrubec
CLIENT
Friendship Cottage Cheese
AGENCY PRODUCER
Mary Miranda
AGENCY
Ogilvy & Mather

331
WRITER
Murray Partridge
CLIENT
Procter & Gamble
AGENCY PRODUCER
Warwick Adams
AGENCY
Grey Advertising/London

332
WRITER
Seth Fried
CLIENT
Miller Brewing/Lite Beer
AGENCY PRODUCER
Zinnian Johnson
AGENCY
Backer & Spielvogel

333
WRITER
Bob Nelson
CLIENT
City Chevrolet
AGENCY PRODUCER
Chuck Dykes
AGENCY
Lane and Huff/San Diego

334
WRITER
Sarah Humphrey
CLIENT
Time Inc./Time Magazine
AGENCY PRODUCER
Justine Mowbray
AGENCY
Young & Rubicam

328

ANNCR: Ladies and Gentlemen...The Return of the Beloved Herring Maven.

MAVEN: "How could we get the head honchos of all the countries in the world to sit down and eat some Vita Herring in real sour cream and Vita Party Snacks in Wine Sauce...it's so delicious, it would make them feel all smiley and good and maybe they would solve the world's problems?" That was the question I hurled at the Serious Person's Society of Roslyn Heights in a talking speech. Quick as a flash some wise guy said: "Hah. A maven from herring you may be. But how are you going to get all those big knockers together?" Thinking quick with my brain, I said I would go on the radio and I would invite all those presidents and prime ministers to write to me, a postal card is fine, in care of this station. What I would tell them is that I would personally rent the big conference room at the Holiday Inn in Nutley, New Jersey, and have a fancy catered affair with all kinds of Vita fish stuff. And it wouldn't be the worst thing if we started off the Vita festivities with our famous song: "Make the world a little bit brighter...eat a piece of pickled herring by Vita."

329

(SFX: TV TURNED ON)

(MUSIC: SOAP OPERA THEME FADES IN)

ACTRESS: Don't leave me, John! How will I know what's on TV?

(SFX: SWITCH CHANNELS)

(MUSIC: BACH SECOND BRANDENBURG CONCERTO UNDER)

HOST:—of course, the only complete listings are in The Herald-Telephone.

(SFX: SWITCH CHANNELS)

(MUSIC: DRAGNET THEME UNDER)

WOMAN:...and that TV Magazine in Saturday's H-T tells you everything that's going to be on for a whole week!

SERGEANT: Yes, ma'm.

WOMAN: And Sergeant—

SERGEANT: Yes, ma'm?

WOMAN: Each day's listings are in that day's paper, too.

(MUSIC: DUM DA DUM DUM!)

(SFX: SWITCH CHANNELS)

ANNCR: (WITH REVERB)...at a subscription price so low, it's worth it for the TV listings alone! And it really, really—

(SFX: SWITCH CHANNELS)

(SFX: STUDIO AUDIENCE LAUGHING)

CELEBRITY: Maybe zey should call it The Herald-Television, Dahling!

(SFX: MORE LAUGHTER, SWITCH CHANNELS)

(MUSIC: ACTION THEME UNDER)

(SFX: AUTOMOBILE FX UNDER)

DRIVER: Have a heart—plug into Bloomington! Pick-up The Herald-Telephone!

(SFX: CAR ZOOMS OFF INTO DISTANCE UNDER)

(MUSIC: THEME UP TOWARDS CLIMAX)

(SFX: TV TURNED OFF, SOUND FADES OUT)

330

MOTHER: Agh!...*what* is this revoltin' development in your refrigerator?

DAUGHTER: *That* is bleu cheese, Ma.

MOTHER: Well you can *have* your mold.

DAUGHTER: Thank you.

MOTHER: I'll take my Friendship Cottage Cheese...sweet, fresh...

DAUGHTER: All you ever talk about is Friendship!

MOTHER: Oh, you wanna talk about who you're dating...?

DAUGHTER: Oh no...

MOTHER: *Speaking of dating...*

DAUGHTER: Ma-a...

MOTHER: Have you *heard*...that some other brands of cottage cheese date their containers for up to 7 weeks?

DAUGHTER: No!

MOTHER: Yeah, but Friendship is dated for only *half* that time. Worth the price, Friendship. Always fresh, sweet and pure as the driven snow.

DAUGHTER: Just like your daughter.

MOTHER: That's right...So tell me, Snow White...whose foot goes in the large gray sock I see peeking out from under the sofa? Eh? Eh?

DAUGHTER: Um, well, you see Ma...um...er...that was there when I moved in!

MOTHER: I'm so sorry I asked.

ANNCR: FRIENDSHIP COTTAGE CHEESE. WHEN YOU KNOW WHAT GOOD IS.

331

MAN: My wife left me with the washing yesterday. I'd heard about this new powder Bold 3...with built-in fabric conditioner...so I thought I'd carry out a little experiment of my own.
I took my wife's favourite dress, washed one half in an ordinary powder and one half in brand-new Bold 3.
She came home just after the experiment had been completed.
She went berserk.
One half of the dress still rather disappointing; the half I'd washed in Bold 3 was clean, soft and fresh.
Unfortunately, she wasn't impressed with the way I'd stitched the two halves back together again. But the experiment had been a complete success.
Bold 3 with built-in fabric conditioner really does clean, soften and freshen all-in-one.
As you can see.
Show them your best side, Margaret.

ANNCR: Mickey Spillane and Rodney Dangerfield for Lite Beer from Miller.

(SFX: TYPING)

MICKEY: I remember the first time I met him. The guy was a mess.

(SFX: TYPING FADES. MOODY MUSIC COMES UP AND CONTINUES UNDER DIALOGUE. DOOR CLOSES, FOOT- STEPS.)

RODNEY: (DESPERATELY) You gotta help me find something.

MICKEY: What's that Pally?

RODNEY: Respect. I dont' get no respect at all. Why, when I was born my father asked the doctor— boy or girl? He said, "Close."

MICKEY: Hmmm, tough case. But I can give you a clue. What you're looking for is a beer.

RODNEY: A beer? I'm looking for respect, I tell ya'. Why, the other day, I had a fight with the dog. My wife said the dog was right.

MICKEY: Like I was saying, start drinking Lite Beer from Miller. Prove you have the smarts to get great taste without getting filled up, maybe you'll find what you're looking for.

RODNEY: But I've been drinking Lite for years. And I still get no respect.

MICKEY: Hmmm. Ever think of trying...comedy?

RODNEY: Geez.

(SFX: MUSIC COMES UP FULL. TYPING FADES BACK IN)

MICKEY: He turned and walked through the door.

(SFX: DOOR CLOSES.)

MICKEY: There were still a lot of questions. Would he ever get respect? Who sold him that tie? And why did he walk into the closet?

ANNCR: Lite Beer from Miller. Everything you always wanted in a beer. And less.

RODNEY: (VOICE ECHOS FROM CLOSET) Boy, this sure is a slow moving elevator.

ANNNCR: Miller Brewing Company, Milwaukee, Wisconsin.

SINGER: *My daddy drove a Chevy,*
His daddy drove one, too.
I'm a third generation City boy,
with a Chevy shiny-new.

I was raised on city driving,
I was raised on Chevrolet,
I'm a third generation City boy,
City by the Bay.
City Chevrolet.

I'll be drivin' these city streets,
In my brand new Chevy,
Drivin' in City style,
Knowin' that these City folks are behind me,
Mile after City mile.

And when it comes time for my children,
To have their very own Chevrolets,
There'll be fourth generation City kids,
City by the Bay
City Chevrolet,
Steady, Chevrolet!

VO: Now, TIME MAGAZINE celebrates its 60th anniversary with a landmark special issue: "The Most Amazing 60 Years in History."
Relive it all through TIME's original stories, written as the events were happening.

(SFX 1: START OF 1920'S/CHARLESTON–STYLE MUSIC UNDER)

VO: From Lindbergh,

(SFX 2): "He's made it!
Charles A. Lindbergh at LeBourget Airport in Paris."

VO: Babe Ruth, the Great Depression, and World War II

(SFX 3: CROWD CHEERING; THEN WITH HITLER IN CHANT:) "Sieg Heil! Sieg Heil!"

VO: To the Beatles, the moon landing,

(SFX 4): "This is base control. The Eagle has landed."

VO: And Watergate.

(SFX 5): "Do I consider resigning? The answer is no. I shall not resign. I have three and a half years to go and I'm going to use every day of these three and a half years."

VO (WITH MUSIC UNDER): They were years of triumph, war, breakthroughs in science, and revolutions in our culture.
Rediscover these amazing years with the magazine that's been there through it all. Find out how we lived, and what we thought about the world through TIME's original words and pictures.
It's a collector's edition you don't want to miss—on sale everywhere...The Most Amazing 60 Years in History.
Pick up your copy today.

335

(SFX: DOORBELL, DOOR OPENING)

LITTLE GIRL SCOUT: Mr Orwell?

ORWELL: Yes?

SCOUT: We're here with the Trailblazer Scout Cookies you ordered.

ORWELL: Good. How much?

SCOUT: Well, you got your Fudgaroonies, your Peanut Butter Buttons and your Mint Doodles. That's twelve bucks, Mr. Orwell.

ORWELL: Are you sure I ordered that much?

SCOUT: Trailblazers never forget, Mr. Orwell. Pay up.

ORWELL: Okay girls. I'll get my checkbook.

SCOUT: Trailblazers don't take checks, Mr. Orwell.

ORWELL: Oh, how did my neighbors pay?

SCOUT: They got fast cash at MPACT.

ORWELL: I don't have MPACT.

SCOUT: It shows. Do you have a credit card?

ORWELL: You take credit cards?

SCOUT: No, but MPACT machines do. You can get cash with your American Express card, or even Teller 24, Paymaster and Money Maker cards.

ORWELL: How does a little girl know all that?

SCOUT: A Trailblazer is always prepared, Mr. Orwell.

ORWELL: But I'm not. Could you come back tomorrow?

SCOUT: We'll wait. (YELLS) Pitch the tents girls.

ORWELL: Oh no.

(SFX: SCOUTS PITCHING TENTS, SOUND UNDER)

ANNCR: MPACT automatic tellers. The shortest distance between you and your money.

SCOUT: And we're not leaving 'til we get paid.

ORWELL: Couldn't you just trust me for it?

SCOUT: A Trailblazer doesn't trust anyone, Mr. Orwell.

336

1ST SINGER: *Don't you just love that Alley Cat?*

2ND SINGER: *He's so cool.*

1ST SINGER: *Don't you just love that Alley Cat?*

2ND SINGER: *Nobody's fool*

1ST SINGER: *He's charming, disarming, knows just where it's at . . .*
Don't you just love that Alley Cat?

(INSTRUMENTAL, FINGER SNAPPING AND WHISTLE UNDER ANNCR)

ANNCR: New Alley Cat brand cat food . . . now available in Buffalo.

1ST SINGER: *He's charming, disarming, knows just where it's at . . .*
Don't you just love that Alley cat
Don't you just love that Alley cat?

(FADE) *Yeah . . .*

337

ANNCR: At CIGNA, our companies insure thousands of works of great art, at hundreds of museums. We'd like to show you some of the artwork. But obviously, we can't. Instead, we'd like you to *listen* to some of the artwork we insure. Toulouse-Lautrec's "At the Moulin Rouge".

(SFX: FRENCH CAN-CAN)

ANNCR: Degas' "Dancers Preparing for the Ballet."

(SFX: SELECTION FROM BALLET "NUTCRACKER SUITE")

ANNCR: Piet Mondrian's "Broadway Boogie Woogie".

(SFX: BOOGIE WOOGIE SAXOPHONE)

ANNCR: Gilbert Stuart's "George Washington".

(SFX: FIFE AND DRUM VERSION OF YANKEE DOODLE)

ANNCR: Hopper's "Early Sunday Morning"

(SFX: PEER GYNT SUITE "MORNING")

ANNCR: Grant Wood's "American Gothic"

(SFX: BLUE GRASS)

ANNCR: And Philippe De Champaigne's "Charles II, King of England".

(SFX: MY COUNTRY 'TIS OF THEE)

ANNCR: Thank you for listening to just some of the artwork insured by CIGNA'S companies. You'll enjoy the artwork even more if you visit one of the 250 American museums for which we provide insurance. CIGNA. We're dedicated to the fine art of insurance.

338

(MUSIC: OPEN ON VOLKSWAGEN THEME. MUSIC CONTINUES AND BUILDS THROUGHOUT).

ANNCR: In 1975, when we introduced the Volkswagen Rabbit, there were over 40 new cars in its class. Millions of dollars were spent to make their names famous. Names like: Pinto, Vega, Pacer, Maverick, Valiant. But the real test of anything is how long it lasts. And one by one, over the years, these cars disappeared—abandoned by their makers.
At Volkswagen we don't change for the sake of change. We change to improve.
And so today,—after over 15,000 improvements—only the Rabbit remains.
He who lasts last, lasts best.
Rabbit. It's not a car. It's a Volkswagen

(MUSIC: UP AND OUT)

339

ANNCR: For every chicken you ever ate,
For every turkey sandwich,
For every duck, quail, and pheasant,
The birds are back and they're fighting mad.
In Phoenix, new for the Atari 2600.
You zig, they zag.
Use your shield, they wait to get you.
Shoot a wing, Phoenix grows another.
Until you face the mother ship.
Phoenix, the arcade hit.
Reach for Atari.

340

INTERVIEWER: We're here again, talking to people who haven't yet discovered Sedgefield Jeans, the 100% cotton jeans that fit forever like they fit in the store. Excuse me, sir...

MAN: No spare change. Get a job. Get a haircut.

INT: No, no... I wanted to talk about your jeans.

MAN: Jeez, if you don't give 'em money, they ask you for your pants. You people are disgusting.

INT: Sir, I just wanted to say your jeans are too short. They look funny.

MAN: Oh, really? (BECOMES SOMBER; A PERSONAL FAILING HAS BEEN UNCOVERED) I washed them a few times... I guess they did shrink.

INT: They sure did.

MAN: Yeah... hey, wait a minute... (BECOMES BELLIGERENT AGAIN)... you're trying to make me feel small and insignificant. That's one of your techniques, right?

INT: No, no...

MAN: Yeah, you're from one of those cults!

INT: What are your talking about?

MAN: Forget it, pal. You'll never get me to join up.

INT: Sir, I'm from Sedgefield Jeans, the 100% cotton jeans guaranteed never to shrink from their original size, no matter how much you wash them. I thought you could use a pair.

MAN: Cotton jeans that don't shrink?

INT: That's right.

MAN: No matter how much you wash 'em?

INT: Sedgefield Jeans fit forever like they fit in the store.

MAN: Gee, what a beautiful concept.

INT: Well, we think so, yes...

MAN: You know, suddenly I feel real calm and peaceful.

INT: Well, that's... great.

MAN: Okay, so first I buy the Sedgefield Jeans, then I shave my head, right?

INT: No, of course not.

MAN: Oh. Well, you want me to panhandle out at the airport for you?

INT: Look, that's crazy.

MAN: Hold it—how stupid of me. Here's all my money.

INT: I don't want your money.

MAN: Here's my bank account.

INT: I just... (FADE)

341

LEAD: *We build our pizza in the pan*

BACKGROUND: *Pizza Hut can,*
Yes we can, yes we can, can
Pizza in the pan, in the pan, pan
Just come on in to Pizza Hut
You can walk, you can run,
You can fly, you can strut
Just bring your body to Pizza Hut

LEAD: *Just bring your body to Pizza Hut*

CHORUS: *You get Aaahh, yes you can*
Oooh, yes you can
Mmmm, yes you can, yes you can, can

LEAD: *The best pan pizza in the land*

BACKGROUND: *Oh, man!*

LEAD: *Pizza Hut can*
yes we can, can
(FADE OUT)

342

HOST: This is Dave Nash with Canada's Wonderland Question Line. Today we're talking about the Season Pass. Go ahead. You're on the air.

CALLER: (THRU PHONE FILTER) Yeah, Dave... about Canada's Wonderland. Are there girls out there?

HOST: (SLIGHTLY UNCOMFORTABLE) Uh, well, yes, uh, I (INTERRUPTED).

CALLER: Are they good lookin', Dave?

HOST: I take it you're asking about the social aspects of the park.

CALLER: No, I'm not. I'm askin' about the girls, Dave.

HOST: Well, Canada's Wonderland is a great place to meet people. And with the Season Pass you can enjoy the different attractions every day, all summer long. Like Wonder Mountain.

CALLER: Wonder Mountain?

HOST: Right.

CALLER: Is that where the girls are?

HOST: And, remember a Season Pass costs just $29.95, that's less than the price of two park passports, and with it you can enjoy all the new live shows, ride the 4 rollercoasters—

CALLER: So the girls are on the rollercoasters?

HOST: Look, you seem to be pre–occupied.

CALLER: No I'm not. Now exactly how many girls are we talking about here? Couple hundred? Couple thousand? What?

HOST: Well, I don't know. You're gonna' have to come out and see for yourself.

CALLER: Oh, I don't know, I don't know... Are the girls out there right now?

HOST: Yes.

CALLER: I'll be there in a minute.

(SFX: PHONE HANGING UP!)

(SFX: BUZZ)

SINGOUT: *I'm going, going, going*
To Canada's Wonderland
Going, going, going
To Canada's Wonderland
Going, going, going... (FADE OUT)

343

HENNY: Hello, friends. This is Henny Youngman. I just flew one of those airlines that make you pay extra for your bags, so I left my wife home.

(VIOLIN)

I gotta tell you about the other day. I ate on an airline that had food fit for a king. Here King, here King!

(VIOLIN)

I went to Florida and got a wonderful tan, then I saw my air fare and turned white again.

(VIOLIN)

Take my stewardess, please.

(VIOLIN)

I just flew in from Vegas. Boy, are my arms tired.

ANNCR: At Northeastern, we believe flying can be a lot better than it is. That's why we offer what every flyer wants, low fares. Then instead of skimping on service, we've actually improved it. You see, we're trying to make flying there as pleasurable as being there.
Northeastern. What flying should be.

HENNY: I paid $800 for an airline ticket. You know where I'm going folks—to the poorhouse.

(VIOLIN)

344

MAN: Well...I think we've worked long enough... wanna call it a night?

WOMAN: Yeh...my eyes are killing me...

MAN: Hmmm. Try taking your glasses off for a minute...maybe you'll feel better...

WOMAN: Good idea...

(SFX: PAUSE, THEN LOVE THEME FROM TCHAIKOVSKY'S ROMEO AND JULIET.)

WOMAN: You're right...that feels a lot better. You know, these glasses feel like they weigh a... what's the matter...

MAN: Nothing...nothing, it's just that I've never seen you without glasses...

WOMAN: Oh...sorry...weird, huh? I'll put 'em back on...

(MUSIC STOPS ABRUPTLY)

MAN: Noo...you look beautiful...please...take them off again...

WOMAN: Really?

MAN: Really.

(SFX: MUSIC AGAIN. LOUDER THIS TIME.)

MAN: I can't believe it...

WOMAN: Are you sure you're okay?

MAN: Fine. Never better...

(MUSIC UNDER AND OUT)

VO: Have you ever known anyone who doesn't look better without glasses? With DuraSoft Brand Contact Lenses you can look great all the time...even if you have astigmatism. And DuraSoft Lenses are so comfortable you probably won't even know you have them on. Ask your Eye Care Professional about DuraSoft Contact Lenses...

MAN: Could you take your glasses off and leave 'em off?

WOMAN: Why not...?

(MUSIC UP AND OVER ANNOUNCER)

VO: DuraSoft...now you can look your best all the time.

345

RADIO TALK SHOW HOST: This is Canada's Wonderland Question Line with Dave Nash. You're on the air.

CALLER: Yeah, is this Question Line?

HOST: (REPEATING) Right, this is Question Line with Dave Nash.

CALLER: Yeah, I want to talk to Dave Nash.

HOST: (REPEATING AGAIN) This is Dave Nash, go ahead with your question.

CALLER: I got a question.

HOST: (GETTING EXASPERATED) Go ahead, please.

CALLER: I want to know about the Canada's Wonderland Season Pass.

HOST: Right, the Canada's Wonderland Season Pass...costs just $29.95.

CALLER: Now exactly how much does it cost?

HOST: (REPEATING) I said, just $29.95...and that's less than the price of two park passports.

CALLER: Ya' know, I just figured it out, and that's less than the price of two park passports.

HOST: I know, but the best thing about the Season Pass is you can enjoy the rides and shows every day all summer long for one low price. It's a great deal.

CALLER: Yeah, and look at it this way: it's a great deal.

HOST: Uh, right, well goodbye and thanks for calling.

CALLER: Look, I'd like to talk longer, but I'm gonna have to say goodbye.

HOST: Goodbye. Goodbye. Goodbye.

VO: Visit Ticketron at Major Eaton Stores or at Sears in the Hillcrest Mall and Mississauga Square One today or just call 766-3271, 766-3271, and use your VISA to order your Canada's Wonderland Season Pass. Only $29.95 for the best days of your summer every day, all summer long.

346

Hello. Um...apparently some of you American type people want to know how to buy Callard & Bowser's rather sophisticated extremely fine British candy. Well...in Britain, you'd stroll to the local sweetshop, push open the oak door with the stained-glass windows, and say "Pray furnish me with a package of your most excellent Callard & Bowser, my man." And the yeoman shopkeeper would reply "Thank you, m'lud. Will that be butterscotch, toffee or the juicy jellies?" And as you quit the emporium, he would fall to his knees calling "Blessings upon you, esteemed highness." Now I understand that in the U.S. of A. it's not quite like this. You have to spend hours zig-zagging up and down supermarket aisles serenaded by pop versions of Bach fugues searching for Callard & Bowser candy. Well, I'm *sorry* it's sometimes so difficult to find. Ah, but I hear you cry "That's all right, old chap. Don't worry. Nothing that's really worthwhile in life is ever that easy to come by." Well, what can I say? Thank you for crying that. You're obviously so intelligent and perceptive that Callard & Bowser will be right up your street, even if it's not right up your aisle.

ANNCR: Today, we've come to a typical shopping mall to serve SPAM Luncheon meat recipes to shoppers who don't know they're eating SPAM. Take a bite and let me know what you think.

1ST MAN: It's not bad. How 'bout another one.

1ST WOMAN: It's good.

1ST MAN: Interesting.

2ND WOMAN: Do you have anything to drink?

2ND MAN: This is very good.

ANNCR: Would it surprise you if I said that that was made from—SPAM?

2ND WOMAN: SPAM? That's SPAM?

3RD WOMAN: You'd never know it.

3RD MAN: Can we go now?

(LAUGHTER)

1ST MAN: Good old SPAM.

4TH WOMAN: This is SPAM? In all of it? I'm surprised.

ANNCR: What surprises you so much? What did you think was in SPAM?

1ST MAN: I don't really know.

4TH WOMAN: Liver? Ya, liver's in it. I think.

3RD MAN: Nobody knows what's in SPAM.

ANNCR: Actually, you see, that's—that's wrong and are you ready for the shock? Ham and pork shoulder.

4TH WOMAN: I'm surprised. (GIGGLES) I really am.

3RD MAN: That's pretty good. I've never appreciated it before.

ANNCR: What do you think of SPAM now?

1ST MAN: I like it.

5TH WOMAN: That's right, that's right. Delicious.

2ND WOMAN: I'm having a party and I would probably make it for the party if I had the recipe—but I'd hide the can.

(LAUGHTER)

ANNCR: (LAUGHING) Come on America. Discover the great taste of SPAM.
It just might surprise you.

1ST WOMAN: If that's SPAM, it's pretty good.

ANNCR: Here's Bob and Ray for Southern California Gas Company.

BOB: It's winter again and although you're already doing things to save gas, here's Ray with three gentle reminders:

RAY: One: to keep heat in on those cold nights, close the drapes.

(SFX: ROAR OF TRAIN.)

RAY: Hold on; we're supposed to hear wind blowing, not a train.

BOB: Ray, it's young Darryl Miller's first day as sound engineer and...

RAY: No relation to Don Miller, our station owner, is he?

BOB: Actually, yes, it's his son...now go ahead, please.

RAY: Two: when not using your fireplace, close the damper.

(SFX TRUMPETING OF ELEPHANTS.)

RAY: For crying out loud, what was that?!

BOB: Ray, it's his first day; give him a chance.

RAY: (ANGRILY) Three! Keep your house at 68 degrees and put on a sweater!

(SFX: BUZZ SAW, FOLLOWED BY CLUNK OF FALLING WOOD.)

RAY: And I suppose that's the sound of someone putting on a sweater.

BOB: Ray, please.

RAY: Well, try this sound on for size!

(SFX: STOMP OF ANGRY FOOTSTEPS AND THEN A DOOR SLAMMING.)

BOB: This is Bob, minus Ray at the moment, telling you you'll find a lot more than gas at the Gas Company.

ANNCR: You've done the right thing by calling. Many creatures of habit won't call because it's too hard, too painful.
So, your call is a fiercely independent act. It's the first step in breaking your habit. Soon, you'll be wearing shoes and eating with utensils. Can you say "u-ten-sils"? Great.
Not all creatures of habit are as bright as you. Many will continue to eat food that's as exciting as the paper it's wrapped in. Some will eat the paper. Some will not know they ate the paper. Now, even though I'm only a recording, I can tell you're special. You really don't want to go to the same place for the same thing. You want desperately to be a functioning—even interesting—member of society. You may already be just a few short years from this goal. Can you say "goal"?
You've said "utensils". You've said "goal". Now say "DEL TACO".
That's it. "DEL TACO." Wasn't that easy?

PROBABLY A SECOND VOICE: This message is brought to you by DEL TACO. Not the same place. Not the same thing.

370

ANNCR: Here's Bob and Ray for Southern California Gas Company.

WALLY: Wally Ballou here, on location with television commercial director, Hackett Barney.

HACKETT: I'm really a movie director—between films.

WALLY: Aren't you directing a commercial telling people that by having their furnace pilot light turned off in the summer, they can save energy and money?

HACKETT: That's right. A very simple message.

WALLY: So why do I see all those bright blue jets overhead?

(SFX: LOUD ROAR OF JETS.)

HACKETT (TALKING ABOVE THE DIN): Those 79 Phantom jets will fly in the formation of a giant pilot light.

WALLY: And that huge chorus gathered on the hillside over there?

(SFX: LOUD GENERALIZED SOUND OF CHORUS.)

HACKETT: 459 thundering voices singing as one... "Call the Gas Company... they'll come out to turn off your furnace pilot light for you!!"

WALLY: Interesting... and what about those 12 snow machines over there?

(SFX: LOUD SNOW MACHINE MOTORS.)

HACKETT: I haven't figured out *what* to do with those things.

WALLY: Hackett, just how long *is* this commercial?

HACKETT: About an hour and a half.

WALLY: Well, I certainly think you're going to get a lot of pilot lights turned off with this one...

HACKETT: You bet.

WALLY: Not to mention a few television sets.

HACKETT: What do you mean by that?

371

(SFX: TWO PEOPLE WALKING)

DAD: You Know, Son, we don't spend enough time together.

SON: I know, Dad.

DAD: So, on the occasion of your birthday, I want to take you to O'Malley's for your very first beer.

SON: Uh, Dad, I uh—

DAD: Now there's a right way and a wrong way to order beer. You can't slouch or mumble like when you talk to me.

SON: (MUMBLE MUMBLE)

DAD: Don't mumble

SON: Sorry—

DAD: You gotta say, loud and clear: I'll have a light beer, please.

SON: Well gee, Dad, I'd rather say: I'll have a Bud Light please.

DAD: Bud Light? Wait a minute—How do you know about Bud Light?

SON: Oh, word gets around... guys talk... ya hear things...

DAD: Well, you can order your Bud Light here at O'Malley's

SON: O'Malley's doesn't serve Bud Light, Dad.

DAD: They don't?

SON: Let's go across the street to O'Leary's.

DAD: How do you know all this?

SON: Oh, word gets around... guys talk... ya hear things...

DAD: Well, okay—A Bud Light in honor of your turning 21!

SON: It's 31.

DAD: Like I said, Gary: we don't spend enough time together.

SON: It's Larry.

DAD: Well, that's pretty close.

ANNCR: Don't just settle for what you get. Ask for Bud Light. Because the best has a taste all its own. Satisfying, but never filling. Anheuser-Busch, St. Louis, Missouri.

SALESMAN: Are you next, Madam?

HE: I think she is.

SHE: Uh, I think you were here first.

HE: Oh, thanks. I'd like that tie to go with this sportcoat, right?

SHE: Oh!... Yeah, that's a nice choice. Boy, that's a pretty tie. What kind of material is that? Boy, that feels nice...

SALESMAN: How would you like to pay for that, sir?

HE: Uh, the American Express Card.

SALESMAN: Excellent.

SHE: Can you... you can use the American Express Card here?

HE: Yeah, watch!

(SOUND OF CARD BEING PUT IN CREDIT CARD MACHINE)

SHE (LAUGHS): I never thought of that, you know... I only use it to go to restaurants and buy airplane tickets and things... That's a good idea...

HE: I shop with it all the time... in fact, anywhere I go, I can't recall a good store that doesn't accept it.

SHE: Hmmmm...

HE: Would you like a further demonstration of its... shopping abilities?

SHE: What?

HE: Well, I have to buy a shirt.

SHE (LAUGHS): You want me to watch you use the American Express Card again?

HE: Would you like to?

SHE: Uh... sure.

HE: Then perhaps I can watch you buy dinners and airline tickets with yours.

SHE: Whoa.... let's just start with your shirt.

HE: What?.... Oh, the shirt!

SHE: The shirt! Right....

ANNCR: Find out what's in store for you when you shop with the American Express Card. Don't leave home without it.

(SFX: MUSIC UNDER THROUGHOUT)

VO: In Narragansett Bay, there is a creature so frightening, so evil, it is incomprehensible to the sane mind. It has neither fins nor gills. Yet it can kill anything in the water. It has been seen as far north as Conimicut Point, and as far south as Newport Harbor. It stalks its prey by day and night. And it's getting more dangerous by the second. It is the deadliest animal in the sea. But it's not a fish. It's a human being. Because it's people that are slowly killing Narragansett Bay. With their toxic chemicals, their industrial waste, their raw sewage. Save The Bay is fighting to end this senseless destruction. But we can't do it alone. So please, call 272-3540 and join Save The Bay. Together, we can do more than make a difference. We can turn the tide.

NELL CARTER: Hello, ladies. I'm Nell Carter. If you're a woman, black and somewhere between the age of 29 and 99—but still sweet, and sort of sassy—I'm talking to you. About breast cancer. How to *detect* it—early—and protect yourself. Oh, I know, I know, you don't want to hear this. And you think it's gonna hurt. Well, honey, it is not the *exam* that hurts. A breast exam takes one half hour, once a year. It's that fast. That easy. And, it's free. And you can get it at the Breast Examination Center in the Harlem State Office Building. Ladies, *I'm* doing it for *my* health. Now, *you* should do it for *yours*. 'Cause the truth is, early detection is the *best* protection—the *only* protection we have. So... If you don't have your breasts examined... Maybe, you should have your *head* examined.

ANNCR: On a clear April morning, an 8 year-old girl ran to the corner of Atlantic Avenue in Brooklyn, and followed all the rules. She stopped... Waited for the "WALK" sign... Then, as she crossed the street, the girl was killed by a driver who ran a red light. If you drive in New York City, please, don't run red lights. It's against the law. And if you break it, you may never be able to put the pieces back together. People who run red lights must be stopped.

ANNCR: New York, 1918. The American Expeditionary Force returns from the continent.

(SFX: PARADE NOISE, STRAINS OF "IT'S A LONG WAY TO TIPPERARY")

ANNCR: 1945. Japan surrenders. The troops come home.

(SFX: SOUSA MARCH, PARADE NOISE.)

ANNCR: 1965. Marty Lewandowski, and thousands like him, come back from Vietnam.

(SFX: WIND BLOWING.)

ANNCR: Vietnam. For those who fought there, there were no parades. No one seemed to care. The New York Vietnam Veteran's Memorial Commission, along with Mayor Koch, thinks it's time we set things right. Time we built a monument to honor every New York veteran of the Vietnam era. Time we started jobs programs. Please, send what you can to the New York Vietnam Veteran's Memorial Fund, one-ten Church Street, one-double-oh-one-three. It's hard enough for any veteran to live with the memory of war. But it's worse to think that, in the end, no one gives a damn. It's time. Give to the New York Vietnam Veteran's Memorial Fund.

Consumer Television
60 Seconds Single

381
ART DIRECTOR
James Woollett

WRITER
John Turnbull

CLIENT
Statewide Building Society

DIRECTOR
Tony Williams

PRODUCTION CO.
Marmalade Films

AGENCY PRODUCER
Karen Godsell

AGENCY
The Campaign Palace/
Australia

382
ART DIRECTOR
Bob Steigelman

WRITER
Charlie Breen

CLIENT
Miller Brewing/High Life

DIRECTOR
Don Guy

PRODUCTION CO.
Dennis, Guy & Hirsch

AGENCY PRODUCER
Sally Smith

AGENCY
Backer & Spielvogel

383
ART DIRECTOR
George Jaccoma

WRITER
Bob Gottron

CLIENT
Burger King

DIRECTOR
Neil Tardio

PRODUCTION CO.
Lovinger, Tardio, Melsky

AGENCY PRODUCER
Tony Silano

AGENCY
J. Walter Thompson

384
ART DIRECTOR
Salvatore Sinare

WRITERS
Robert Black
Salvatore Sinare
Rich Pels

CLIENT
Pacific Telephone

DIRECTOR
Rick Levine

PRODUCTION CO.
Levine/Pytka

AGENCY PRODUCER
Flo Babbitt

AGENCY
Foote, Cone & Belding/
San Francisco

381

EXECUTIVE (BEING DYNAMIC): Next, the bank.

(DICTATING): "Dear Baldy...ah...you...fat...
old skinflint...ah...fed up with getting no
interest on my cheque account...sick of your
absurd bank charges...closing my account...
you're fired...I'm opening a Statewide Intercheque Account...pays all my bills...heaps of
interest...no bank charges...get lost,"

(TO SECRETARY): Read that back, please Jane.

JANE (SWEETLY): "Dear Mr. Flint, because my
Statewide Building Society Intercheque Account
pays my bills and pays me up to 12½% interest a
year, I regret I must close my account with you.
Thank you for everything, yours most
sincerely..."

EXECUTIVE (PLEASED WITH HIMSELF):
That's telling him!

MALE V/O: Statewide Intercheque.
It pays your bills and pays you interest.

382

(MUSIC UNDER)

(SFX: Car, alley cat)

ANNCR VO: That kid's out there again
But he's not alone.
He's got a dream with him, and every night after
work he chases that dream, the one that says
someday you're going to watch him run 400 meters
faster than any other man in the summer games.

(MUSIC UP)

In the past it probably would have been just a
dream but we have an Olympic training center
now in Colorado Springs.
And he can go there and learn how to run faster
than he's ever run before. So maybe he'll become
as good as he believes he can be.
And maybe one summer day when you're watching
the 1984 games you just might say...
that kid's out there again.

(CHANT: USA...USA...USA)

ANNCR VO: This American Dream was brought
to you by Miller High Life...
Sponsor of the U.S. Olympic Training Center

383

ANNCR: Burger King presents...the Battle of the Breakfasts. A look behind the lines...

GUY: Ok, I'm in...now let's see...they have omelettes, something called a Cr...Croissan'wich. Whoap...make that three Croissan'wiches... eggs 'n cheese with either sausage, ham or mmmmmm crispy bacon.
Uh oh, they're giving away free coffee refills, guys.
And, what's this? The Burger King Breakfast Bar. It has hot blueberries that *everyone's pouring* over their pancakes, along with hot apples, maple syrup...and there's hollandaise for the omelettes plus cheese sauce, creole sauce...mushrooms... And there's fresh melon...watermelon, honey-dew, cantaloupe...There's grapefruit and pineapple (MUNCH) oranges...

(DIALOGUE FADES TO EATING SFX)

ANNCR ("AYH" HOOK UNDER): The all new breakfast. From Burger King

(MORE EATING SFX)

384

(MUSIC UP.)

(SFX: BIRDS, OUTDOORS SOUNDS.)

PRIEST: Monsignor? There's a phone call for you. A Will McDonough?

MONSIGNOR: Will...

PRIEST: ...says you played football together...

MONSIGNOR: That we did, that we did...

SINGER (VO): *Drift away, drift away,*
How the time disappears.
Just the blink of an eye
And the days turn into years
Drift away, drift away...

MONSIGNOR: Will!

ANNCR (VO): Think of all the times you thought about calling old friends and haven't done it. Then think about how good it would make them feel. Old friends are only as far away as you let them be.

SINGER (VO): *There's so much left to say...*

WILL (VO): Can you still catch a pass, Patrick?

MONSIGNOR: If you can still throw it, Will.

SINGER (VO): *Don't drift away...*

(MUSIC OUT.)

told *Rudy* to pick us up.

**Consumer Television
60 Seconds Single**

388
ART DIRECTOR
Martin Mayhew
CLIENT
Martini & Rossi/Rosso
DIRECTOR
Mike Berkofsky
PRODUCTION CO.
RobersonBerkofskyHutchins
AGENCY PRODUCER
Jacci Barrett
AGENCY
McCann-Erickson/London

389
ART DIRECTORS
Brent Thomas
Lee Clow
WRITER
Steve Hayden
CLIENT
Apple Computer
DIRECTOR
Ridley Scott
PRODUCTION CO.
Fairbanks Films
AGENCY PRODUCER
Richard O'Neill
AGENCY
Chiat/Day - Los Angeles

390
ART DIRECTOR
Mary Martin
WRITER
Mary Ann Quick
CLIENT
United Airlines
DIRECTOR
Norm Griner
PRODUCTION CO.
Griner/Cuesta
AGENCY PRODUCER
Michael Birch
AGENCY
Leo Burnett/Chicago

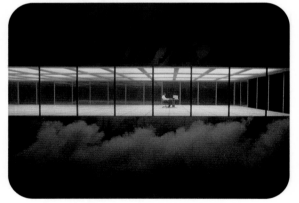

388

(MUSIC)

vo: This is the Martini time of day...

(MUSIC CONTINUES)

vo: Martini Rosso...

(MUSIC CONTINUES)

vo: anytime...
anyplace...
anywhere–
because
Martini is...
the right one.

389

(SFX: SOLO CLARINET)

ANNCR (VO): Some business people don't have
their best ideas sitting at a desk.

(SFX: GUY MAKING NOTES.)

(SFX: MORE CLARINET.)

ANNCR (VO): At Apple, we understand that
"business as usual" isn't anymore. That's why we
make the most advanced personal computers in
the world. And why, soon, there'll be just two
kinds of people.
Those who use computers.
And those who use Apples.

SING: *You're not just another face*
Along the way to another place.

AGENT: Where are you headed today, Private... Zeleski?

MARINE: Home!

AGENT: Home... that's one of our most popular destinations.

SING: *You're the pride of United's Friendly Skies.*

MARINE: Thank you, sir.

SING: *So before you go, my friend, we want you to know, my friend,*
You are not just flyin, you're flyin' The Friendly Skies.

FLIGHT ATTENDENT: You must have been starving.

MARINE: You run a great mess hall here.

SING: *Flying high across the land*

CAPTAIN: Don't worry son, *yours* will grow back.

SING: *We're givin' you everything we can* (ECHO)
and we've got more to give along the way.

F.A.: Private Zeleski?
Private Zeleski!

MARINE: Yessir!

F.A.: You're home.

MARINE: Home?

SING: *You're not just flyin'*

MARINE: I'm Home!

SING: *You're flyin' The Friendly Skies.*

391
ART DIRECTOR
Jim Bruch
WRITER
Rob Conrad
CLIENT
United Airlines
DIRECTOR
Joe Pytka
PRODUCTION CO.
Levine/Pytka
AGENCY PRODUCER
Dave Musial
AGENCY
Leo Burnett/Chicago

392
ART DIRECTOR
Karen Zateslo
WRITER
Jack Smith
CLIENT
McDonald's
DIRECTOR
Rob Lieberman
PRODUCTION CO.
Harmony Pictures
AGENCY PRODUCER
Dave Musial
AGENCY
Leo Burnett/Chicago

393
ART DIRECTOR
Trevor Kennedy
CLIENT
Martini & Rossi/Bianco
DIRECTOR
Ken Turner
PRODUCTION CO.
Clearwater Films/London
AGENCY PRODUCER
Anni Cullen
AGENCY
McCann-Erickson/London

391

ANNCR: In this Olympic year, United Airlines salutes the best friends any up and coming athlete could ever have: Mom and Dad.

SING: *Come run with me.*

DAD: Time for practice, son.

SING: *Fly with me.*
Spread your wings and reach up to the sky with me.
Together, we can go the world just one better.
Climb with me
Soar with me
Reachin' higher than you ever been before
With me
Together we'll reach out
And together we can climb.

ANNCR: At United, we know how important it is to have a friend standing by you every step of the way...
and we're proud to be the official airline of the nineteen-eighty-four Olympic Games.

SING: *You're not just flyin'*
You're flyin' The Friendly Skies.

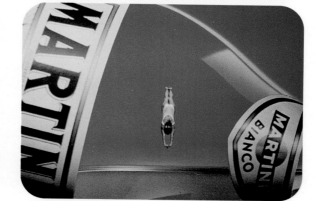

392

SING: *I remember when, little sister, you were two...*
I was ten...
Baby sister you tried desperately...for attention from me...
Would you settle for a french fry for now, little baby sister of mine.

ALL SING: *You grew up together...McDonald's and you, and you grew...*
and you grew, and you grew.

SING: *You were just a me-too tag along tomboy...*
Making a scene. Then I turned around...
And found a Homecoming Queen.
Little sister...
Ooooohhhh...
You know I'm gonna miss her...
Cause we grew up...together...

ALL SING: *McDonald's and you.*

393

(MUSIC THROUGHOUT)

SUNG VOCAL: *Martini Bianco*

(MUSIC THROUGHOUT)

SUNG VOCAL: *Martini Bianco*

(MUSIC THROUGHOUT)

MVO: **Martini.**
The Right Bianco

394
ART DIRECTOR
Ron Condon
WRITER
Greg Taubeneck
CLIENT
United Airlines
DIRECTOR
Joe Pytka
PRODUCTION CO.
Levine/Pytka
AGENCY PRODUCER
Dave Musial
AGENCY
Leo Burnett/Chicago

395
ART DIRECTOR
Bob Engel
WRITER
Rory Monaghan
CLIENT
McDonald's
DIRECTOR
Rob Lieberman
PRODUCTION CO.
Harmony Pictures
AGENCY PRODUCER
Jim McAward
AGENCY
Leo Burnett/Chicago

394

GRANDPA (VO): Yep. Nineteen-thirty-two. Never
been so excited. The Olympics were in Los
Angeles.
Well sir... my Dad and I flew there... in a big
United Airlines plane... least we thought it was
big then.
They served coffee out of a silver urn. I got a big
glass of Bosco.
What a time we had cheering for Babe Didricksen.

(SFX: CROWD ROAR)

GRANDPA (VO): And Eddie Tolan winning the
hundred...
I was yelling my head off. So I figured, I take my
grandson to L.A. in eighty-four in the same
style... bigger United plane, but the same nice
people.

STEW.: How about something to celebrate?

KID: Got any chocolate milk?

GRANDPA: Sounds pretty good to me, too.

ANNCR (VO): United *has* gotten bigger since we
flew to the games in thirty-two.
But we're still flying on the same belief—

KID: Grandpa! Look!

ANNCR.: Making friends, and keeping them.

GRANDPA: I think we've come to the right place.

SINGERS: *You're not just flying
You're flying The Friendly Skies.*

ANNCR (VO): Official Airline of the nineteen-
eighty-four Olympics.

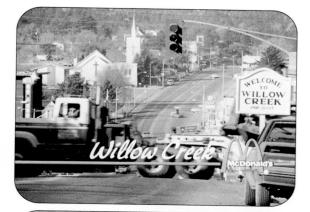

395

(SFX: DIESEL TRUCK ON HIGHWAY.)

SING: *Something is coming...*
A place all your own.

BARBER: Heard what they're building up the street?

CUSTOMER: Isn't that something!

(SFX: CONSTRUCTION WITH BULLDOZER AND CREW.)

MAN #1: They said it was a choice between building it here, or building it over in Pleasant Valley.

MAN #2: Poor old Pleasant Valley. Heh, Heh, heh!

(SFX: OF CONSTRUCTION)

KID: And they got the greatest french fries!

KIDS: Yeahhhh!

WOMAN: Guess who won't be cooking dinner every night?

(SFX: MORTAR AND BRICK–BUILDING ON WALL.)

GIRL: Guess what, Bobby's going to be working there!

GIRLS: Bobby!

(SFX: OF CONSTRUCTION)

GIRL: You think they'll ever finish?

(SFX: CRANE ENGINE PULLING UP SIGN.)

SING: (SOFTLY) *McDonald's and you...*

MAN #1: It'll be nice havin' a place where everyone can get together.

MAN #2: Poor old Pleasant Valley.

SING: (BUILD) *McDonald's and you...*
Sharing the good times
Like good neighbors do
Together...
McDonald's and you

410
ART DIRECTORS
Martha Holmes
Don Schneider
WRITER
Martha Holmes
CLIENT
Pepsi Cola/Diet Pepsi
DIRECTOR
Adrian Lyne
PRODUCTION CO.
Jennie
AGENCY PRODUCER
Ed Pollack
AGENCY
BBDO

411
ART DIRECTOR
F. Paul Pracilio
WRITERS
Jeff Atlas
Robert Neuman
CLIENT
American Express
DIRECTOR
Bob Eggers
PRODUCTION CO.
Eggers Films
AGENCY PRODUCER
Ann Marcato
AGENCY
Ogilvy & Mather

412
ART DIRECTOR
Lou Zaffos
WRITER
Dean Weller
CLIENT
WCBS-TV
DIRECTOR
Michael Ulick
PRODUCTION CO.
Michael Ulick Productions
AGENCY PRODUCER
Milda Misevicius
AGENCY
Korey, Kay & Partners

413
ART DIRECTOR
Jim Liggett
WRITER
Joan Trojak
CLIENT
Brooklyn Bridge Centennial
DIRECTOR
Alex Fernbach
PRODUCTION CO.
Sunlight Productions
AGENCY PRODUCER
Sandra Breakstone
AGENCY
Ogilvy & Mather

410

SHE: Says here the temperature on Venus averages 800 degrees.

HE: So let's go to the beach instead.

SHE: 29 million miles away...

HE: The beach is closer...

SHE: Here, finish this off before your ice cubes melt.

HE: Is that what I've been drinking?

SHE: Yeah. They improved it.

HE: One calorie? Oh, it's got that new sweetener in it.

SHE: It's sweeping the planet.

HE: Which planet?

SHE: You know...the one with the beach.

411

(MUSIC UNDER)

MILLER: Do you know me?
You may know my *"Do Wacca Do Wacca Do Wacca Do"*
But my "Do Wacca Do" don't do me no good when I'm travelin'.
So I just got myself an American Express Card. That makes me the *"King of the Road."*

ANNCR: To apply for the Card look for an application and take one.

MILLER: The American Express Card (SFX) don't leave home without it.

412

ANNCR V.O.: Early in his life, Warner Wolf showed an avid interest in sports...

RADIO V.O.: Five seconds left and they're gonna run out the clock. But the ball is stolen. One second to go, he puts it up from the mid-court line and he made the BASKET!

YOUNG WARNER: Swish!!!

ANNCR V.O.: And an unusual grasp of the language.

RADIO V.O.: It's a long one, deep into right field. It's a HOMERUN!

YOUNG WARNER: Boom!!!

ANNCR V.O.: Nobody speaks sports like Warner Wolf...

RADIO V.O.: Ball at the 25, 13 seconds left in the half. There's the snap. It's a quarterback sneak. He breaks free. He's at the 20, the 10, the 5, TOUCHDOWN!

YOUNG WARNER: Let's go to the videotape!

FATHER: The what?

ANNCR. V.O.: Warner Wolf, on Channel 2 News.

413

DICK CAVETT: For sale: Gothic style suspension bridge.

BOB ELLIOTT: I'll buy that.

RAY GOULDING: He'd buy anything.

DICK CAVETT: Sleek lines, classic styling.

ANDY WARHOL: A work of art.

DICK CAVETT: Fully equipped with 14,000 miles of steel wire...

MARILYN MICHAELS: That's what I call an extension, Oooh!

DICK CAVETT: Owned for 100 years by millions of New Yorkers.

ALAN KING: And we wouldn't sell it for the world.

MISS PIGGY: On May 24th, the Brooklyn Bridge celebrates it's 100th birthday with parades, fireworks and light shows. The bridge will be almost as exciting as moi!

DICK CAVETT: Join the party. After all, it's your bridge.

**Consumer Television
30 Seconds Single**

426
ART DIRECTOR
Doug Lew
WRITER
Terry Bremer
CLIENT
Cub Foods
DIRECTOR
Steve Griak
PRODUCTION CO.
Wilson-Griak
AGENCY
Chuck Ruhr Advertising/
Minneapolis

427
ART DIRECTOR
Boyd Jacobson
WRITER
John van der Zee
CLIENT
Wells Fargo Bank
DIRECTOR
Boyd Jacobson
PRODUCTION CO.
Chandler Studios
AGENCY PRODUCER
Jim Allen
AGENCY
McCann-Erickson/
San Francisco

428
ART DIRECTOR
Bill Hoo
WRITER
Charles McAleer
CLIENT
Health Stop
DIRECTOR
Bill Hoo
PRODUCTION COS.
Kim & Gifford
Howard Schwartz
Soundtrack
AGENCY PRODUCERS
Bill Hoo
Jon Goward
Charles McAleer
AGENCY
Clarke Goward Fitts/Boston

429
ART DIRECTOR
Robert F. Donnellan
WRITER
Jim Herbert
CLIENT
Timex
DIRECTOR
Sid Myers
PRODUCTION CO.
Myers Films
AGENCY PRODUCER
Edgar C. Kahn
AGENCY
J. Walter Thompson

426

VO: There isn't just one reason the prices at Cub Foods are lower than the prices at a regular supermarket. There are thousands of reasons.

(SYMPHONIC MUSIC UNDER)

VO: Everything we buy, we buy in volume. So everything we sell, we sell for less.

VO: Cub Foods. More than you'd expect. For less.

427

MAN: Here's the kitchen. Close to the well.

ANNCR (VO): Even when the west was mostly made of dreams, there was Wells Fargo helping people turn a vision of life...

MAN: And over here'll be the root cellar.

ANNCR (VO): ...into life itself.

WOMAN: And over here could be the nursery.

ANNCR (VO): It's something we still do. If you need money to buy or build or become something, talk to the bank that's been lending money to Westerners longer than any other bank.
WELLS FARGO BANK

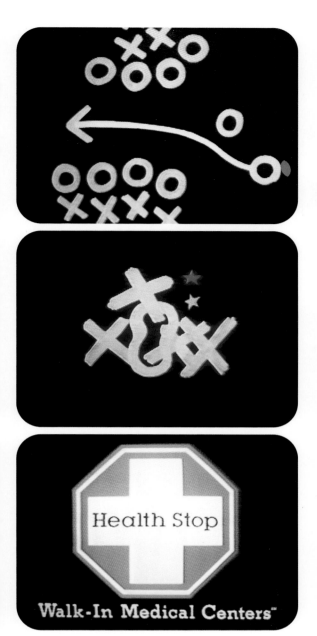

428

(SFX: FOOTBALL HUDDLE)

VO: Accidents can happen just like that.

(SFX: CR-R-ACK! THEN: SCREAM.)

VO: Now there's a place that can fix them. Just like that. Health Stop. Your minor-disaster area.

429

(MUSIC)

1ST MAN: I spent a fortune on a computer. Know what I found out? I hate computing.

1ST WOMAN: Computing. I love it.

2ND MAN: I hate it.

2ND WOMAN: It's terrific. (SFX: WOMAN LAUGHS)

3RD MAN: She loves it.

4TH MAN: Computing? Uhhh.

ANNCR: Why spend a fortune to find out how you feel about computing when you can do it on a Timex Sinclair 1000 for $49.95?
Who knows, you might love computers.
Or maybe not.
The Timex Sinclair 1000.

5TH MAN: I thought I'd hate it, but *tah dah!*

(MUSIC OUT)

430
ART DIRECTOR
Nick Gisonde
WRITER
Charlie Breen
CLIENT
Miller Brewing/Lite Beer
DIRECTOR
Bob Giraldi
PRODUCTION CO.
Giraldi Productions
AGENCY PRODUCER
Eric Steinhauser
AGENCY
Backer & Spielvogel

431
ART DIRECTOR
John R. Evans
WRITER
Melissa Huffman
CLIENT
Del Taco
DIRECTOR
Joe Sedelmaier
PRODUCTION CO.
Sedelmaier Films
AGENCY PRODUCER
Barbara Gangi
AGENCY
keye/donna/pearlstein -
Los Angeles

432
ART DIRECTORS
Howie Cohen
Frank Perry
WRITER
Brian Sitts
CLIENT
Burger King
DIRECTOR
Steve Horn
PRODUCTION CO.
Steve Horn Productions
AGENCY PRODUCER
Gary Bass
AGENCY
J. Walter Thompson

433
ART DIRECTOR
Alan Chalfin
WRITER
Larry Vine
CLIENT
Luden's
DIRECTOR
Geoffrey Mayo
PRODUCTION CO.
Geoffrey Mayo Films
AGENCY PRODUCER
Dorothy Franklin
AGENCY
Geers Gross

430

UECKER: . . . it was one of my bigger days.

MAN: Let me buy you a beer.

UECKER: Sure.
Ah, these fans, I love 'em.
When I came in, they didn't recognize me at
first. But then when I told them who I was,
next thing you know they're buying me my
favorite beer. Lite Beer from Miller. They know
us ex-big leaguers drink Lite because it's got a
third less calories than their regular beer. It's
less filling, and it tastes great.
Thanks.

MAN: Hey, it's a pleasure to buy a beer for a great
pitcher like Whitey Ford.

UECKER: So I lied.

ANNCR VO: Lite Beer from Miller.
Everything you always wanted in a beer. And
less.

MAN: Hey Whitey, I thought you were a lefty.

UECKER: Ooo, that's right.

431

MR. HERN: Excellent, excellent, just excellent. How
about lunch?

MAN 1: Same place?

HERN: Same place.

MAN 2: Same thing?

HERN: Same thing.

ANNCR: Creatures of habit. That's what people
become when it's time to eat.

OLD LADY: Same place?

HERN: Same place.

YOUNG LADY: Same thing?

HERN: Same thing.

YOUNG LADY: Same thing.

ANNCR: Time to get out of the rut and into Del Taco,
where everything we make is habit breaking.

TED: Same place?

HERN: Same place.

TED: Same thing?

HERN: Same thing.

ANNCR: Don't be a creature of habit. Come into
DEL TACO. Not the same place. Not the same
thing.

432

ANNCR VO: Burger King presents a love story.
Separately they won the hearts of America. Now
finally they found each other. Burger King and
Pepsi, two winning tastes together at last.

SINGERS: *Have a Pepsi at Burger King now!*

433

(MUSIC UP)

SPOKESMAN: Today, a refresher course in sore
throats. There's the one from smoking.

(SFX: COUGH)

SPOKESMAN: The dry tickly kind.

(SFX: COUGH) The burning sore throat.

(SFX: COUGH)

SPOKESMAN: Fortunately, there's great tasting Luden's
Cough Drops.

SPOKESMAN V/O: Luden's help replace pain. With
pleasure. They quickly dissolve to coat irritated,
inflamed tissue with soothing, cooling relief.

SPOKESMAN: So for minor sore throat problems

(SFX: COUGHS) get major relief.

SPOKESMAN V/O: From Luden's

(MUSIC OUT.)

434
ART DIRECTOR
Houman Pirdavari
WRITER
Brent Bouchez
CLIENT
Yamaha
PRODUCTION CO.
Director's Consortium
AGENCY PRODUCER
Richard O'Neill
AGENCY
Chiat/Day - Los Angeles

435
ART DIRECTOR
Nick Gisonde
WRITER
Charlie Breen
CLIENT
Miller Brewing/Lite Beer
DIRECTOR
Bob Giraldi
PRODUCTION CO.
Giraldi Productions
AGENCY PRODUCER
Tom Dakin
AGENCY
Backer & Spielvogel

436
ART DIRECTOR
Beth Pritchett
WRITER
Kathy McMahon
CLIENT
Kids 'R US
DIRECTOR
Greg Weinschenker
PRODUCTION CO.
Grand Street Films
AGENCY PRODUCER
Sid Horn
AGENCY
J. Walter Thompson

437
ART DIRECTOR
Gary Gibson
WRITER
John Crewley
CLIENT
Texas Power & Light
DIRECTOR
Roger Flint
PRODUCTION CO.
Flint Productions
AGENCY PRODUCER
George Klein
AGENCY
The Richards Group/
Richards, Sullivan, Brock
& Associates/Dallas

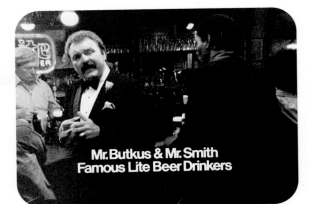

434

(MUSIC: UP AND UNDER.)

ANNCR (VO): Ever wonder why three-wheelers have
chain drive instead of shaft drive?

(SFX: AUTO REPAIR SHOP SOUNDS.)

ANNCR (VO): After all, how many chain driven cars
have you seen lately?

CUSTOMER: That's the way the guy sold it to me.

ANNCR (VO): Which is why Yamaha is proud to
introduce the world's first three-wheelers with
shaft drive.

(SFX: TRI-MOTO ENGINE.)

ANNCR (VO): No more chain to lube...
...or adjust...
...or break.
So all you have to do is ride.
The new Yamaha Tri-Motos with *shaft drive.*
Because anything else...just doesn't work
quite as well.

435

(SFX: BAR SOUNDS)

BUTKUS: I tell ya, trying to get cultured isn't easy.
We just went to the opera, and we didn't
understand a word.

SMITH: Yeah. That big guy in those tights sure could
sing.

BUTKUS: Well, at least we still drink a very civilized
beer. Lite Beer from Miller. Lite tastes great.

SMITH: But us impresarios drink it because it's less
filling.

BUTKUS: We can't afford to get filled up. Tomorrow
night we're going to the ballet.

SMITH: Yeah, I sure hope they do it in English.

BUTKUS: Me too.

(SFX: CROWD LAUGHS)

ANNCR V.O.: Lite Beer from Miller.
Everything you always wanted in a beer. And
less.

436

SINGERS: *Kids are big*
Kids are small
Kids "R" Us!
Now there's a place
that suits them all
Kids "R" Us!
Now there finally is
Kids "R" Us!
A clothing store just for kids
Kids "R" Us!
Kids "R" Us
Kids are hot
Kids are cool
Kids are chic
Kids are us
Kids are tops
Kids are now
Kids are neat
Kids are us
Kids look nice
At a price you can't beat
Every style for a child there is
at Kids "R" Us
The clothing store just for kids.
Kids "R" Us!

437

(SFX: CRACK OF LIGHTNING, RUMBLE OF THUNDER.)

(BABY (VO): CRYING, INCREASING IN INTENSITY.)

(SFX: RUMBLE OF THUNDER.)

(SFX: DOOR OPENING.)

MOTHER (VO): Shhh. It's O.K. It's just thunder. Shhh.
You're O.K.

ANNCR. (VO): We're there when you need us. Texas
Power and Light Company.

(BABY (VO): GURGLE. COO.)

438
ART DIRECTOR
Earl Cavanah
WRITER
Larry Cadman
CLIENT
Volvo
DIRECTOR
Henry Sandbank
PRODUCTION CO.
Sandbank Films
AGENCY PRODUCER
Dane Johnson
AGENCY
Scali, McCabe, Sloves

439
ART DIRECTOR
Gary Ennis
WRITER
Seth Werner
CLIENT
The Stroh Brewery
DIRECTOR
Rick Levine
PRODUCTION CO.
Levine/Pytka
AGENCY PRODUCER
Paula Dwoskin
AGENCY
The Marschalk Company

440
ART DIRECTOR
Mark Drossman
WRITER
Ted Trautwein
CLIENT
MGM/UA
DIRECTOR
Bob Reagan
PRODUCTION CO.
Film Tree & Reagan
AGENCY PRODUCERS
Pam den Hertog
Lisa Paillet
AGENCY
Drossman Lehmann Marino
Reveley

441
ART DIRECTOR
Paul Jervis
WRITER
Neil Drossman
CLIENT
Airwick Industries
DIRECTOR
Paul Jervis
PRODUCTION CO.
Tulchin Studios
AGENCY PRODUCER
Rhoda Malamet
AGENCY
Drossman Lehmann Marino
Reveley

438

(SFX UNDER)

ANNCR. (VO): Two years ago, Volvo introduced the Turbo. A four cylinder car that could blow the doors off a V-8. (SFX) Now there's something new, a Turbo that *Car & Driver* has shown can go from 0 to 55 in a scorching 6.8 seconds. They call it a missile. The intercooled Turbo from Volvo. It does everything the Turbo can do... (SFX: CAR CRASHES THROUGH GARAGE DOOR) only faster.

439

POKER PLAYER: I'd sure like another Stroh's.

HOST: No, wait. (TO THE DOG) Alex, (DOG BARKS) two cold Stroh's. (DOG BARKS AGAIN)

(TO HIS BUDDIES.) Wait till you see this.

(SFX REFRIGERATOR DOOR OPENING.)

He just opened the refrigerator.

(SFX BOTTLE OPENING.)

He just opened one bottle.

(SFX BOTTLE OPENING.)

He opened the other.

(SFX STROH'S BEING POURED.)

Now he's pouring yours.

(SFX OTHER STROH'S BEING POURED.)

Now he's pouring mine.

(SFX DOG DRINKING.)

(TO THE KITCHEN) Alex! You better be drinking your water.

(MUSIC)

ALAN THICKE'S SECRETARY

THICKE OF THE NIGHT

BEFORE

AFTER

440

SECRETARY: A lot of people think Mr. Thicke's a success because of his music or comedy. But I think it's his ability to deal with a crisis. Like yesterday? I told him we ran out of staples? (IMPRESSED) Without even batting an eye, he says, just like this, he says, "Well, order more." Imagine that. "Order more." What a guy! No wonder he's almost a household name.

VO: Thicke of the Night. A late night comedy series starting September 5th.

441

VO: You've seen what plastic surgery can do for people.
But have you seen what it can do for plastic?
This is a Stick Up concentrated air deodorizer before plastic surgery.
Stick Ups air deodorizers now have a slimmer, trimmer design and a controlled release system to last longer, up to 6 weeks. Well?

GUY: Ahhhh
This is a good place for a Stick Up.
Isn't it wonderful what plastic surgery can do?

CLUB MED
The antidote for civilization.™

442

VO: To run the Hat of the Month Club
in a businesslike way,
the boss has to keep the books,
organize the files, write the letters,
be creative and still keep on top of things.
The boss could bring home a tool for modern times,
the IBM Personal Computer.
It can help the businessperson
wear many hats, and sell even more.
The IBM Personal Computer.
Try one on at a store near you.

443

ANNCR (VO): Here's what you can do on the average
vacation at no extra cost.
Here's what you can do at Club Med at no extra
cost.

SONG: *The Club Med vacation.*
The antidote for civilization.
The Club Med vacation.
The antidote for Civilization.

ANNCR (VO): At Club Med, if you ever find yourself
doing absolutely nothing, it'll be a matter of
choice.

444

RADIO ANNCR: Here's a KFWB weather update. Sixty percent chance of rain today with continued thunder showers...(FADE).

RADIO ANNCR: The Traffic Monitor reports potholes on Pico Boulevard. Watch out for lane number 2 because these potholes are reported to be quite large. Some motorists...(FADE).

RADIO ANNCR: Scientists announced that Halley's Comet is nearing its closest point to the planet Earth in 76 years. This remarkable Comet... (FADE).

VO: KFWB NEWS 98. Have we got news for you.

445

(MUSIC AND SFX: VIDEO GAME-LIKE SOUNDS)

AVO: A snack attack can sneak up on anyone... anywhere...(SFX: VIDEO GAME-LIKE SOUND) ...anytime.
To combat snack attacks, reach for new Superman Raisins.
Plump...juicy...100% natural.
They've earned the Good Housekeeping Seal.
Superman Raisins are snacks you can feel good about because they're nutritious.

(SFX: SNACKS DISAPPEARING FROM SCREEN)

(SFX: BANG, BANG, BANG)

New Superman Raisins: Fighting a never ending battle against the snack attack.

(SFX: BANG)

446
ART DIRECTORS
Anthony Angotti
Ralph Ammirati
WRITER
Tom Thomas
CLIENT
BMW of North America
DIRECTOR
Dick James
PRODUCTION CO.
James/Stern
AGENCY PRODUCER
Ozzie Spenningsby
AGENCY
Ammirati & Puris

447
ART DIRECTOR
Chet Sailor
WRITER
Jack Ouzts
CLIENT
Mrs. Winner's Chicken
& Biscuits
DIRECTOR
Joe Sedelmaier
PRODUCTION CO.
Sedelmaier Films
AGENCY
Les Hart Advertising/
Nashville

448
ART DIRECTORS
Dean Stefanides
Ralph Ammirati
WRITERS
Stephen Smith
Martin Puris
CLIENT
BMW of North America
DIRECTOR
Robert Brooks
PRODUCTION CO.
Brooks, Fulford, Cramer,
Seresin
AGENCY PRODUCER
Ozzie Spenningsby
AGENCY
Ammirati & Puris

449
ART DIRECTOR
Brian Fandetti
WRITER
Ted Charron
CLIENT
Etonic
DIRECTOR
Patrick Pittelli
PRODUCTION CO.
Pittelli Productions
AGENCY PRODUCER
Ted Charron
AGENCY
Impecunious/Massachusetts

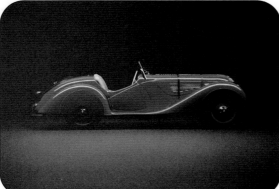

446

ANNCR (VO): BMW unveils a truly advanced automobile.
With graceful aerodynamics...
an ingenious independent suspension...
and hemispherical combustion chambers...
for peak performance.
But what's truly remarkable about all this
technology is that it appeared...
on a 1936 BMW.
Before you buy a car claiming to have leaped into
the future... we suggest you find out when it
began leaping.

447

ANNCR: Ohhh... the things people do to sell chicken.
Like spices... They've pelletized it.

TV PITCHMAN: Ummm-Ummm! Chewy Chicken
Chunks! Don't they look good?

ANNCR: And even stranger things...

(SFX: SOUNDS OF CHICKENS)

WOMAN: Leon, I think we're supposed to choose our
chicken.

ANNCR: At Mrs. Winner's, we've devoted our time to
having the most delicious fried chicken around...
just like homemade.

And more customers every week tell us they
wouldn't have it any other way.

448

ANNCR (VO): In the rarefied world... of forty-thousand-dollar luxury sedans... the BMW 733i is rare indeed.
For it not only offers a host of luxury appointments... it also offers something quite uncommon in this class.
High performance.
Perhaps that's why chauffeur-driven BMW's... are seldom driven by... their chauffeurs.

449

ANNCR: If you think any running shoe will protect you from injuries, you're in for a shock. Because only the Etonic Alpha One has this fiberglass plate to disperse shock and provide stability, Dr. McGregor's Foot Cradle for comfort, and a rear lacing system for a snug fitting heel.

(SFX: WHOCK!!!)

(SFX: WHOCK!!!)

ANNCR: So when you think about running more injury-free, think about Etonic.
We're a step ahead.

**Consumer Television
30 Seconds Single**

450
ART DIRECTOR
Axel Chaldecott
WRITER
Steve Henry
CLIENT
Holsten Distributors
DIRECTOR
Richard Sloggett
PRODUCTION CO.
Brooks, Fulford, Cramer,
Seresin
AGENCY PRODUCER
Diane Croll
AGENCY
Gold Greenlees Trott/London

451
ART DIRECTOR
Jack Mariucci
WRITER
Marvin Honig
CLIENT
Polaroid
DIRECTORS
Jack Mariucci
Michael Ulick
PRODUCTION CO.
Michael Ulick Productions
AGENCY PRODUCER
Mary Ellen Pirozzoli
AGENCY
Doyle Dane Bernbach

452
ART DIRECTOR
Bob Tabor
WRITER
Jeff Frey
CLIENT
Frito-Lay
DIRECTOR
Bob Eggers
PRODUCTION CO.
Eggers Films
AGENCY PRODUCER
Lewis Kuperman
AGENCY
Foote, Cone & Belding

453
ART DIRECTOR
Joe Genova
WRITER
Richie Kahn
CLIENT
National Car Rental
DIRECTOR
Dick Loew
PRODUCTION CO.
Gomes Loew
AGENCY PRODUCER
Bob Schenkel
AGENCY
Campbell-Ewald

450

GRIFF RHYS JONES: Help me Herbie.

BOGART: He's out on the ledge below, trying to make the fire escape.

GRIFF RHYS JONES: Sorry Herbie. Got stuck coming back with my Holsten Pils.
Most of the sugar turns to alcohol, you know.

BOGART: Take it easy now Rico.
Reach my hand.

GRIFF RHYS JONES: Oh no, I've dropped them.

(SFX: CRASH!)

GRIFF RHYS JONES: Hey, Herbie—don't leave me here. Herbie?

MVO: Holsten Pils.
The original Pils.

451

(MUSIC THROUGHOUT)

MAN: I love my new cowboy hat, can we see these pictures right away?

GIRL: No, we're not in a Polaroid Instant camera.

DAD: Is my hat on straight?

GIRL: I wouldn't worry about it.

VO: But with a Polaroid Instant camera, you get something you don't get from an ordinary camera, you get a second chance.

ALL: Oh boy! Wow!

MOM: Beautiful color.

DAD: Hey pardner, you look good.

MOM: He loves that hat.

GIRL: I know.

KID: This is a great looking family.

GIRL: Especially me.

DAD: Who's that funny face?

VO: Polaroid. Why in the world wait?

452

ANNCR: New GrandMa's Rich'n Chewy Chocolate Chip Cookies.

AGGIE: D'you know what bugs me about some of them chocolate chip cookies, Bessie?

BESSIE: Uh-uh.

AGGIE: They're hard and dry.
But yours are delicious.
Crispy on the outside and moist and chewy on the inside.

BESSIE: (GESTURES) Oh.

AGGIE: And loaded with chocolate chips.

AGGIE: The amazin' part is, you're the worst cook in Crawford County—what happened?

BESSIE: Just a late bloomer I s'pose.

ANNCR: New GrandMa's Rich'n Chewy Chocolate Chip Cookies taste suspiciously close to homemade.

453

WEEKEND RENTER: Where'd you get this price? That's not the weekend rate you promised me.

COMPETITOR'S COUNTERGIRL: Of course it is, sir.

MAN: No way.

COMPETITOR'S COUNTERGIRL: Would I lie?

MAN: Are you sure?

COMPETITOR'S COUNTERGIRL: Oh, I'm positive, sir.

NATIONAL SPOKESMAN: Only National guarantees weekend rates. Just $19.95 a day or less on any car up to this Olds Cutlass...
Guaranteed.
And if we don't deliver, you'll get $50 off your next rental.
We give you National attention, and that's the truth.

454
ART DIRECTOR
Frank Sobocienski
WRITER
Seumas McGuire
CLIENT
Massachusetts State Lottery
DIRECTOR
Joe Sedelmaier
PRODUCTION CO.
Sedelmaier Films
AGENCY PRODUCERS
Maggie Hines
Steve Fox
AGENCY
Hill, Holliday, Connors,
Cosmopulos/Boston

455
ART DIRECTOR
Paul Frahm
WRITER
Michael Robertson
CLIENT
National Railroad Passenger/
Amtrak
DIRECTOR
Steve Horn
PRODUCTION CO.
Steve Horn Productions
AGENCY PRODUCER
Peter Cascone
AGENCY
Needham, Harper & Steers

456
ART DIRECTOR
Jim Scalfone
WRITER
Jim McKennan
CLIENT
Volkswagen
DIRECTOR
Sol Goodnuf
PRODUCTION CO.
Lee Rothberg
AGENCY PRODUCER
Liza Leeds
AGENCY
Doyle Dane Bernbach

457
ART DIRECTOR
Clive Loxton
WRITER
Mike Golding
CLIENT
American Swiss Watch
DIRECTOR
Mike Hodges
PRODUCTION CO.
James Garrett
AGENCY PRODUCER
Penny Fry
AGENCY
Bernstein, Loxton, Golding
& Klein/ South Africa

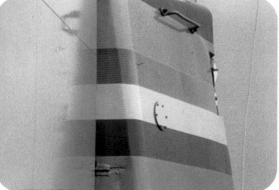

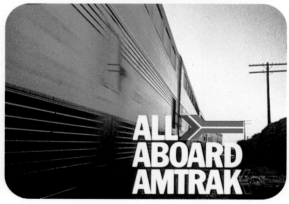

454

(SFX: CONFERENCE ROOM AMBIANCE; PHONE)

1ST VP: Who . . . who . . . who called this meeting.

ALL VPS: (MUMBLED AND CONFUSED) Not me. I don't
know. I don't know.

(SFX: DOOR OPENS AND CLOSES)

WOMAN JANITOR: I did.

ALL VPS: She did. She did. She did.

WOMAN JANITOR: Have you all heard of
Megabucks?

ALL VPS: Megabucks? Megabucks? Megabucks?
Oh, Megabucks.

ANNCR: In the lottery's Megabucks game, the
jackpot keeps growing every week until someone
wins.

WOMAN JANITOR: Gentlemen, I've enjoyed
working for all of you. *And* I'm sure you'll *all*
enjoy working for me.

ANNCR: Megabucks. The game that dreams are
made of.

455

ANNCR: Next time you're planning to fly
somewhere, consider going with a carrier who has
spent the last seven and a half years rebuilding its
entire fleet, a fleet that now offers you some of the
newest, most technologically advanced equipment
in the world.
Not surprisingly, it's also among the most
comfortable.
Next time, see what a thrill it is to fly on a train.

CONDUCTOR: All Aboard . . . !

SINGERS: *All Aboard, All Aboard, All Aboard
Amtrak.*

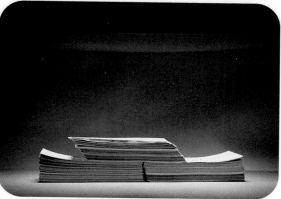

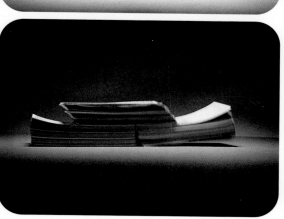

NOW R375 excl.

456

457

ANNCR: Your Bay Area Volkswagen Dealers have
some money for you. Until April 30th, you can
drive off in a selected new Volkswagen and get
$500 to $2,000 back from Volkswagen of America.
That's up to $2,000 on a Scirocco, Jetta, Quantum,
Vanagon or Camper Diesel.
And with 10.9% financing, you can pile up even
more.
But you should move fast. Money like this doesn't
sit around for long.

(SFX: LIBERACE PLAYING CHOPIN FUNERAL MARCH.)

LIBERACE: Hi, you beautiful people, I've got wonderful news. It's the diamond sale at American
Swiss... with 25% off every piece of diamond
jewellery... at all their stores.

ANNCR: There's twenty-five percent off the diamond
ring of your dreams.

LIBERACE: Can you believe it?

ANNCR: Not to mention a gorgeous diamond pendant.

LIBERACE: It's wonderful. And cruel.
Because unlike you lucky peole... I can't be there.

(SFX: CRASH OF KEYBOARD.)

Consumer Television
30 Seconds Single

458
ART DIRECTOR
Warren Greene
WRITERS
Herman Davis
Barry Udoff
CLIENT
Norcliff-Thayer/NoSalt
DIRECTOR
Phil Marco
PRODUCTION CO.
Phil Marco Productions
AGENCY PRODUCER
Ivan Molomut
AGENCY
Cadwell Davis Partners

459
ART DIRECTOR
Bill Bartley
WRITER
Jack Foster
CLIENT
California Milk
Advisory Board
DIRECTOR
Elbert Budin
PRODUCTION CO.
Ampersand
AGENCY PRODUCER
Len Levy
AGENCY
Foote, Cone & Belding/
Los Angeles

460
ART DIRECTOR
Jay-Mo Lo
WRITER
Peter Lyell
CLIENT
General Motors Holden
Camira SJ
DIRECTOR
Henry Meinesz
PRODUCTION CO.
The Film House
AGENCY PRODUCER
Kenneth Brinkworth
AGENCY
McCann-Erickson/Australia

461
ART DIRECTOR
George Halvorson
WRITER
Bill Johnson
CLIENT
The Barbers
PRODUCTION CO.
Filmhouse
AGENCY PRODUCERS
Bill Johnson
George Halvorson
AGENCY
Halvorson/Johnson-Minnesota

458
ANNCR VO: Are you a saltaholic?
Sure you are, because salt hides in most everything.
Even where you don't expect it.
Most Americans get twenty times the salt their bodies need.
So why salt the salt?
NoSalt flavors like salt without salt.
Cook with NoSalt.
Shake with NoSalt.
Since there's salt in most everything, who needs more salt?
NoSalt.
And shake the salt habit.

459
VO: Hooray for the red, white and blueberry.
For the pineapple fruit-on-the bottom.
They're all light and good from the dairy.
And you can spoon 'em and top 'em and plop 'em.
Yogurt's great for a snack or a lunch. For a breakfast, a dip, or a dressing. So go out and pick up a bunch, 'cause they're oh so good and refreshing. You may think that this is the end. Well it is.

460

(EXCITING ROCKY MUSIC THROUGHOUT, RISING TO
CRESCENDO, DIMINISHING UNDER VO.)

(SFX: ENGINE REVVING)

ANNCR (VO): Now there's a Holden Camira on the
wild side . . . the new SJ. Your mother will hate
it.

461

(MUSIC THROUGHOUT)

OFFICE MANAGER: Love your new hairstyle, Marcia.
It's so . . . foreign.

SALESMAN: Let me guess—"Bride of Frankenstein,"
1935! Right?

ANNCR (VO): Sometimes, a new hairstyle attracts a
little too much attention.
The Barbers believe that a good hairstyle makes
you look terrific without making others look
twice.

MAILBOY: No matter what anyone says, Marcia, I
don't see anything wrong with your haircut.

ANNCR (VO): The Barbers. We cut your hair so there
are no cutting remarks.

**Consumer Television
30 Seconds Single**

462
ART DIRECTOR
Dan Krumwiede
WRITER
Ron Sackett
CLIENT
Northland Ford Dealers
Advertising Federation
DIRECTOR
John Denny
PRODUCTION CO.
Producers Services
AGENCY PRODUCER
Julie Sadeghi
AGENCY
Carmichael-Lynch/
Minneapolis

463
ART DIRECTOR
George Halvorson
WRITER
Bill Johnson
CLIENT
The Barbers
PRODUCTION CO.
Filmhouse
AGENCY PRODUCERS
Bill Johnson
George Halvorson
AGENCY
Halvorson/Johnson-Minnesota

464
ART DIRECTOR
Dennis Strickland
WRITER
Palmer Pettersen
CLIENT
Pizza Haven
DIRECTOR
Gary Noren
PRODUCTION CO.
Daye-Smith
AGENCY PRODUCER
Palmer Pettersen
AGENCY
John Brown & Partners/
Seattle

465
ART DIRECTOR
Pat Burnham
WRITER
Tom McElligott
CLIENT
Country Kitchen
DIRECTOR
Jim Hinton
PRODUCTION CO.
Wilson-Griak
AGENCY PRODUCER
Judy Carter
AGENCY
Fallon McElligott Rice/
Minneapolis

462

(INSTRUMENTAL MUSIC)

ANNCR: The Ford F Series Pickups.
The Ford Ranger.
The Ford Bronco.
The Ford Bronco II.
No wonder they're the best selling trucks in the Northland. After all, you don't *Chevy* a stream. You *Ford* a stream. Tough Ford Trucks. Only at your hometown Northland Ford Dealers.

463

(MUSIC THROUGHOUT)

ANNCR (VO): When you buy a bad-looking suit, or an ill-fitting shirt, you can always return it. Unfortunately, it's not that way with every-thing...

MELVIN: I'd like to return this haircut, please.

ANNCR (VO): The Barbers will never give you a haircut you'll want to return. Because we talk to you to find out what kind of hairstyle fits your kind of lifestyle.

MELVIN: Well, if I can't return the haircut, could I at least exchange it...for a different color?

ANNCR (VO): The Barbers. Where there are no unpleasant surprises.

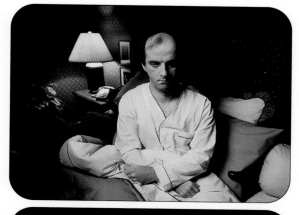

464

(MUSIC: HARP UP AND UNDER.)

ANGEL: I'm here to remind you of Pizza Haven's heavenly new offer: it's our hot, delicious medium pizza topped with fresh, pure Canadian style bacon, for only three dollars and ninety nine cents. And you get two large Pepsis free, just for being good.
That's the best deal anywhere on earth, so when you're hungry, come to Haven.

DEVIL: It's a tasty little devil.

ANGEL & DEVIL: (SINGING) *Haven, you're in Haven...*

465

VO: Do you ever wake up with an appetite that's so big, you just can't control it?
At Country Kitchen we understand big appetites. That's why we're offering...three new hearty skillet breakfasts...steak and omelet skillet...skillet scramble...and Southern skillet. Country Kitchen's newest skillet breakfasts. Big breakfasts...
for big appetites. Without big prices.

466
ART DIRECTORS
Richard Kushel
Bill Shea
WRITER
David Weinman
CLIENT
Olin HTH
PRODUCTION CO.
EUE/Screen Gems
AGENCY PRODUCER
Nick Lemesh
AGENCY
Grey Advertising

467
ART DIRECTOR
Pat Burnham
WRITER
Tom McElligott
CLIENT
WTCN-TV
DIRECTOR
Jim Hinton
PRODUCTION CO.
Wilson-Griak
AGENCY PRODUCER
Judy Carter
AGENCY
Fallon McElligott Rice/
Minneapolis

468
ART DIRECTOR
Michelle Farnum
WRITER
Christine Osborne
CLIENT
Clairol
PRODUCTION CO.
Film Consortium
AGENCY PRODUCER
Ellen Epstein
AGENCY
Doyle Dane Bernbach

469
ART DIRECTOR
Pat Burnham
WRITER
Bill Miller
CLIENT
WTCN-TV
DIRECTOR
Jim Lund
PRODUCTION CO.
James Productions
AGENCY PRODUCER
Judy Carter
AGENCY
Fallon McElligott Rice/
Minneapolis

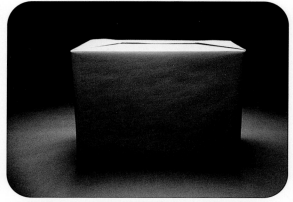

466

ANNCR (VO): This woman is putting HTH pool
   chlorinator through a truly grueling test. A
   test designed to prove how easy it can be to have
   the most crystal-clear water.
   Everyday. You see, no chlorine in any form is
   stronger, more effective than HTH.
   Here's the proof.

(SFX: EFFECT)

WOMAN: Is your pool clear enough that they could
   have filmed this commercial in it?

ANNCR (VO): HTH. Water so clear . . . (SFX) it's
   startling.

467

ANNCR (VO): There are subjects that some people
   would rather keep under wraps. Herpes simplex
   is one of them. A social disease affecting the sex
   lives of over three hundred and fifty thousand
   Minnesotans.
   A disease that will continue spreading as long
   as people are uninformed about it.
   Only one Minnesota television station had the
   courage to take the wraps off of Herpes . . . in one
   of the most-watched and critically acclaimed
   news specials of the year.
   NewsCenter 11. We not only cover the news,
   we uncover it.

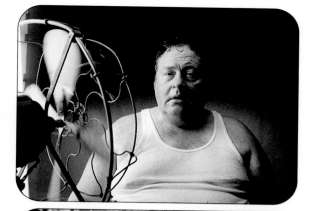

468

(MUSIC THROUGHOUT)

vo: If you've ever seen the play of light on hair...
you've seen highlights.
They're subtle, yet spectacular.
And they're yours with Light Effects from Clairol.
Highlighters that don't change the color, but give
it radiance.
Light Effects. The application of light to selected
strands of hair.
Choose the kit for your natural color.
Light Effects. Just the right effect...from Clairol.

469

mvo: Just because you don't like hot...

(SFX: FAN BLOWING.)

mvo: ...doesn't mean you have to settle for cold.

(SFX: WIND AND CHATTERING TEETH.)

wvo: Just because you don't like busy...

(SFX: WHIRRING.)

...doesn't mean you have to settle for boring.

mvo: Just because you don't like up...

(SFX: WHISTLING UP-SCALE.)

...doesn't mean you have to settle for down.

(SFX: WHISTLING DOWN-SCALE AND BOOM! BANG!)

mvo: Just because you don't like in...
doesn't mean you have to settle for out.

wvo: Just because you don't like wet...

(SFX: SPLASH OF WATER HITTING FACE.)

...doesn't mean you have to settle for dry.

(SFX: BLOWDRYER.)

vo: Just because you don't like the news on
Channel 4
...doesn't mean you have to settle for the news on
Channel 5...

(SFX: GORILLA ROAR.)

Now you have a third choice for news. Channel
11. Maybe you don't need a first.

470
ART DIRECTOR
Deborah Shulman
WRITER
Gregory Sheppard
CLIENT
Eastern Air Lines
DIRECTOR
Gregory Sheppard
PRODUCTION CO.
Dalton/Fenske & Friends
AGENCY PRODUCER
Gregory Sheppard
AGENCY
Campbell-Ewald/Canada

471
ART DIRECTOR
John Coll
WRITER
Bob Hoffman
CLIENT
KYUU FM Radio Station
DIRECTOR
Richard Chambers
PRODUCTION CO.
Chambers & Associates
AGENCY PRODUCER
Carol Tanner
AGENCY
Allen & Dorward/
San Francisco

472
ART DIRECTOR
Dean Hanson
WRITER
Tom McElligott
CLIENT
Minnesota Federal
Savings & Loan
DIRECTOR
Steve Steigman
PRODUCTION CO.
Big City Productions
AGENCY PRODUCER
Judy Carter
AGENCY
Fallon McElligott Rice/
Minneapolis

473
ART DIRECTOR
Howard Alstad
WRITER
Gregory Sheppard
CLIENT
Stella Pharmaceutical/
Slim-Fast
DIRECTOR
Gregory Sheppard
PRODUCTION CO.
Partners Films
AGENCY PRODUCER
Angela Carroll
AGENCY
Campbell-Ewald/Canada

470

(SFX: WINTER. SLUSH. BLIZZARD. FOOTSTEPS IN THE SNOW.)

(MUSIC: PACED TO THE FOOTSTEPS, BUILDING AS PACE
QUICKENS.   TONE–URBAN. TENSE.)

(SFX: SEA. SURF. SEAGULLS. CHILDREN LAUGHING,
PLAYING.)

(MUSIC: UPBEAT. TROPICAL. HAPPY.)

ANNCR (VO): Eastern Super 7's present one
glorious week in the sun including hotel, rental car
and return airfare for as little as $455 or $473.
Call Eastern or your Travel Agent now.

471

HE: Hello, my name is Bob.

THEY: (SILENCE)

HE: (EXASPERATED) Hmm... Today's word is radio.

THEY: (SILENCE)

HE: 99.7... That's KYUU.

THEY: (SILENCE)

HE: The hit music station. (SINGS TO HIMSELF) *Who
can it be now.*

(MUSIC BEGINS)

THEY: (SINGING) *Who can it be now...*

ANNCR: For the best variety of hit music, listen
to 99.7 FM. KYUU.

472

ANNCR: For years banks and savings and loans have been singing the same old song.

BANKER #1: *"I can't give you anything but love, Baby..."*

BANKER #2: *"That's the one thing I've got plenty of, Baby."*

ANNCR: They tell you how much they love you, but they never seem able to loan you money. At Minnesota Federal we love you, too, but we also have money to loan...at very competitive rates.

(SFX: MUSIC UP.)

Minnesota Federal. Money to loan without the song and dance.

473

(MUSIC: STOCK. PERCUSSION)

WOMAN #1: To my ex-husband Robert who used to tell people how much he loved my baby fat. Bye bye baby!

VO: (FEMALE WHISPER) Slim-Fast

WOMAN #2: To my dearest Ronnie who always used to say there was so much of me to love. So long!

VO: (FEMALE WHISPER) Slim-Fast

WOMAN #3: Arthur. Sweet little Arthur. You always said I should wear loose dresses. Get lost!

VO: (FEMALE WHISPER) Slim-Fast

ANNCR VO: Slim-Fast Meal Replacement and Reducing Plan. Helps say good–bye to extra pounds...and hello to a whole new you.

474
ART DIRECTOR
Nancy Rice
WRITER
Tom McElligott
CLIENT
Gold 'n Plump
DIRECTOR
Jim Hinton
PRODUCTION CO.
Wilson-Griak
AGENCY PRODUCER
Judy Carter
AGENCY
Fallon McElligott Rice/
Minneapolis

475
ART DIRECTOR
Donna Weinheim
WRITER
Cliff Freeman
CLIENT
Wendy's
DIRECTOR
Joe Sedelmaier
PRODUCTION CO.
Sedelmaier Films
AGENCY PRODUCER
Susan Scherl
AGENCY
Dancer-Fitzgerald-Sample

476
ART DIRECTOR
Pat Burnham
WRITER
Bill Miller
CLIENT
WTCN-TV
DIRECTOR
Jim Lund
PRODUCTION CO.
James Productions
AGENCY PRODUCER
Judy Carter
AGENCY
Fallon McElligott Rice/
Minneapolis

474

(MUSIC OVER)

VO: Time again for Gold'n Plump news.
Following their victories across the Midwest, a
new Gold'n Plump army prepares to move out.

(MUSIC UNDER)

Thousands of Minnesota-fresh troops are ready to
roll at a moment's notice. (MUSIC UNDER)
Fighting under the motto "to protect and be
served," these dauntless birds will stop at
nothing... (MUSIC UNDER)
as they make their way to your supermarket in
record time. (MUSIC BUILDS)
Gold'n Plump chickens...freshness marches on!

(MUSIC FANFARE)

475

MILDRED: It certainly is a *big* bun.

ELIZABETH: It's a *very* big bun.

MILDRED: A big *fluffy* bun.

ELIZABETH: (weaker) A...very...big...fluffy...
bun.

CLARA: Where's the beef?

ANNCR (V/O): Some hamburger places give you a lot less
beef on a lot of bun.

CLARA: Where's the beef?

ANNCR (VO): At Wendy's, we serve a hamburger
we modestly call a "Single"—and Wendy's Single
has more beef than the Whopper or Big Mac. At
Wendy's, you get more beef and less bun.

CLARA: Hey, where's the beef? I don't think
there's anybody back there!

ANNCR (VO): You want something better, you're
Wendy's kind of people.

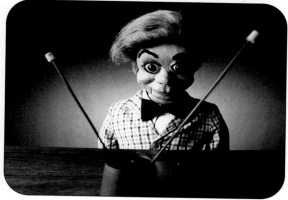

476

MVO: Just because you don't like left...

(SFX: BOOM)

VO: ...doesn't mean you have to settle for right.

(SFX: BOOM)

VO: Just because you don't like little...

(SFX: SQUEAK)

...doesn't mean you have to settle for big.

(SFX: LARGE DOG GROWLING)

VO: Just because you don't like slow...
...doesn't mean you have to settle for fast.

(SFX: CATSUP "GLUG GLUGGING" OUT OF BOTTLE)

WVO: Just because you don't like shaggy...

(SFX: DOG PANTING)

...doesn't mean you gave to settle for shaved.

(SFX: DOG WHIMPERING)

MVO: Just because you don't like heights...

(SFX: BOARDS BREAKING)

MVO...doesn't mean you have to settle for
depths.

(SFX: SOUND OF OXYGEN TANK/BUBBLES.)

VO: Just because you don't like the news on
Channel 4...

(SFX: "CLICK" OF CHANGING CHANNELS ON TV)

VO...doesn't mean you have to settle for the news
on Channel 5.
Now you have a third choice. Channel 11.
Maybe you don't need a first.

477
ART DIRECTOR
Michael Tesch
WRITER
Tom Messner
CLIENT
Travelers Insurance
DIRECTOR
Dick Loew
PRODUCTION CO.
Gomes-Loew
AGENCY PRODUCER
Maureen Kearns
AGENCY
Ally & Gargano

478
ART DIRECTORS
Jim Scalfone
Mark Hughes
Gary Goldsmith
WRITERS
Neal Gomberg
Rhonda Peck
Steven Landsberg
CLIENT
Volkswagen
DIRECTORS
Willi Patterson
John St. Clair
Jim Johnston
PRODUCTION COS.
Petersen Communications
Fairbanks Films
Johnston Films
AGENCY PRODUCERS
Sheldon Levy
Jim Debarros
AGENCY
Doyle Dane Bernbach

479
ART DIRECTOR
Clyde Hogg
WRITER
Rob Ingalls
CLIENT
KGO-TV
DIRECTORS
Paul Henman
Jean Maxine Perramon
PRODUCTION COS.
Kaleidoscope
Richard Williams Animation
AGENCY PRODUCER
Randy Rennolds
AGENCY
Davis, Johnson, Mogul
& Colombatto/Los Angeles

480
ART DIRECTOR
Michael Tesch
WRITER
Patrick Kelly
CLIENT
Federal Express
DIRECTOR
Patrick Kelly
PRODUCTION CO.
Kelly Pictures
AGENCY PRODUCER
Maureen Kearns
AGENCY
Ally & Gargano

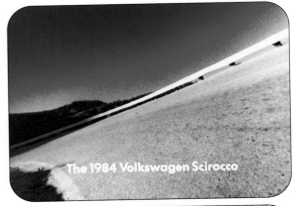

477

(MUSIC UNDER THROUGHOUT)

ANNCR (VO): Ah, the proud owner of a spanking
new car.
When you get a new car, talk to an independent
Travelers agent.

(SFX: CAR CRUNCH)

See if you qualify for the Travelers repair or
replacement collision coverage.
It insures you for up to five years for the full
purchase price of the same type of car you just
bought.
There are more expensive things The Travelers
insures.
But, to the guy whose midsized car was just
turned into a compact, none more important.

478

(SFX: HEARTBEAT.)

VO: Introducing the 1984 Volkswagen Scirocco.

VO: You get the idea.
Scirocco. It's not a car. It's a Volkswagen.

479

(MUSIC: EERIE ELECTRONIC TONE, UP, THEN UNDER,
RISING AGAIN AT END)

(SFX: AMBIENT CASINO NOISES UNDER THROUGHOUT)

THE GRIM CROUPIER (VO): Ladies and gentlemen, place
your bets.
Round and round and round they go,
Who will get them? Nobody knows...
Round and round and round they go,
Who will cure them? Nobody knows...

ANNCR (VO): Diseases...for which there are no known
causes or cures. What are the odds your
number will come up? Find out. Watch "Mystery
Illnesses." This week at six on Channel Seven.

THE GRIM CROUPIER: The house wins again.

(SFX: OUT)

(MUSIC: OUT)

VO: Mystery Illnesses
At 6 on Channel 7

480

JOHN (VO): To get ahead in business these days,
you've got to be fast.
You not only have to be fast, you have to be
faster than the next guy.
And as fast as you are, there's always someone
else who thinks he's faster than you.
And the faster you go, the faster everyone else
tries to get ahead of you, and the faster you have
to go to keep up with the fastest.
And no matter how fast you go, everyone
everywhere is always trying to be faster.
So you have to be really fast, tremendously fast,
incredibly fast, or you'll fall behind someone
else who is faster.
Faster than Jimmy,
faster than Joey,
faster than Janie
and faster than Johnny...

ANNCR (VO): To get ahead in business these days, go
with a company who invented the whole idea of
fast.
Federal Express.
Why fool around with anyone else?

JOHN (VO): ...hoppity toe, whickity whack, flippity
flop, jimminy criminy, whoopity scoopity, zoom
it, move it, whoom it, floom it, rock it, sock it...

481
ART DIRECTOR
Wayne Gibson
WRITERS
Kerry Feuerman
Bill Westbrook
CLIENT
Richmond Newspapers
DIRECTOR
Martin Beck
PRODUCTION CO.
Bridge Productions
AGENCY PRODUCER
Kerry Feuerman
AGENCY
Westbrook/Virginia

482
ART DIRECTORS
Jan Hawkins
Mary Moore
WRITER
Karen Larson
CLIENT
Kendall Company
DIRECTORS
George Gomes
Peter Cooper
PRODUCTION COS.
Gomes-Loew
Cooper & Company
AGENCY PRODUCERS
Lisa Page
Amy Mizner
AGENCY
Humphrey Browning
McDougall/Boston

483
ART DIRECTOR
Jerry Box
WRITER
Jim Copacino
CLIENT
Alaska Airlines
DIRECTOR
Joe Sedelmaier
PRODUCTION CO.
Sedelmaier Films
AGENCY PRODUCER
Virginia Pellegrino
AGENCY
Livingston & Company/Seattle

484
ART DIRECTORS
William Morden
Todd McIntosh
WRITERS
Jim Thomas
Michael Stocker
CLIENT
Ford
DIRECTORS
Bill Tannen
Tim Newman
PRODUCTION COS.
The Film Consortium
Jenkins Covington Newman
AGENCY PRODUCER
Jerry Apoian
AGENCY
J. Walter Thompson/Detroit

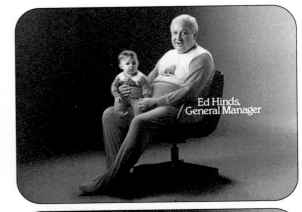

481

SPOKESMAN: Studies show that people who subscribe to the daily newspaper don't usually read the whole thing.
In fact, most only read...a quarter.
But even if you only read a quarter of the newspaper, look how much you get.
Comics...sports scores...recipes...classifieds, "roommate wanted, call Wendy." Editorials...
There's more than news in the Richmond Newspapers. To subscribe call 649-6600.

482

ED: I'm Ed Hinds from Curity, and we make sleepers.
I knew that details make a big difference in comfort and quality...
But I wanted to make sure.
So I had these made. And you know what?
Curity's fabric is not only soft...it's sturdy.
And these vinyl soles really don't skid...
And triple-stitched elastic really keeps a guy's pants up.

VO: We put extra detail into everything we make. Which is why the best reasons for Curity Sleepers and Bedding are little ones.

ED: In these, I could sleep like a baby.

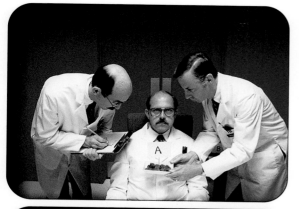

HONDA 750 MILEAGE IS OBTAINED FROM EPA EMISSIONS TESTING, AND IS NOT AN OFFICIAL RATING.

BASED ON EPA INTERIOR VOLUME INDEX.

483

484

ANNCR (VO): Before you try anything new on an Alaska Airlines flight, we try it first.

MAN #1: Too spicy

MAN #2: Too spicy

MAN #3: Too spicy

MAN #1: More.

MAN #2: More.

MAN #3: More.

MAN #1: Too far.

MAN #2: Too far.

MAN #3: Too far.

MAN #1: Still too spicy.

MAN #2: Still too spicy.

MAN #3: Still too spicy.

MAN #1: Louder.

MAN #2: Louder.

MAN #3: Louder.

MAN #1: Too loud.

MAN #2: Too loud.

MAN #3: Too loud.

ANNCR (VO): Why does Alaska Airlines go to all this trouble?
So you won't have to.

ANNCR (VO): Ford Escort.
It's engineered with 4-wheel independent suspension for a smoother ride than *this* Japanese import. It's engineered with more passenger room for more comfort than *this* Japanese import. Plus, Escort has more standard features than *this* Japanese import.
And now, with the new available 2-liter diesel engine, Ford Escort is engineered for better mileage ratings...than *this* Japanese import.

(SFX: ORIENTAL GONG.)

ANNCR (VO): Have you driven America's best-built cars?
Have you driven a Ford...lately?

(SFX: CAR HORN.)

485
ART DIRECTOR
Sam Scali
WRITER
Ed McCabe
CLIENT
Perdue
DIRECTOR
John Danza
PRODUCTION CO.
Levine/Pytka
AGENCY PRODUCER
Carol Singer
AGENCY
Scali, McCabe, Sloves

486
ART DIRECTOR
Beth Prichett
WRITER
Kathy McMahon
CLIENT
Eastman Kodak
DIRECTOR
Joseph Hanwright
PRODUCTION CO.
Kira Films
AGENCY PRODUCER
Sid Horn
AGENCY
J. Walter Thompson

487
ART DIRECTOR
Axel Chaldecott
WRITER
Steve Henry
CLIENT
Holsten Distributors
DIRECTOR
Richard Sloggett
PRODUCTION CO.
Brooks, Fulford, Cramer, Seresin
AGENCY PRODUCER
Diane Croll
AGENCY
Gold Greenlees Trott/London

488
ART DIRECTORS & WRITERS
Donal Swift
Jim Falconer
CLIENT
Minties
DIRECTOR
Donal Swift
PRODUCTION CO.
Motion Pictures of Wellington, New Zealand
AGENCY PRODUCER
Jeff Clark
AGENCY
J. Walter Thompson/New Zealand

485

FRANK PERDUE: Hot Dogs, only 25¢.

KID: Only 25¢ for a hot dog? How good could it be?

(SFX: LAUGHTER)

FRANK PERDUE: I'm making it easy for people to try Perdue Chicken Franks.

KID: *Chicken* Franks? Free would be a lot easier.

FRANK PERDUE: Perdue Chicken Franks cost less, and have 25% less fat than regular hot dogs.

KID: All right, I'll bite.

FRANK PERDUE: So?

KID: Tastes as good as a real hot dog.

FRANK PERDUE: This kid's got good taste and good looks.

ANNCR (VO): Try Frank's Franks. They're good in every way.

486

SINGERS: *Watch out world*
I'm going click, click, click
I'm gonna get you with the Kodak Disc
I'm gonna get you with the Kodak Disc
As sure as shootin' I'm not gonna miss.
Not when it's as easy as this
I'm gonna get you with the Kodak Disc!

VO: The Kodak disc camera, with it's automatic advance and built-in flash, is just about the easiest camera in the world to use. No matter who you want to hound. Smile.

SINGERS: *You can oink, you can moo, you can cock a doodle do. I'm gonna get you with the Kodak disc!*

487

GRIFF RHYS JONES: Hullo Nobby, I've brought you
   some Holsten Pils. Most of the sugar turns to
   alcohol, you know?

RAFT: (Looking longingly at the bottle).
   Funny—us three back together again.

GRIFF RHYS JONES: Yup—you, me and a bottle of
   Holsten Pils.
   I'll save this for you 'till you get out—when is
   that?

RAFT: 9 more years and 6 months in this hole.

GRIFF RHYS JONES: Oh well—seems a shame to let it
   go flat.

GUARD: Time's up.

GRIFF RHYS JONES: I'll bring you another one to look
   at next week, Nobby.

MVO: Holsten Pils.
   The original Pils.

488

(THEME MUSIC)

(APPROPRIATE SFX)

VOCALS: *It's moments like these you need Minties.*

489
ART DIRECTOR
Mike Faulkner
WRITER
Patti Dennis
CLIENT
Arizona Bank
DIRECTOR
Ken Berris
PRODUCTION CO.
River Run Productions
AGENCY PRODUCER
Marc Malvin
AGENCY
Benton & Bowles/Los Angeles

490
ART DIRECTORS
David Stickles
Bruce Kramer
WRITERS
Ed Smith
Bruce McCall
Jon Stone
CLIENT
Mercedes-Benz of
North America
DIRECTORS
Michael Werk
John St. Clair
PRODUCTION CO.
Petersen Communications
AGENCY PRODUCER
Sherry Rousso
AGENCY
McCaffrey & McCall

491
ART DIRECTOR
Kevin Jones
WRITER
Paul Hodgkinson
CLIENT
British Telecom
DIRECTOR
Paul Weyland
PRODUCTION CO.
Paul Weyland Productions
AGENCY PRODUCER
Sandy Watson
AGENCY
KMP Partnership/London

489

BOB: Guess how much The Arizona Bank has in
assets.

RAY: Big bank. Must be a lot.

BOB: Over 2 billion dollars.

RAY: How's our bank ever gonna beat that?

BOB: Hey, they have good rates for loans, let's get
one from them.

WOMAN: Would you like a consumer or business loan?

RAY: A home improvement loan.

BOB: We're redoing our kitchen.

WOMAN: How much will you need?

RAY: 2 billion dollars.

WOMAN: 2 billion dollars?

BOB: It's a big kitchen.

RAY: We're gourmet cooks.

WOMAN: What do you have for collateral?

BOB: We own a bank.

VO: For loans...The Arizona Bank.
It's pretty hard to beat.

490

ANNCR (VO): This is the automobile you probably
didn't expect from Mercedes-Benz.
On the test track it moves comfortably at more
than 100 miles an hour.
Its unique rear suspension provides extraordinary
handling. Its quick reflexes exemplify legendary
Mercedes-Benz performance. From the engineers
of Mercedes-Benz, a new *class* of automobile.
The Mercedes-Benz 190 Class.

491

MISS PRINGLE: Yes, Mr. Sedgwick. He'll see you now, Colin.

SEDGWICK: Come in.

VO: As every business man knows, getting extra business depends on chasing up sales–leads quickly.

SEDGWICK: What's this, Crawley? Still no sales from these 27 prospects?

CRAWLEY: I do keep writing to them, Mr. Sedgwick, Sir–

SEDGWICK: Consolidated Gum.

CRAWLEY: I got young Higgins to pop round the other day, Sir, but they were out—

SEDGWICK: Incorporated Stair Carpets?

CRAWLEY: Expecting a reply any day now, Sir—

SEDGWICK: Acme Elastic?

VO: And a word over the phone can often get results faster than words on paper.

HINCHCLIFFE: OK, then, that's settled, you want 2000 at the original price...

CRAWLEY: I could use first–class mail next time, Sir?

SEDGWICK: But I want action now!!

VO: So if it can be said, phone instead.

492

ANNCR (VO): There's a new personal computer from
Commodore,

(SFX: APPLE BEING BITTEN INTO)

with a third more built–in memory than the
Apple II, at half the cost.

(SFX: APPLE)

The Commodore 64.

493

MAN: The next time you're sending two packages to
the same place, send one by Federal. The other
by Airborne. See which one gets there first.
Watch out Federal! Here comes Airborne.

ANNCR: Airborne Overnight.

494

ANNCR (VO): The way some radio stations select music, you never know what you're going to hear.

(MUSIC UNDER)

But 97 WYNY selects only the truly great songs. From the truly great artists.

495

(SFX: AIRPORT EFFECTS CONTINUOUS CAMERA CLICKING.)
VO: Who's that drinking Campari?

496
ART DIRECTOR
Ron Arnold
WRITER
Peter Levathes
CLIENT
Saab-Scania
DIRECTOR
Sid Avery
PRODUCTION CO.
Avery Film Group
AGENCY PRODUCER
Jerry Haynes
AGENCY
Ally & Gargano

497
ART DIRECTOR
Jordin Mendelsohn
WRITER
Jeff Gorman
CLIENT
Raging Waters Theme Park
DIRECTORS
Jordin Mendelsohn
Jeff Gorman
PRODUCTION CO.
Avery Film Group
AGENCY PRODUCER
Michelle Miller
AGENCY
Mendelsohn Advertising/
Los Angeles

498
ART DIRECTOR
Michael Tesch
WRITER
Patrick Kelly
CLIENT
Federal Express
DIRECTOR
Patrick Kelly
PRODUCTION CO.
Kelly Pictures
AGENCY PRODUCER
Maureen Kearns
AGENCY
Ally & Gargano

499
ART DIRECTORS
Jeff Roll
Greg Clancey
WRITER
Dale Richards
CLIENT
7-Eleven
DIRECTOR
Mark Coppos
PRODUCTION CO.
Director's Consortium
AGENCY PRODUCER
Bill Bratkowski
AGENCY
Chiat/Day-Los Angeles

496

(SFX: TRUCKS PASSING)

ANNCR (VO): What is it that makes Saabs different
from other cars?

(SFX: CAR PASSING)

For one thing, people are buying them.

497

VO: "No matter where you are, watch out for
Raging Waters."
Coming June 18.

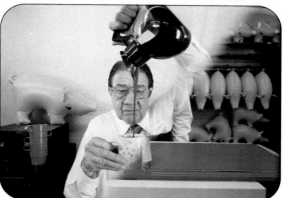

498

ANNCR (VO): If you have to work Saturdays, you're not alone. Now somebody else is working too.

(SFX: BOOM, BOOM, BOOM)

GUY: Who is it?

VOICE: Federal Express. Saturday pick up.

499

BOXER: Play 7-Eleven's Pepsi–Big–Gulp–Peel–and–Win–Game and you could win a trip for two to the fights.
Y'just peel off this little thing here...
y'just...just...

(SFX: POW.)

Public Service
Television Single

504
ART DIRECTOR
Cheryl Hall
WRITER
Pat Sutula
CLIENT
NYC Department of
Transportation
DIRECTOR
Don Guy
PRODUCTION CO.
Dennis, Guy & Hirsch
AGENCY PRODUCER
Diane Jeremias
AGENCY
The Marschalk Company

505
ART DIRECTOR & WRITER
Al Zerries
CLIENT
National Highway Traffic
Safety Administration
DIRECTOR
Steve Horn
PRODUCTION CO.
Steve Horn Productions
AGENCY PRODUCER
Maura Dausey
AGENCY
Grey Advertising

506
ART DIRECTOR
Trevor McConnell
WRITER
David Hayward
CLIENT
Alberta Human Rights
Commission
DIRECTOR
Jon Anderson
PRODUCTION CO.
Frame 30 Productions
AGENCY PRODUCERS
David Hayward
Trevor McConnell
AGENCY
Hayhurst Communications
Alberta Ltd./Canada

507
ART DIRECTOR
John Morrison
WRITER
Jarl Olsen
CLIENT
Projects With Industry
DIRECTORS
John Morrison
Jarl Olsen
PRODUCTION CO.
Wilson-Griak
AGENCY PRODUCER
Judy Carter
AGENCY
Fallon McElligot Rice/
Minneapolis

504

(MUSIC UNDER AND THROUGHOUT.)

VO: In the first half of this test, this driver drove
this course, perfectly. Then, he had 3 drinks.
Only 3 ounces of alcohol. Not enough to consider
him legally drunk.
Not even enough to make him act drunk.
Just enough to make him drive drunk. Fortunately,
this is just a test.
But all too often, it's not. You don't have to *be*
drunk to *drive* drunk.

505

(SFX: CARS GOING BY ON HIGHWAY, BIRDS...)

POLICEMAN: No matter how tough a policeman
thinks he is, he's never ready for the first highway
fatality he sees. Mine was here 11 years ago. I had a
six-year old die in my arms. It still wakes me up
some nights. She'd be about 17 today if her mother
had her wear her safety belt.
Safety belts can save more than 16,000 lives each
year. In all those 11 years, I've never once
unbuckled a dead man.

506

(MUSIC THROUGHOUT)

(SFX: DOORBELL)

BOY: Want to come out and play?

FRIEND: My Mom says I can't play with you anymore.

BOY: Why not?

FRIEND: She says I have to play with my own kind.

BOY: What's your own kind?

FRIEND: I don't know. I thought you were.

(VO): People aren't born racist. They learn it. So please be aware of what your children are learning. Alberta is for all of us.

507

(MUSIC UP: 30'S NEWSREEL)

VO: In 1932, the people of the United States voted for Franklin Delano Roosevelt for president.
They voted for him again in 1936.
And in 1940. Nobody asked if he could climb stairs or do heavy lifting.
Please, if you have a position to fill, find out if a disabled person could do it.
Call 1-800-328-9095. HireAbility. It's not a new idea. Just a good one.

FDR: "We have nothing to fear but fear itself."

508
ART DIRECTORS
Mickey Tender
John Byrnes
WRITER
Susan McFeatters
CLIENT
The United States Army
DIRECTORS
Lear Levin
Don Guy
Neil Tardio
PRODUCTION COS.
Lear Levin Productions
Dennis, Guy & Hirsch
Lovinger, Tardio, Melsky
AGENCY PRODUCER
Jim McMenemy
AGENCY
N W Ayer

509
ART DIRECTOR
Len Fink
WRITER
Lou Linder
CLIENT
Ad Council
DIRECTOR
Phil Marco
PRODUCTION CO.
Phil Marco Productions
AGENCY PRODUCER
Herbert Miller
AGENCY
Leber Katz Partners

510
ART DIRECTOR
John Doyle
WRITERS
Ted Charron
Phillippa Ewing
CLIENT
Blue Cross/Blue Shield
of Rhode Island
PRODUCTION CO.
WGBH Productions
AGENCY PRODUCER
Phillipppa Ewing
AGENCY
Impecunious/Massachusetts

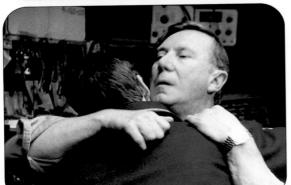

508

FATHER: I thought you had practice today.

SON: Nah, the field was too wet.
Dad, do you have a minute?

FATHER: What's up?

SON: Dad I've decided...

(SFX: WHIRR OF TV)

DAD: What?

SON: I've decided to join the Army.

DAD: Wooa!

SON: I think it's right for me.

DAD: What about college.

SON: I'm still gonna go to college after the Army.

DAD: I thought you wanted to be an electrical
engineer.

SON: I'll be learning about electronics and that will
help me with my engineering.

DAD: It's a big step, Tom.

SON: Dad, listen, I can qualify for the Army
College Fund. So the government will help me pay
for my tuition when I get out. That way I can help
you out for a change.

(MUSIC UP.)

ANNCR: If you qualify, the Army College Fund will
help you accumulate as much as $20,100 for
tuition.

FATHER: So, you're gonna be a soldier.

SON: Yeah.

SINGER: *Be All That You Can Be...*

SON: and an engineer.

FATHER: Be a good one.

SINGERS: *You Can Do It in the Army.*

ANNCR: Call for your copy of this free booklet.

509

When friends don't stop friends from drinking and driving (SFX) friends die from drinking and driving (SFX) friends die from drinking and—

Drinking and driving can kill a friendship (SFX)

510

VO: Now the nice weather's here, Why not do a little jogging? It's very good for your health. And when you've got your health...you've got everything.

511
ART DIRECTOR
Gary Horner
WRITER
Indra Sinha
CLIENT
Shell
DIRECTOR
Barry Kinsman
PRODUCTION CO.
Kinsman Taylor
AGENCY PRODUCER
Sue Bethell
AGENCY
Ogilvy & Mather/London

512
ART DIRECTOR
Bob Needleman
WRITER
Jim Murphy
CLIENT
AT&T
DIRECTOR
Steve Horn
PRODUCTION CO.
Steve Horn Productions
AGENCY PRODUCER
Gaston Braun
AGENCY
N W Ayer

513
ART DIRECTOR
Dennis D'Amico
WRITER
Bob Montell
CLIENT
MCI Telecommunications
DIRECTOR
Michael Seresin
PRODUCTION CO.
Brooks, Fulford,
Cramer, Seresin
AGENCY PRODUCERS
Jerry Haynes
Linda Kligman
AGENCY
Ally & Gargano

514
ART DIRECTOR
Terri Small
WRITERS
Kevin Threadgold
Jim Copacino
CLIENT
Pacific Northwest Bell
DIRECTOR
Terri Small
PRODUCTION CO.
Midocean Motion Pictures
AGENCY PRODUCER
Virginia Pellegrino
AGENCY
Livingston & Company/Seattle

511

(SFX: NATURAL THROUGHOUT.)

MVO: No nation has ever been as inventive as the
    British.
    Which is why British industry has been winning
    around 90% of the orders created by our work
    in the North Sea.
    Our orders have been earning British companies
    one million pounds per day.
    Hundreds of British companies have now
    worked alongside Shell in the North Sea.
    Without their ideas and skills

(SFX: CRASH OF DROP FORGE.)

    and the craftmanship of their people...

(SFX: CRASH OF DROP FORGE.)

    and their willingness always to rise to a new
    challenge...
    ...this would still be a wilderness.
    Thank you Britain.
    Shell can be sure of you.

512

(MUSIC UNDER THROUGHOUT)

VO: More than 50 years ago, a scientist at AT&T's
    Bell Laboratories discovered the principle that
    led to all solid state technology.
    His discovery won him the 1937 Nobel Prize.
    Nineteen years later, the Nobel Prize was again
    awarded to Bell Labs' scientists for the
    transistor... the key that opened the entire
    computer age.
    The creativity of AT&T people has been
    recognized with more Nobel Prizes than any
    other company on earth.
    Over the years, people have come to expect a lot
    from us.
    And now... you can expect even more.
    We're the new AT&T. And we're reaching out
    to find even newer ways to improve your life.

SCIENTIST: There's nothing to be nervous about. Just
    be great, man. Good luck.

VO: AT&T. We're reaching out in new directions.

513

(MUSIC UNDER)

ANNCR (VO): Some people think MCI just offers long distance savings to big cities.

But MCI can now reach every single town.

We mean every town.

Towns like Happy Jack, Arizona.

Embarrass, Wisconsin.

Point Blank, Texas.

From most areas you can reach the most remote phone in any other state and save over Bell.

On every call.

Not just to every metropolis...

...but every tiny town.

Call MCI. Now you can reach every phone from coast to coast.

514

ANNCR VO: Pacific Northwest Bell is constantly working to keep your telephone constantly working.

No matter what problem befalls you...we're there. With the people, the equipment and the service. Where you need it, when you need it. Pacific Northwest Bell. Above and beyond the call.

515
ART DIRECTOR
Gary Johns
WRITER
Jeff Gorman
CLIENT
Nike
DIRECTOR
Mark Coppos
PRODUCTION CO.
Director's Consortium
AGENCY PRODUCERS
Morty Baran
Richard O'Neill
AGENCY
Chiat/Day - Los Angeles

516
ART DIRECTOR
Ralph Price
WRITER
Michael Wagman
CLIENT
Atlantic Richfield
DIRECTOR
David Stern
PRODUCTION CO.
Associates & Toback
AGENCY PRODUCER
Paul Babb
AGENCY
Foote, Cone & Belding/
Los Angeles

517
ART DIRECTOR
Gary Johns
WRITER
Jeff Gorman
CLIENT
Nike
DIRECTOR
Bob Giraldi
PRODUCTION CO.
Giraldi Productions
AGENCY PRODUCER
Morty Baran
AGENCY
Chiat/Day - Los Angeles

515

CARL: My first jump was a joke. Nine feet even. But I said to myself "don't give up." In high school, I kept coming in second. I could have called it quits. But I believe you should never give up. When that's your philosophy, there's no telling how far you can go.

516

SPORTS ANNCR: Representing the United States of America in the 200 meter event...

ANNCR V/O: No one knows what a child will grow up to be. But whatever it is, it takes a lot of energy to guide and encourage him to strive for excellence. And it's excellence that leads to success. That's why for 20 years, ARCO, Atlantic Richfield, has helped children pursue excellence with the ARCO Jesse Owens Games. A track program for youngsteres who just love to run, jump, dash—and a program that inspires those youngsters whose goal is to run, jump and dash in the Olympics. That's why ARCO is an official sponsor of the Los Angeles Olympics. Because ARCO is committed to using its energy to help our children become the best they can be.

SPORTS ANNCR: And the gold medal winner from the United States of America is...

ANNCR V/O: ARCO. We put our energy into excellence.

517

(SFX: ECHO OF BALL BOUNCING AND GRUNTS OF MAN.)

MALONE: At the age of 14, I discovered the secret.
  Pick the one thing you do best. And work at it.
  So, while every other kid was trying to be the
  next Ice Man, I was hitting at the boards.
  Because I figured if you ain't got the ball...you
  can't shoot the ball.

(SFX: SLAM OF BALL BEING DUNKED.)

Index

Artists

Photographers

Directors

Agency Producers

Clients

We won't send you flowers if we promised you a rose garden.

© PhotoUnique
New York — Los Angeles